Christine de Pizan
Her Life and Works

Christine de Pizan
Her Life and Works

Charity Cannon Willard

Persea Books / New York

For information, address the publisher:

Persea Books, Inc.
60 Madison Avenue
New York, New York 10010

Library of Congress Cataloging in Publication Data

Willard, Charity Cannon.
Christine de Pizan.

Bibliography: p.
Includes index.
1. Christine, de Pisan, ca. 1364–ca. 1431.
2. Authors, French—To 1500—Biography. I. Title.
PQ1575.Z5W55 1984   841'.2 [B]   84-1081
ISBN 0-89255-084-8 (hc)
ISBN 0-89255-152-6 (pbk)

Designed by Peter St. John Ginna
Set in Garamond by Keystrokes, Lenox, Mass.

Printed in the United States of America

First paperback printing, 1990

Contents

❧

Illustrations

Preface

It has now been many years since I first made the acquaintance of Christine de Pizan and her works. Recalling the circumstances, it is interesting to consider that it was around the time when Virginia Woolf was writing *Three Guineas,* complaining about the difficulties faced by the daughters of educated men in acquiring good educations themselves. Being quite unaware of the problem, I was already launched on advanced studies in medieval French literature. So it was that one spring evening, while preparing for a final examination, I read in Bédier and Hazard's *Illustrated History of French Literature* that a number of this interesting writer's works still remained unedited. Almost immediately it became one of my great ambitions to edit one of those works. Good fortune (and a shortage of academic appointments during the Great Depression) permitted me to edit Christine's *Livre de la Paix (The Book of Peace)* for the doctorate in Romance Philology at Radcliffe College under the direction of Professor J. D. M. Ford, whose unfailing kindness to and interest in his women students should not be forgotten.

During the long, hot summer of 1939, as I was typing and checking the text, Christine's observations about the political climate in France in 1412 and 1413 often seemed to be editorial comment on the news broadcasts concerning the deteriorating situation of Europe on the brink of World War II. This revealed to me, as little else could have, the authenticity of Christine's writings, an impression which was renewed as I recalled in Paris during May 1968 what she had to say about an earlier French popular uprising.

My thesis was defended the day the Belgian king surrendered to advancing enemy tanks, and my degree was awarded the week France fell to German occupation. Further serious research had to be postponed for more than ten years until it was once more possible to travel freely in Europe and to work in libraries there. Since 1951, however, it has been possible for me to spend time in Europe almost every year and, with more rapid transportation available, sometimes more frequently. Boarding 747s in recent years, I have enjoyed recalling that as a child I traveled to Europe for the first time with my parents by ship the same week that Charles Lindbergh made his flight in "The Spirit of St. Louis."

In the early years after the war, I also discovered the resources of New York's Morgan Library, where I soon made the acquaintance of Dr. Curt Bühler, then Curator of Early Printed Books. He was working on his edition of Stephen Scrope's Middle English translation of Christine de Pizan's *Epître d'Othéa (Othéa's Letter)*, and he claimed that we were the only two people in the United States interested in Christine. We soon discovered that the late Millard Meiss was also working on Christine, reconstructing the workshops where her earliest manuscripts were illustrated. This research was eventually published in his monumental volumes, *French Painting in the Time of Jean de Berry.*

In Europe, I was fortunate to encounter other scholars interested in Christine de Pizan, first of all the late L. M. J. Delaissé, then on the staff of the Bibliothèque Royale in Brussels. He encouraged me to examine and to try to understand the border decorations and the script, as well as the illustrations, of the Christine de Pizan manuscripts, especially those from Burgundian collections. Over a period of years, I was able to profit from his expertise in codicology, not only in Brussels but also at Harvard, where he was a visiting professor during the same period when I held a research grant at the newly-established Radcliffe Institute (now the Bunting Institute), and finally at Oxford, in the Bodleian Library or in his study at All Souls College. I count myself among his many friends and students who have felt his untimely loss keenly.

Another loss has been Franco Simone, the gracious editor of *Studi Francesi,* with whom I was able to discuss Christine and her intellectual background, both in Turin and in the United States. I remember these missing friends with affection and gratitude for their important contributions to my understanding of the late Middle Ages.

There still exists, however, a considerable network of Christine scholars with whom I have been frequently in contact, from Kenneth Varty and Angus Kennedy at the University of Glasgow to Liliane Dulac at the University of Montpellier and Gianni Mombello at the University of Turin, not to mention Eric Hicks at the University of Lausanne, Gilbert Ouy and his *équipe* at the Centre de la Recherche Scientifique in Paris, and, nearer to home, Christine Reno at Vassar College. Encounters with these scholars, and others too numerous to mention here, have greatly lightened long hours spent in libraries and archives.

These have been happy and profitable associations, but we would all agree that the time has now come to make Christine de Pizan better known to a wider readership. This is the purpose of the present book. Besides giving as many details of Christine's life as can be reasonably confirmed from her work and from external sources, it attempts to describe the period in which she lived. The text includes many passages from her work, some never before translated into modern English. Except where credited to another, these translations are my own. It is hoped that the accompanying illustrations will give some further insight into the period and suggest Christine's association with manuscript illustrators of her day. The book was undertaken at the suggestion of its editor, Karen Braziller, and carried to completion under her competent supervision.

It would be ungrateful of me to fail to mention the benefits I have gained from conversation with two distinguished art historians who have been unfailingly generous with their time and advice: Eleanor Spencer, the friend of so many visiting scholars in Paris, and Walter Gibson of Case Western Reserve University. I also think with gratitude of the help given by Major Miguel Ruiz, U. S. A., who took off time from his studies at the Ecole de Guerre in Paris to procure in record time the color photograph needed for the jacket of this book, and of the assistance of my faithful typist, Nancy Reed Swenson.

Needless to say, I have enjoyed and profited from the resources and hospitality of a number of libraries, not only the Morgan Library, but the Harvard Library, where much of my basic research on the Middle Ages was carried out; also the Bibliothèque Nationale in Paris, the Bibliothèque Royale Albert Ier in Brussels, and the British Library in London. It has been my good fortune to be able to examine all but a very few of the known Christine de Pizan manuscripts and working in these great libraries has made me appreciate all the more Christine's "long road of learning."

Finally, I must express once more my affectionate appreciation of the continuous help given me by my husband, Brigadier General (Ret.) Sumner Willard. Friend and companion of graduate school days, he has more recently accompanied me from Pizzano to Poissy, with longer sojourns in Paris, Brussels, and London. He has also discussed with me and proofread uncounted pages, possibly the most important contribution of all.

C. C. W.

Cornwall-on-Hudson, New York
May 1984

Christine de Pizan
Her Life and Works

A View of Venice

A View of Paris

1

A Child of Two Worlds

Christine de Pizan, France's first woman of letters, would have been an unusual person in any era; at the time in which she lived and wrote, at the end of the Middle Ages, when womankind in general was held in singularly low esteem, she was a phenomenon who would not have an equal for nearly another century. Left a widow at the age of twenty-five and with a family to support and care for, she managed to make her way through exceptionally troubled times and achieve for herself a much-desired renown, an ambition she mentioned often in her writings.

Not the least noteworthy aspect of her career is that she left behind her a detailed record of her inner life and her struggle for recognition and of the "long road of learning" that prepared the way for her achievement. Writing at a time when there was almost no model beyond Petrarch for such introspective writing, she nevertheless provided a remarkable self-portrait, although leaving out enough details to provide ample opportunity for speculation by readers in later centuries.

In addition to the autobiographical elements that form the basis for several of her works, Christine left a lively description of the world in which she lived, especially in her biography of the French king Charles V, at whose court she spent her childhood, and in her book of advice to the women who were her contemporaries, *Le Livre des Trois Vertus (The Book of the Three Virtues)*. Although sometimes accused of seeing the French court in an unduly rosy light because of nostalgic recollections of her childhood, and occasionally guilty of inaccuracy in some detail, she has at least recorded an interesting view of late medieval French society as seen by one who was living in it. Taken together with certain contemporary artists who were the first illustrators of her works, she gives a fascinating glimpse of life and thought during the troubled years of civil strife leading up to the appearance of Joan of Arc, who seemed to crown Christine's hopes for France as well as her ambitions for womankind, and who was the inspiration for her last known work.

One surprising circumstance of Christine's life is that she was not born in Paris but in Venice. Although she left her native city too early to have any direct memories of it, she took great pride in her Italian origin, which most certainly exercised an important influence on her outlook on life. Nearly forty years later, while contemplating the miseries of the world around her, she paused to speak fondly of Venice as "a rose among thorns . . . sitting in the midst of the sea,"[1] recalling with pride its Trojan origin, its place of distinction as a power upon the seas, and its republican form of government.

Venice in the fourteenth century was, indeed, an extraordinary city, unlike any other of its day. It can be claimed that the Venetians were both democrats before the age of democracy and capitalists before the capitalistic era. The noblemen who governed the city were primarily businessmen who built up an important position in trade and a commercial empire that extended from the Middle East to the Alps. Venetians were thus exceptionally cosmopolitan, although they owed much of their cultural heritage to Byzantium. The beauty of the city was, of course, legendary.[2]

At the time of Christine's birth, around 1364, the city was just recovering from a series of misfortunes. A great earthquake in January 1348 had been followed by an initial outbreak of the bubonic plague, the dreaded Black Death, that had carried off as much as half of its population before sweeping on across Europe.

Although such doctors as were available were able to observe the course of the disease with admirable accuracy, its behavior was totally incomprehensible to them, and the population was generally overwhelmed with a sense of inevitable doom. It seemed obvious that the affliction was airborne, and it was taken for granted by doctors and other learned men that a primary cause was the corruption of the atmosphere, so it was commonly agreed that the change in the composition of the air might have been brought about either by the putrid fumes of decaying matter or by the movement of the stars.

Few contemporary chroniclers failed to point out that this plague was an affliction ordained by the Almighty as a punishment for the wickedness of the times. Venice had been involved in expensive wars with northern neighbors as well as in maritime rivalry with Genoa. Ten years earlier, there had been the grisly history of the rise to power of the Doge Martino Faliero, which had ended in his execution. Many portents of disaster were later recalled. The earthquake had set the bells of St. Mark's pealing without the touch of human hand. Other signs of what was in store had been observed in the skies, so it did not seem surprising that the movements of the planets were the means by which God had chosen to carry out his punishment.[3] In the fourteenth century, astronomy was by far the most advanced branch of scientific knowledge, astrology was near the peak of its prestige, and few were capable of distinguishing between the two.[4]

In 1348 Christine's father was not yet living in Venice, but these events already had begun to influence his subsequent career there. He was still a lecturer in astrology at the University of Bologna, the most important center in Europe for such studies; he had finished his medical studies there four years earlier. Tommaso di Benvenuto da Pizzano was a native of Bologna, born there in the early years of the century. His family owed its origin to the village of Pizzano in the foothills to the southeast of the Emilian capital; it was only in the sixteenth century that French printers gave the family a spurious connection with the city of Pisa and so began to misspell the family name using the letter *s*. The region of Pizzano had suffered from hostilities between Bologna and Ferrara at the end of the thirteenth century, which may account for the family's decision to seek a greater security in the city.[5]

The course of study that Tommaso had pursued at the celebrated University of Bologna toward the degree of doctor in medical studies normally would have included the study of astrology, as the constellations were thought to govern not only the destiny of the individual but also the various members of one's body at specified seasons of the year. He would also have taken the prescribed preliminary studies in the Faculty of Arts. Future physicians were expected to master, in particular, the art of rhetoric in order to be able to persuade their patients to submit to the treatments they prescribed. Logic and natural philosophy were also considered necessary preparation for the study of medicine.

At the time, Bologna was not only one of the great intellectual centers of Europe along with Paris but it was one of the two most important centers for book production. Unlike the University of Paris, however, Bologna's faculties did not rest on religious foundations, and from the beginning many of its professors were laypersons. To have studied at the University of Bologna implied having been exposed to some of the best and most progressive thought available, and to have rubbed elbows with some of the most intelligent people of the day.

For example, during this same period, Coluccio Salutati, future humanist and chancellor of the Republic of Florence, not to mention Petrarch's chief disciple and correspondent with Europe's leading intellectuals, was pursuing notorial studies in Bologna. The French canonist Jean André was also teaching at the university, so Tommaso could have known his learned daughter Novella, who was said to have been allowed to lecture to his classes, albeit from behind a protective screen so as not to distract the students with her beauty. (Novella would later figure in Christine's *Livre de la Cité des Dames {Book of the City of Ladies}*.)[6] In this stimulating intellectual atmosphere, Tommaso spent his formative years.

The course of study leading to the doctorate normally required five years, and the final examination concluded with a colorful ceremony in which the candidate for the degree was conducted to the cathedral by his sponsors. There the candidate delivered an oration defending a thesis about which he was then questioned by teachers and fellow students. It was expected that a successful candidate would now spend a certain number of years lecturing at the university; and as such a person would probably be at least twenty years old at the time of finishing his studies, it is reasonable to suppose that Tommaso remained in Bologna until he reached his early thirties. In 1357, he left Bologna for Venice.

Tommaso went to Venice primarily at the urging of a friend from university days, Tommaso Mondino da Forlì. It has been suggested that he was a member of the same family as the celebrated anatomist at Bologna, Mondino de Luzzo, but this is not certain. In any case Mondino helped establish his friend in Venice, and Tommaso da Pizzano eventually married Mondino's daughter. So it was that Christine was born in Venice.

Although Christine could scarcely have had personal memories of her native city, Venice became part of her heritage through the tales she heard her father tell during later years in Paris. She speaks of both her father and grandfather as "salaried counselors" of the Venetian Republic, which probably means that they belonged to the civil service. Christine's father surely must have been employed in the health services of the city, which had been organized in 1344, the first of their kind in Italy.

At the time Tommaso took up residence in the city, the Procurators of St. Mark, the administrators of large public bequests, were also the supervisors of several almshouses and hospitals. One result of the Black Death had been a heightened interest in the conduct of such hospitals and in the medical profession in general. The Venetian merchants, in particular, gave great importance to the quality of their medical service, and from the first appearance of the plague in the city, they had hired doctors to enforce special sanitary regulations; the affliction continued to appear at intervals for the next century, however. Petrarch wrote of one of these epidemics at the end of 1363: "Everywhere you hear weeping and lamentations; everywhere you see corpses that are still warm; everywhere you see the carrying of coffins."[7] Petrarch was then dividing the year between Venice and Padua, and during the spring of 1363, while in Venice, had received a three-month visit from Boccaccio. Around the same time, Christine's father, as well as Petrarch, had occasion to become acquainted with Philippe de Mézières, a Frenchman who was the chancellor of Peter I, king of Cyprus. After the king's assassination in 1369, Philippe returned to Paris to the court of Charles V, where he and Christine's family would meet again.[8]

It is uncertain how well Tommaso would have been acquainted with Petrarch, the most important figure of his day, but they could scarcely have avoided meeting in Venice, either at civic festivities, where the poet was always an honored guest, or through intellectual associations, both being former students of the University of Bologna. It was true, of course, that Petrarch had little use for either medicine or astrology, as he made clear repeatedly, not only in his *Invectivae contra Medicum (Invectives against a Doctor)* but also in letters to various friends, and Tommaso must have been aware of the discussions Petrarch was carrying on with four friends on the relative merits of science and literature around the time Christine was born.[9]

The issue is interesting in that it reveals a difference of opinion that must have divided educated men of the time, although its merits have been obscured by Petrarch's wide acceptance by later generations as the "first modern man." Two of Petrarch's friends who were involved in the discussions had probably also studied at the University of Bologna, and a third had been at the University of Paris. Their training was based primarily on commentaries of Aristotle's writings, whereas Petrarch's view of the world was that of an Augustinian Platonist. One of these friends, Guido da Bagnolo, was an eminent physician and quite possibly an associate of Christine's father.

Although Petrarch's viewpoint, later developed in his treatise *On His Own Ignorance and That of Many,* is generally assumed to represent a more "modern" view than the traditional scholasticism of his adversaries, this tradition was upheld by physicians and others who dealt with the observation of scientific phenomena and represented a positivistic attitude that was uncongenial to Petrarch's poetic outlook. Furthermore, the teaching in the secular Italian universities had exposed their students to the Arabic interpretation of Aristotle's system of the universe, notably through the commentaries of Averroes (1126–1198), which had ruled out the intervention of divine Providence, thus permitting an astrological basis for human behavior. Petrarch disapproved of the skepticism of the Averroists and was influenced, rather, by Saint Augustine's concept of Christian philosophy as a moral and ethical guide to a better life. In his treatise Petrarch berated his friends for their learned ignorance, insisting that they denied Catholic faith and Christian teachings.[10]

Tommaso would have sided with Petrarch's adversaries, although in her writings Christine was always careful to insist that her father's astrology did not carry him beyond the limits set by Christian dogma. This discussion was undoubtedly still in progress when Tommaso was called back to Bologna not long after Christine's birth to look after personal affairs. He and his family were never to return to Venice, a decision that may have been influenced by the death, in July 1365, of the enlightened doge Lorenzo Celso and the succession of the wealthy, octogenarian Marco Corner, whose interests appear to have been more commercial than intellectual. His leadership could well have created an atmosphere less congenial to the concerns of an ambitious man such as Christine's father.

Shortly after his return to his native city, moreover, Tommaso was given the opportunity to choose between two attractive possibilities, an appointment at either the court of France or of Hungary. Christine later saw fit to attribute this good fortune to her father's professional reputation,[11] but it would probably be nearer to the truth to suppose that it was the prestige of the University of Bologna that was solicited. Monarchs wanted astrologers at their courts as advisers, a precedent having been set in the thirteenth century by Frederick II of Hohenstaufen and Alfonso the Wise of Spain.

Although Louis II of Hungary was well known as a patron of the arts and had ambitions to found a university at Pecs, Tommaso judged the offer of the French king Charles V more attractive because, as Christine later explained, he wanted to become acquainted with the University of Paris as well as the French court. Therefore, establishing his family on his "possessions and inheritance" in Bologna, he set out alone for Paris with the intention of spending a year or two there and then returning to Italy. At the end of the first year, he was persuaded to stay on and finally, after three years and with the tempting prospect of "possessions, rents, and pensions to maintain his estate honorably," Tommaso decided to have his family join him in France.[12] So it was that in December 1368 Charles V received at the Louvre the newly arrived family of Tommaso, now transformed into Thomas de Pizan.

What sort of person was Thomas de Pizan? There are a few portraits of men of his profession that can be considered impartial. He was, of course, a contemporary of Chaucer's Physician, but he bears little resemblance to him. Chaucer's character was a man greatly versed in astrology, who knew well Aesculapius, Avicenna, Averroes, and Galen, but who devoted little time to reading his Bible, and whose greed corresponded to Petrarch's view that doctors were noted for their propensity for making money. Christine's father may indeed have been ambitious, but her only complaint about him was that he had no financial talent, and the critics of astrology at the French court were quick to point to shortcomings in his science. [13]

Still, since Bologna was a serious intellectual center throughout the Middle Ages and the court of Charles V had a greater concern for learning than most other European courts of the day, some credence must be given to Christine's references to her father's accomplishments. In *L'Avision-Christine (Christine's Vision),* she spoke of his "high understanding of the sciences," and in her biography of Charles V she called her father "philosopher, servant, and counselor" to the king. Elsewhere she praised his competence as "astronomer and mathematician." [14] All of these could readily apply to a scientist of his day whose learning would have had a strong mathematical base and whose central interest was natural philosophy or what the modern world calls physics. From the beginning of the fourteenth century, natural philosophy formed an integral part of medical education. Thus the image of Thomas that evolves from his daughter's writings corresponds rather well to what is now known about the scientists of his era.

The French king to whom the four-year-old Christine was presented soon after the family's arrival in Paris was then in the fourth year of his reign and about thirty years old. From his youth, he demonstrated unusual intellectual qualities and followed with interest the scientific discussions of his time. His passion for collecting a library also dated from before his accession to the throne, and he had already begun to cultivate relationships with outstanding members of the faculties at the University of Paris. It was through such contacts that Charles V had commissioned Nicole Oresme, a Norman by birth who had studied at the celebrated College of Navarre before returning to Rouen as dean of Notre Dame and eventually serving as bishop of Lisieux, to translate into French the known works of Aristotle. In the late fourteenth century, it was still a rarity to find serious works of scholarship available in a vernacular language. Over a period of years, Oresme translated the *Ethics,* the *Politics,* and the pseudo *Ethics* and wrote a commentary on Aristotle's cosmography, the *De Caelo (Book of the Sky).* In this last work, he developed the ideas of an early fourteenth-century professor at the University of Paris, Jean Buridan, whose theories of universal dynamics, discussed in his *Quaestiones de Caelo et Mundo (Questions of the Sky and the World)* in some respects foreshadowed the scientific revolution of the seventeenth century.[15] It was through such commentaries and questions that scientific knowledge progressed from the thirteenth century onward, stirring the imaginations of even such laymen as Charles V. The king also had his first official astrologer, Pelerin de Prusse, compose for him a treatise on the use of the astrolabe, along with the translation of a treatise on the influence of the planets, both of which were dedicated to Charles while still dauphin, around 1362. To this manuscript were later added horoscopes prepared for the king and four of his children. Charles V was so devoted to Pelerin de Prusse that he had him live in the Royal Palace so that he could frequently enjoy his company.[16]

The king's interest in astrology was not just the result of pure superstition. His perpetually fragile health and the traumatic experiences of his youth after his father's capture by the English at the Battle of Poitiers and the resulting outbreaks of violence in Paris might well have raised questions in his mind about conventional beliefs in God's will ordaining events. One senses in him a perpetual search for a fuller explanation of the mysteries of the universe, with the result that his whole reign represents a tactful maneuver to establish a secular government, one basically removed from the clerical influence of the University of Paris.[17] This preoccupation is reflected in other translations he commissioned that stress the supernatural origin of the monarchy. For instance, *Le Traité du Sacre (Treatise on Consecration)*, which Jean de Golein, one of the king's favorite translators, inserted into his translation of Guillaume Durand's *Rationale Divinarum Officiorum (Rationale of Divine Offices)*, made a great point of the divine authority conferred on the king by the anointing with holy oil during the coronation ceremony. Still another translator, Raoul de Presles, in the prologue to his translation of Saint Augustine's *City of God*, insisted on the miraculous origin of the French royal lily.[18] Such interests as these suggest the reason for Charles V's concern with ideas from Italian universities, with their predominantly lay faculties. Thomas de Pizan, moreover, could bring with him not only the fruits of his intellectual training at Bologna but also his experience as a public servant of the Venetian Republic. The king could consult him about his ever more debilitating afflictions, take courage in Thomas' astrological predictions, and discuss with him scientific questions for which he could not find satisfactory explanations in Paris.

Through his love of learning for its own sake, his essentially secular spirit that accompanied a conventional respect for religion, his striving for the ideal of good government, and his love of beauty in the material world surrounding him, Charles V already had some of the traits of a Renaissance prince. Certainly, he was one of the outstanding personalities of his day, and Thomas de Pizan had no reason to regret his decision to remain at his court.

Christine recalled gratefully the king's generosity toward her family, saying, "In my youth and childhood, with my parents, I was nourished by his hand," and adding on another occasion, "The foresight of the good king would not allow any need in his friend's household to go unfulfilled."[19] Among the gifts her father received, in addition to a generous stipend, was an annual income of twenty Parisian pounds from property he had been given at Orsonville in the Forest of Fountainbleau, not far from the king's favorite country residence, the Château de Beauté. Thomas was also given the Château de Mémorant in the same region, a property that Christine later sold to Philippe de Mézières. And in May 1380, Thomas was given possession of the Barbeau Tower in Paris, which had formerly marked the limit of the thirteenth-century wall that dated from the reign of Philip Augustus on the Right Bank of the Seine, but was now within the new city wall and near the king's residence of St.-Paul.[20]

Christine thus grew up in favored circumstances, living on the flourishing Right Bank of the Seine and perhaps even in one of the rambling buildings that made up the king's favorite residence. This collection of buildings of which the Hôtel St.-Paul was composed had been acquired by Charles when he was still dauphin, shortly after his father's return from English captivity. He was no doubt suffering from a certain amount of frustration at the time, being forced to take a secondary position after having rescued the country from the perils to which his father's absence had exposed it. He was, furthermore, saddened by the deaths of two small daughters within a few weeks of each other. At this time Charles bought a *hôtel* belonging to the count of Estampes, near the Church and Cemetery of St.-Paul. To this building he eventually added others, connecting them by a series of galleries and passages. The whole was soon surrounded by gardens and orchards, and there was even a zoo to house the exotic birds, not to mention the boars and lions fancied by the king. Special guards were appointed to care for these creatures, and the royal accounts detail payments to the "keeper of the lions" and the "keeper of the nightingales."

St.-Paul housed not only the royal family, but also a large number of its retainers. It was also a favorite residence of the queen Jeanne de Bourbon, whose exemplary life no doubt inspired Christine's portrait of the ideal queen in *The Book of the Three Virtues*. The dauphin, the future Charles VI, and his younger brother Louis also had apartments there. The queen's apartments were especially impressive, including a long gallery whose walls were painted from floor to ceiling to represent a forest of shrubbery and fruit-bearing trees. In the midst of this verdure, children were depicted gathering the flowers and picking the fruit. The sky over their heads was painted the blue and white of a summer's day. In the little passage that allowed the queen to pass directly from her oratory into the Church of St.-Paul were painted myriads of angels holding back a curtain decorated with the royal coat of arms, while other angels descended from on high, singing and playing musical instruments.

A great novelty and luxury for the times were the palace baths, which were entered through a trellised door bordered in Irish wood. The tubs were fashioned from this same wood, ornamented with gilded knobs and bound by metal rings attached to the wood with gilded copper nails. The adjoining warming rooms were constantly maintained at an agreeable temperature, a popular arrangement during the rainy Parisian winters. The vogue for baths and bathing was encouraged by the interest in Roman baths evoked by Valerius Maximus, whose Roman history was partially translated by Simon de Hesdin in 1375. Fifteenth-century copies of the text were sometimes illustrated by rather explicit scenes of bathing in mixed company, although surely proper Christian decorum was observed in the baths of Charles V and his virtuous queen.

The palace's Council Chamber was large enough to hold 200 people comfortably, and there was also a Charlemagne Room and a Theseus Room, presumably named after the decorations on the walls. The whole establishment was served by a vast kitchen paved with stone blocks, the ceiling supported by nine pillars arranged in lines of three. Four huge fireplaces at the corners of the room were provided for cooking. The food preparation was also supported by a series of domestic offices that surrounded the kitchen court: the conciergerie, bottling room, sauce room, pantry, falconry, fruit room, buttery, and poultry room, the cellars, and finally, the laundry.

Christine's familiarity with life at the court was such that she was able to describe in some detail the daily activities and to give portraits of members of the royal family, notably the king and queen, the dauphin and his brothers, the royal uncles, as well as the exotic ambassador from the sultan of Cairo who visited the court during Christine's childhood.[21]

She also recalled with admiration, twenty-five years after his death, seeing Charles V riding through the streets of Paris as she had known him in her youth. She described the scene not only in her biography of the king but also again some years later in *Le Livre de la Paix* (*The Book of Peace*), written for his grandson Louis de Guyenne:

> His accustomed manner of bearing himself was very noble as he rode in the midst of a great company of barons and gentlemen, well mounted and richly dressed. He sat among them on his own elegant horse, always dressed in royal attire so that anyone who saw him, be he stranger or any other, would know at once that he was the king. He rode accompanied not only by his courtiers but also by men-in-arms in battle dress, the fleur-de-lys borne before him, and he was immediately surrounded by his brothers and other members of the royal family. Thus accompanied, nobody approached him unless summoned, but wherever he went, within Paris or beyond the city walls, he was joyously greeted and he greatly impressed his subjects.[22]

The Paris of Charles V where Christine spent her childhood was undergoing important transformations. The large domains that had originally belonged to the nobility were being divided into smaller plots where houses were being constructed for merchants and artisans. The increasingly prosperous middle class was interested in investing its wealth in real estate and lost no time in acquiring the land that former owners were selling to finance their growing taste for luxury. The Crusades had been at the root of this trend, but it had been further encouraged by the war years, during which those who could moved into the city for protection.

This expansion called for a new city wall to replace the one dating from the reign of Philip Augustus that had suffered considerable damage from the years of warfare with the English. Charles V's new wall was cited by Christine and her contemporaries as a major accomplishment of the early part of his reign. It was greatly admired, with its crenelations, its moat, and its guard walk along the inside. Possibly the wily king, ever suspicious of English intentions, saw fit to strengthen the city's defenses; perhaps he even foresaw his own project of retaking territories lost to England through the Treaty of Brétigny and wanted to be prepared for a counterattack.

The traditional center of the city continued to be the island in the middle of the Seine, the Ile de la Cité. There the king shared his authority with the archbishop of Paris, just as Notre Dame, with the archbishop's palace beside it, divided the territory with the old Royal Palace. In addition to Notre Dame, there were sixteen other churches and religious foundations on the island, including the king's Ste.-Chapelle in the palace enclosure. In front of Ste.-Geneviève-la-Petite, there was a market where all sorts of poultry were sold, and nearby, in front of St.-Christophe, was an egg and cheese market. In addition, many individual houses had shops on the ground floor, arranged at the front of the building in such a manner that the customers could make purchases across an outdoor counter without entering the shop, unless, of course, they wanted to watch the craftsmen at work inside. Here could be found bookbinders, booksellers, and apothecaries, or, in the shadow of the palace, where a growing luxury trade flourished, glovemakers, furriers, and goldsmiths.

The Royal Palace occupied essentially the same space as the modern Courts of Law. Charles V abandoned it as a residence in favor of St.-Paul partly because he considered the new setting in spacious gardens more beneficial to his fragile health. Furthermore, after the tumultuous events of 1358 when Etienne Marcel and his cohort had attempted to seize power by instituting a reign of terror and had pursued him to his very apartments in the palace, and after the death there of his infant daughters in the fall of 1361, the king had been glad to escape from a spot so haunted by unhappy memories. There were other drawbacks, too. The main part of the structure dated from the reign of Saint Louis and was inconvenient by fourteenth-century standards. Parliament, however, continued to administer justice there, and other royal officers carried on their duties in its confines.

There, too, was the Ste.-Chapelle with its astonishing collection of relics, which Charles V delighted in showing to important visitors. There were, of course, the fragments of the True Cross and of the Crown of Thorns brought back from the Holy Land, which the chapel had originally been built to house, but there were also such curiosities as a large griffin's foot, admiringly spoken of by Guillebert de Mets in his description of Paris in 1407. Such novelties were not uncommon at the time, and Guillaume Durand, in his *Rationale of Divine Offices,* recommends suspended ostrich eggs and unicorn horns as a means of attracting people to holy places, thus disposing them to piety.[23] In another part of the palace was a new clock, the first public clock in Paris, which has sounded the hours from 1370 onward. Charles V was so pleased with it that he had two others constructed, one for the Château de Vincennes and the other for the Hôtel St.-Paul. Then he required all the churches of Paris to ring their bells in accord with the royal clocks, ensuring a constant tempo of life throughout Paris and secularizing it by measuring the day according to mechanically regulated time rather than the traditional canonical hours. This was a subtle way of asserting his independence from ecclesiastical domination in worldly affairs.

During this time, as in a later day, the Right Bank of the Seine was the administrative and commercial part of Paris, whereas the Left Bank was the center of intellectual life. Although the king preferred his new residence of St.-Paul, he continued to make use of the Louvre, transforming it from a medieval fortress into a more modern and comfortable habitation, a process he initiated by having the crenelations and defense curtains removed and by adding the towers and gardens that can be recognized in the miniature from the duke of Berry's *Très Riches Heures*. The Valois kings were already noted for their patronage of the arts, but Charles V was to eclipse the family's earlier accomplishments and set an example that his younger brothers and heirs would all try to follow. Christine qualified Charles V as *"vrai architecteur,"* but it was really the talent of his master builder, Raymond du Temple, that made of the Louvre one of the outstanding artistic accomplishments of the reign.

In the principal courtyard could be seen the donjon, cylindrical in form, with walls thirteen feet thick at the base, surrounded by a deep moat. This enclosure could be entered only by crossing a narrow bridge and passing under a single arch. The upper stories were each lighted by eight grilled windows. On these upper levels were several rooms and a chapel. Of particular note was the vaulted room set aside for the royal treasury, a spot that could be reached only by way of a narrow staircase and through a thick door reinforced by several intricate locks. Before the existence of a trustworthy banking system, the royal treasure consisted to a large extent of jewels and gold and silver plate that could be melted into bullion or put up to guarantee loans when the occasion required. It was also the source of lavish gifts distributed as *étrennes* on New Year's Day, or whenever political expediency dictated. Although the Valois princes were notable for their display of material wealth, Charles V's treasure outshone all others. In spite of the sobriety of many aspects of his life, he showed a taste for collecting precious objects from an early age. An inventory made when he was still dauphin, in 1363, listed nearly a thousand objects in this collection, including a cup that reputedly had belonged to Charlemagne and another assigned, with perhaps greater authenticity, to Saint Louis. Another inventory made near the end of his reign, in 1379, listed the astonishing number of 3,900 objects. The treasure kept in the Louvre included twenty-six crucifixes for use in his chapels, sixty-three sets of chapel furnishings, more than two hundred pieces of gold plate, and among the numerous jewels, forty-seven crowns. All of this, and much more, was stored in cupboards reaching from floor to ceiling. From time to time in leisure hours, the king would visit this stronghold to admire his possessions. Christine describes him "visiting his jewels and other riches" at the end of the day, or receiving merchants who came to show him all sorts of "curious beautiful objects which he had shown also to the connoisseurs of his circle, including members of his family."[24]

It was in another tower, joined to the donjon by a gallery, that Raymond du Temple's masterpiece was to be seen. This was the remarkable stairway leading from the ground floor to the royal living quarters. The great spiral was four stories high, beginning with a large flight of eighty-three steps, passing to a smaller one of about half that number, and ending in a terrace. Even more impressive than the structure itself were the ten statues that adorned it, each with its own base and canopy, the work of a group of artists who seem to have aspired to faithful portraiture. Jean de Saint-Romain was responsible for two representations of sergeants-at-arms who guarded the entrance to the royal apartments and also the Virgin with Saint John that decorated the gable. Between these two groups were likenesses of the king's three brothers: the duke of Berry, by Jacques de Chartres; the duke of Burgundy, by Guy de Dammartin; and the duke of Anjou, by Jean de Saint-Romain; along with a statue of their uncle, the duke of Orleans, by Jean de Launay. The most important figures were naturally those of Charles and his queen, Jeanne de Bourbon, which were the work of Jean de Liège. These figures, the sergeants at the bottom (it is interesting to note that Raymond du Temple was himself a sergeant-at-arms at court) and the sacred images at the top, were obviously part of a hierarchic plan. The king was intent upon calling attention to the stability of the monarchy at a time when there was no direct heir to the throne. Until 1368, the king's oldest brother, Louis of Anjou, was next in line of succession. The birth of a dauphin occurred during the same autumn when Christine reached Paris.[25]

The part of the palace that would have the most significant influence on Christine's future was the *Librairie,* established about this same time in still another tower. Christine later described this collection of books as "all the most notable volumes that had been compiled by sovereign authors, either of Holy Scriptures, of theology, philosophy, and all the sciences, very well written and richly decorated, always by the best scribes occupied by his order at this work."[26] Supervised until 1411 by a trusty and especially favored member of the royal household, Gilles Malet, it was unequaled by anything in Europe except the Visconti Library in Pavia. Many of the works were intended to support the king's concept of the political and moral role of the monarchy, although they also nourished his personal interest in learning.

Christine speaks not only of Charles V's books, but also of the study, a room arranged on the floor above the collection itself, where visitors might come to consult the manuscripts. It is not certain at what point Christine became acquainted with this spot, but she wrote of it as if from personal knowledge. Desks and benches were provided, the walls were paneled in Irish wood, the gift of the seneschal of Hainaut, and the ceilings had inlays of cypress wood. The windows provided to light the room were protected with iron grills designed to keep birds from flying in and out.

The library was intended to make an important contribution to the king's program of enhancing the prestige of the French monarchy, and it was to this end that he commissioned the translation of Latin treatises on kingship and good government. Although he was reputed to understand Latin himself, he wanted others to have the benefit of the knowledge of earlier ages. These translations were usually provided with commentaries that underscored the practical applications of the ideas set forth. Christine was familiar with the most important of these translations, and they frequently were an important source for her own writings.

The king's desire to present himself as a patron of learning is shown not only by his collection of manuscripts but also by the dedication miniatures that are a feature of the most important ones. There is, for instance, the *Livre des Neuf Juges d'Astrologie (Book of the Nine Judges of Astrology)* prepared for him in 1361, while he was still dauphin.[27] The portrait of the prince is recognizable, for it corresponds closely to Christine's description of his appearance. In an unusual detail, the prince appears to be addressing himself directly to Aristotle, one of the judges who is expected to answer his questions. At this date, the idea of conferring directly with the ancients could only have been inspired by Petrarch's letters to the ancient writers he particularly admired. The year before Petrarch had indeed been at the French court as Galeazzo Visconti's ambassador, sent to congratulate John II on his release from English captivity. Charles had heard the oration Petrarch delivered on the occasion and was greatly impressed by it. Every effort had been made to persuade the famous Italian humanist to remain at the French court, though to no avail.

The nature of the king's relationship with his translators is depicted at the beginning of his copy of Aristotle's *Ethics,* where the king is shown smiling as he leans forward to receive the volume Nicole Oresme holds out to him.[28] The scene is especially human and communicates well the importance to Charles V of his books, a relationship that served as a model to his younger brothers and other literary and artistic patrons in the fifteenth century, those to whom Christine would dedicate some of her own works.

Charles V's desire to understand better the physical world led him to acquire such a great quantity of scientific works that it became necessary to add a third floor to his library. He is known to have possessed most of the texts that had been translated from Arabic, as well as treatises on atmospheric pressure, classification of animals, plants, stones, and other branches of nature. He owned sixty volumes devoted to medicine and surgery. The question naturally arises as to where all these volumes came from, for the sources in Paris could scarcely have provided them all. Little has been done to identify and study the scientific texts listed in the royal inventories, the first of which was prepared by Gilles Malet himself, but it has recently been noticed that a number of manuscripts seem to have come from Bologna.[29] This would scarcely be surprising in view of the Italian city's importance as a center of book production, and it also leads to the speculation that Christine's father might have been involved in the selection and acquisition of such books for the library. If he had indeed been a sort of scientific adviser for the library, it would account in large measure for the high regard in which Christine insisted he was held by the king, and it would clarify several little understood aspects of Christine's own career, in particular her relationship with Gilles Malet and her access to the royal library.

It would also account for Christine's connections with the Paris book trade in general, and especially with the workshops where the early translations of Boccaccio, for instance, were produced. It might even throw welcome light on how she came to know the talented Italian illustrator who has come to be so closely associated with her works that he has been called the Epître d'Othéa Master because of his illustrations of a copy of one of her early works.

The growing importance of the University of Paris, which flourished under the king's special patronage, had brought into being a whole world of copyists, illuminators, binders, booksellers. These were concentrated around the Rue de la Parcheminerie near the Rue St.-Jacques, just behind the Church of St.-Séverin. This industry of bookmaking flourished from about the middle of the thirteenth century until the establishment of the first printing presses.[30] The books produced for the university were strictly controlled; the *pecia,* or sections of a given manuscript to be copied, were rented out by authorized stationers, and these folios had to be examined and approved in advance by a university committee. If the process was interrupted in the middle of a term, instruction would inevitably suffer. But along with this official book production there developed a parallel commerce, sponsored in large measure by the king and his younger brothers and further encouraged by the increasing group of literate Parisians, many of them from the developing middle class of lawyers and administrative officials in the government. Such as these were especially open to new literary ideas that were beginning to come from Italy. Notable in this group were the secretaries of the royal chancellery, some of whom would eventually be in direct contact with counterparts in Italian chancelleries.

It was this bookish environment that made Christine's career as a writer possible. The sources of her inspiration came from a combination of influences from the two worlds that formed her. Recollections of Venice and Bologna blended with the interests of the French royal court and the large group of counselors and administrators surrounding it. All these must be taken into account to follow the ideas of this extraordinary woman, who left behind her a record of her inner life as well as a record of the life of a whole society.

An Astrologer Lectures to Students

Le premier chapitre parle des
qualites des quatre elemens.

Et sont quatre ele
mens et quatre
qualites sont tou
corps sont compos
materielement
et espciannment
le corps humain
le quel est ce plus

ortune mere
de tristesse
de doulour
dafflicton
mettre ma faut
en ma vieillesse
on estude et mentension

The Wheel of Fortune

2

The Wheel of Fortune Turns

There have been speculations about the nature of Christine's education, but information beyond what she herself said is almost entirely lacking. Indeed, little is known about the education of young girls before the Renaissance. By the second part of the fourteenth century, more girls were literate than had been the case earlier, especially young noblewomen and also the wives and daughters of Italian merchants, who were frequently taught to read and write so that they could assist the men of their families with bookkeeping and correspondence. The correspondence of Francesco di Marco Datini with his wife Marguerita, better known than most, gives a good idea of the capabilities of such a woman.[1] In other instances, however, spiritual education was considered of primary importance, so that many girls appear to have learned to read from their Books of Hours or from primers based on the same sort of religious material that was to be found in the Books of Hours. The next consideration was that they should know how to manage their households, and once they were married, raise their children. Christine herself made a considerable point of this in *The Book of the Three Virtues*, although elsewhere she complained that she had not been able to spend her early years learning what would have been useful to her later on, particularly how to look after her husband's financial affairs after his death.[2] Furthermore, at an early age, Christine had shown an interest and aptitude for intellectual pursuits, and her father, recognizing her ability, was inclined to encourage her. His views on the education of women were notably liberal for his day, believing as he did that women were none the worse for acquiring knowledge. Christine's mother was more conventional in her outlook and believed that her daughter should tend to her spinning.[3] It is evident that her mother won her point because Christine explained that she had been obliged to gather up such crumbs of knowledge as she could from her father's wisdom.

In view of the fact that one of the usual methods of teaching the young seems to have been through telling them edifying stories, one may suppose that the foundations of Christine's later intellectual development might have been the tales her father told her about his youth in Italy, his studies at Bologna, and, especially, what he had learned about the literary classics he had read there and also what he knew about the physical universe. Echoes of all these matters are to be found in her writings. Her actual contact with the books that became her most important sources did not occur until after her widowhood. She was, in a very true sense, self-educated, though the inspiration must have come from her father and perhaps also from her husband, an educated man who seems to have taught her something about writing, at least the sort of writing that was useful for a notary. It must have been from him that she learned the notorial script now identified as hers.

The period of her youth available for intellectual pursuits was brief, since, according to accepted custom, by the time Christine was fifteen years old a husband had been chosen for her. She speaks rather coyly of the suitors who sought her hand because of the favor her father enjoyed at court, but their identities are not known. In the end, Thomas chose for his daughter a promising young man, a university graduate from a Picard family of northern France. Christine herself commented that he was more notable for his character and intelligence than for his worldly goods, though he did come from a good family.[4]

This young man, Etienne de Castel, was most probably the son of a court official of the same name who served as "armorer and embroiderer" to Charles V even before he was king, perhaps as early as 1351.[5] As armorer, he would have supplied arms to the king and his knights, an important undertaking at the time, since Charles V was bent on regaining French territories lost to the English by the Treaty of Brétigny. Furthermore, payments recorded in the royal accounts for the purchase of tapestries supplied by Etienne's father suggest that he was a man of some substance. Unfortunately, by 1371 he was dead, leaving his son, who could not have been more than sixteen at the time, to make his way in the world. Of course, in the fourteenth century, sixteen would have been considered a mature age.

One of the executors of the father's will was Gilles Malet, who would later perform the same service for his king.[6] It is apparent that the son had graduated from a university, for he is referred to in official documents as Maître Etienne Castel. But the records of the University of Paris yield no information. The title of Maître would imply at least a certain exposure to the liberal arts as preparation for legal or notorial training, and the young man was a notary by profession. About twenty-five at the time of his marriage, he was in the same year made a royal secretary, a lifetime appointment. During this period, royal secretaries were the intellectual elite of Paris. Intimately associated with the royal household, they were in a good position to profit from royal favors. They were charged with the preparation of letters and acts emanating directly from the king, and they frequently represented the king on diplomatic missions. Highly successful careers in the royal service were often initiated in the chancellory. The future must indeed have seemed rosy to Etienne and his bride in the early months of 1380.

The marriage turned out to be very happy, and in her writings Christine never failed to speak of her husband with tenderness and affection. At the beginning of the long, partially autobiographical, allegorical poem entitled *La Mutacion de Fortune (The Mutation of Fortune),* she included an account of her ten happy years at the Court of Hymen.[7] During this time, three children were born, a daughter Marie, a son Jean, and another child whose name is not known, who died in childhood. Perhaps he was another Etienne.

Soon after this decade of personal happiness, the family fortunes were threatened by the untimely death of Charles V. Christine later said of this event: "Now was our door opened to misfortune and I, still young, passed through it."[8] She and her family were not alone in their distress, for the king's death marked the beginning of one of the darkest chapters in French history.

Certain disturbing indications of problems in store became immediately apparent. Even during the funeral services for the dead king, a portentous incident occurred. The members of the university, in full regalia and led by the rector, appeared to take their place in the funeral procession, only to be told by Hugues Aubriot, the provost of Paris and the marshal of the ceremony, that they were not to have the prominent position to which they felt entitled. In previous years, when there had been altercations between the colleges and the Paris police, the king had frequently interceded in person and had usually taken the part of the scholars. Whether this led to unfounded presumption on the part of the university or to a deep-seated resentment among the city police officers is not clear, but a scuffle between the two groups broke out, and it was only with the greatest difficulty that the royal regent, the duke of Anjou, was able to restore sufficient order for the ceremony to proceed.[9]

The following day, as the king's casket was being transported from Notre Dame to the royal mausoleum in the Abbey of St.-Denis, there was a repetition of the incident. By this time the university was sufficiently aroused to decide that it would avenge its honor and dignity. Joining forces with others who had grievances against Hugues Aubriot, they denounced him for heresy. Aubriot was brought to trial before the inquisitor so suddenly that he did not even have time to organize the suit he was intending to bring against the university for disturbing the peace, in a disgraceful fashion, on such a solemn occasion. At a trial that claimed to expose scandalous aspects of the provost's private life, his enemies were able to find sufficient grounds to have him excommunicated. He was accused, among other sins, of not believing in the sacrament of the altar, but rather mocking it, and of not keeping Easter and not going to confession. Aubriot escaped being burned at the stake only because the royal princes decided that the affair had gone too far. Instead, he was shut up in an ecclesiastical prison, from which he was fortunate enough to be liberated two years later through the good offices of another of Charles V's former officials. By then, the university apparently felt that its dignity had been restored and had turned its attention to other matters.

In the meantime, another power struggle had developed.[10] Charles V, having foreseen the dangers of a regency that might result from his own poor health and the tender age of his heir, had made every effort to provide legislation to cover such a contingency. As early as 1374 he had passed an ordinance establishing fourteen as the age at which a dauphin could be crowned king of France. As it turned out, however, when the king's life ended on September 16, 1380, the dauphin was not yet twelve. It had been stipulated that in such a situation the duke of Anjou, the oldest of the uncles, was to be regent with the assistance in financial matters of Bureau de la Rivière, one of Charles V's most trusted advisers. The dukes of Burgundy and Bourbon were to act as the young prince's guardians.

This was an excellent plan but unfortunately it did not take into account the personal ambitions of the uncles. Quarrels broke out almost immediately. According to the chronicler Froissart, Charles V had scarcely drawn his last breath when the duke of Anjou took possession of the whole royal treasure, putting it into a safe place for his own purposes. Moreover, he seized a large sum of money the king had kept in the Château de Melun and helped himself to some eighty of the most precious manuscripts in the royal library. He lost no time in making it clear to his younger brothers that he intended to take charge of every aspect of the regency.

When the duke of Burgundy, for his part, insisted that the ordinance of 1374 should be respected, the disagreement was so sharp that there was danger of a show of arms. Finally, it was agreed that the prince should be crowned immediately. The coronation took place on November 4, and by the end of the month a new arrangement had been worked out that considerably reduced the duke of Anjou's influence in the government. Undoubtedly, Anjou's ambition to organize an expedition to Italy in order to make good his claim to the kingdom of Naples facilitated his agreeing to the new arrangement.

At the same time, France was afflicted by a series of popular uprisings against what was seen as unjust taxation. These protests culminated in a Parisian riot known as the Maillotin Revolt, taking its name from a rather nasty two-headed leaden hammer. A supply of these weapons was seized by the mob from the Hôtel de Ville, where they had been stored against a possible English raid on the city. The disturbance was soon brought to an end by the duke of Burgundy, who was experienced in dealing with urban revolts because of a similar contestation with his Flemish subjects in Ghent only a short time before. As a result, when the duke of Anjou departed for Italy soon thereafter, the duke of Burgundy's authority in Paris was undisputed.

In the long run, however, the remaining royal uncles divided France between them, and each pursued individual ambitions in his own sphere. Philip of Burgundy's activities were inevitably bound up with the Duchy of Burgundy and also Flanders, of which he became the count after his father-in-law's death in 1384. Fortunately for him, Paris, where he now spent at least half his time, afforded him a good vantage point from which to oversee his scattered territories. He was especially interested in guiding France's foreign policy toward peace with England in order to protect the prosperity of the Flemish wool trade, and also in promoting good relations with the Holy Roman Empire, to which some of his territories were attached. It was with this particular interest in mind that he arranged the marriage between the young king and Isabeau of Bavaria, which was celebrated in the Cathedral of Amiens on July 17, 1385. The bride was the daughter of the duke of Bavaria, a member of the extensive German Wittelsbach family into which Philip had already married two of his own children.

The duke of Berry, to whom Charles V had assigned no role at all in the projected regency, managed to have himself designated governor of the southern provinces of Guyenne and Languedoc. This, in addition to the territories he already possessed (Macon, Berry, Poitou, and Auvergne), made him master of about a third of France and gave him the opportunity to exploit the region in his own fashion. His political ambitions were limited, but he was the most enthusiastic builder and collector in the entire Valois line. He was thus able to make impressive strides in his program of building and refurbishing his numerous residences and of increasing his collections of rare and precious objects. In Paris he persuaded his nephew to give him the Hôtel de Nesle on the Left Bank of the Seine, formerly the home of some of Charles V's most devoted servants, the Orgement family, whose fortunes had considerably diminished during his son's reign. This now became, after a series of embellishments, one of the duke's principal residences. He also devoted himself enthusiastically to building his palace in Poitiers, with its great hall, which still stands, and its monumental fireplace ornamented by statues of himself, his second wife Jeanne de Boulogne, and Charles VI with his new wife Isabeau. As his marvelous château at Mehun-sur-Yèvre, near Bourges, was nearing completion, he turned his attention to his tomb and to his Sainte-Chapelle in the Cathedral of Bourges, destined to house not only his tomb but also a piece of the True Cross, a fragment of the famous relic deposited by Saint Louis in the Parisian Sainte-Chapelle and given to the duke by Charles V in 1372.[11] Taxes extracted from the duke's unfortunate subjects paid for many of these luxuries.

Although France during these years was governed, in theory, by a royal council that still included some of Charles V's most trusted officers, in fact their role was minimal. Almost none of the men who had been favored by the late king continued to prosper, and it is scarcely surprising that Thomas de Pizan's fortunes also waned. He was retained as a member of the king's household, but with a diminished income that was irregularly paid.

Furthermore, Thomas was growing old, and in 1385 he had the misfortune to become involved in an altercation with a German alchemist, Bernard Thomas of Trier, that scarcely did him credit. To a treatise addressed to this alchemist, Thomas appended a note begging him for protection against certain detractors. It seems that Thomas had prescribed a medicine involving mercury that had brought on him the accusation of trying to poison a member of the royal court. Bolognese doctors had used mercury salts in drugs for more than a century—mercury ointments being especially popular as cures for certain skin diseases—but perhaps Thomas had done some experimenting that had gone awry, or perhaps the remedy was less well known in France.[12] No serious consequences seem to have resulted from the affair, yet whenever Christine had occasion to speak of alchemists, she paid her disrespects to her father's colleague in Trier. Far more serious was the fact that the astrologer fell into a period of infirmity for which he was not prepared financially, and the Pizan family fortunes suffered accordingly. Although records of the royal household carry Thomas de Pizan's name in the accounts at the beginning of 1387, it is missing the following year. It may be supposed that he had died in the meantime, "at the hour he had predicted in advance," as his daughter explained, adding that her father was "such a man that his own had cause to mourn his passing" and praising him for "his great knowledge of mathematical science and astrological judgments."[13]

Christine's husband, Etienne, now became the head of the household. Being young and well established in his position as royal secretary, he seemed to have every reason to face the future with high hopes, but he, too, was soon lost to the family. In the fall of 1390, while in Beauvais on a mission with the king, he suddenly died in an epidemic. When this disaster overtook them, Etienne was thirty-four and Christine was twenty-five. Understandably, Christine was overwhelmed by grief at her loss.[14]

The first of the practical difficulties that beset her was that she was left not only with the responsibility for her three children but also for her widowed mother and a niece. As she explained, she was "six times one person." Her two brothers, Paolo and Aghinolfo, had left France after their father's death to claim an inheritance in Bologna. They are known to have sold there, for instance, a house that was part of this heritage, which also included Thomas de Pizan's interest in a mill he had inherited in Pizzano some years earlier. So it was that Christine had no relatives in Paris to whom she could turn in this moment of distress.[15]

To her personal problems were soon added a variety of economic disasters. Christine felt considerable bitterness at the custom that denied women adequate information concerning their husband's financial affairs, and as she was not even with her husband when he died, she had no real idea of his financial situation. When she tried to collect money due his estate, she was met by deception and dishonesty and also was burdened by a series of lawsuits. This, as she ruefully acknowledged, was all too often the lot of widows. Perhaps Christine's difficulties were compounded because her husband was normally entitled to a "purse," a kind of bonus awarded to certain royal secretaries deriving from a tax on official documents that they prepared. Since Etienne had been away from Paris when he died, he would not have been given this extra money for the period of his absence; yet he should have been reimbursed separately and directly by the king for time spent on a special mission.[16] Given the habits of greed of so many public officials of the day, it is easy to understand that Christine could have had trouble collecting the money due her. She was also involved in a suit with the royal accounting office over a piece of property her husband had acquired. Possession of the property had reverted to the Crown upon her husband's death, but she was still obliged to pay rent on it. Although the details of the suit are not clear, Christine was probably suing to be released from responsibility for the property. Worse still, the money set aside for the children's future had been invested with a merchant who turned out to be dishonest. Later, Christine complained that she had been involved in suits in four Parisian courts at one time. Fourteen years and large sums of money were required to extricate her from her predicament, and even then she was not entirely free from financial troubles. [17]

Writing *Le Livre du Corps de Policie* (*The Book of the Body Politic*) some years afterward, Christine urged princes to have pity on "poor gentlewomen, widows, and orphans." In her time of need, she had found few friends to whom she could turn, a problem of widowhood about which she had more to say in *The Book of the Three Virtues*. There she explicitly warns widows not to count on friends who might have seemed affectionate and trustworthy during the lifetime of their husbands, and above all, never to become involved in lawsuits, however legitimate the claim, without good legal advice and unlimited resources to pay the costs. [18]

By 1392 Christine had apparently been able to rescue her fortune to some extent by selling to Philippe de Mézières the property she had inherited from her father near Melun. The "old pilgrim," whom her family had formerly known in Venice, was by then living in retirement at the Celestine convent near the royal residence in Paris. Yet even now her troubles were not ended. She then fell ill, perhaps the victim of one of the epidemics that constantly swept through Europe and certainly exhausted by her struggles. As she described it, she "succumbed like Job to a long illness." [19]

The year 1392 was scarcely more fortunate for France. In August Charles VI, then twenty-four years old, suffered the first attack of the insanity that would plague him intermittently until his death thirty years later. His mental and physical health had already given cause for concern. The duke of Burgundy had remonstrated against the excesses of the intense social life that characterized the court after the marriages of the king and his younger brother Louis, but in 1388 Charles had declared his independence from his royal uncles and, with the help of some of his father's former advisers, had undertaken to rule for himself. His brother was also of an age to want to play an important role at court, an ambition that was probably encouraged by the French constable Olivier de Clisson, to whom the king and his brother were devoted. In addition, several others among Charles V's former officers were waiting in the wings for an opportunity to regain the power they had lost in 1380: along with Olivier de Clisson, there were Bureau de la Rivière, Jean Mercier, and Jean de Montaigu, capable and experienced administrators who wanted nothing better than to take charge of the government while the king and his brother amused themselves.

The arrangement would have had considerable merit had it not been for the progressive deterioration of the king's health. Already in April 1392 he had suffered from a disturbing illness from which he had not entirely recovered by August when he insisted on making an expedition to Brittany to sustain Olivier de Clisson in a private war his constable was carrying on with the duke of Brittany. So it came about that as the king was riding through a forest in full armor on a hot summer day, he was startled by the sudden appearance of an eccentric stranger in his path, just at the moment when a drowsy page allowed a lance to fall against the metal helmet of a nearby horseman. The startled king became hysterical and attacked some of his companions who were riding near him, killing at least one of them before he could be restrained and disarmed. As a consequence, Charles VI's personal rule came to an end, for even during periods of lucidity thereafter, his intelligence was never more than childish, and he was usually willing to agree to almost anything his relatives might propose to him. At the same time, however, between attacks of insanity, Charles gave the appearance of carrying on his duties, which prevented the establishment of a true regency and instead opened the way for an unremitting struggle around him for control of the real power of government.

From 1392 until the time of his death in 1404, the duke of Burgundy was able, albeit with increasing difficulty, to maintain predominant power. He found an ally in Isabeau, the queen, who came to be regarded as the official ruler during her husband's "absences," but who was by no means old or experienced enough to govern the country. Her activities were also constantly hampered by the births of her many children, most of whom did not survive to maturity.

The most serious challenge to the duke of Burgundy's authority came from the king's younger brother Louis, who at the age of twenty was already embarking on his ambitious program of personal aggrandizement, although many of his efforts were thwarted by his uncle's superior political skill and experience.

In spite of internal weaknesses, however, during the final years of the fourteenth century, France enjoyed a period of great splendor. Philip of Burgundy, a marriage maker *par excellence,* was instrumental in bringing about a twenty-eight-year treaty with England based on the marriage of Richard II, a widower since 1394, with Charles VI's six-year-old daughter Isabelle. The marriage was celebrated and the treaty signed in November 1396, permitting Philip to pride himself on having ensured peace for France while promoting the prosperity of his Flemish subjects.

The prospect of a lasting peace with England also served to encourage the frivolity of the French court. Led by the queen and Louis of Orleans, the court devoted itself to a revival of the more superficial aspects of chivalry, renewing a fashion that had not been seen since the reign of John II. Unfortunately, these chivalric practices bore all too little relationship to the realities of the day.

It is probable that Christine, absorbed as she was by her own troubles, was not aware of the true sources of unrest in France. Her first literary contacts were with this frivolous court, where writing poetry was one of the principal social accomplishments. Yet it is evident that she knew well that beneath the brilliant surface of Parisian society were concealed a cruelty and a selfishness that were both shocking and disconcerting. This knowledge is reflected in the poetry she began to write, in part as an outlet for her grief. Her lyrical recollections of happier days during the reign of Charles V may have been inspired by her own memories of a more secure and agreeable personal life, but they correspond to a reality well documented by other testimony.

Once Christine recovered from her illness, her fortunes seem to have improved somewhat, possibly through the intervention of Jean de Montaigu. In her biography of Charles V, Christine speaks of Montaigu with gratitude, noting that he was generous to those in need both with his wealth and with his word.[20] Gilles Malet, who continued to occupy his post as guardian of the royal library in the Louvre and who otherwise enjoyed royal favor, would also have been in a position to help her, at least by giving her access to books and possibly by introducing her into the court of Louis of Orleans. Christine also knew Bureau de la Rivière and his wife and she speaks of them with affection. After 1392, to be sure, the influence of these men was diminished, yet they were able to retain some of their former wealth and authority. It was probably through such people as these that she met the earl of Salisbury, who was in Paris on a diplomatic mission in the fall of 1398: Christine's poetry was beginning to be known, at least in limited circles, and provided the basis for her meeting with the English nobleman.[21] He, too, was something of a poet as well as a patron of literature, and Christine did not hesitate to accept his offer to take her son Jean into his household in England as a companion for his own son, only slightly younger than Jean. It is likely that she believed that she had thus secured her son's future because Salisbury enjoyed an especially favored place at Richard II's court.

There remained the problem of her daughter's future. Christine was certainly unable to provide the dowry she would require for a suitable marriage, but an alternative presented itself, probably also through the influence of powerful friends: in 1397 her daughter was given the opportunity to enter the royal Dominican convent at Poissy, in the outskirts of Paris. In the autumn of that year, at the age of five, Charles VI's daughter Marie had taken the veil and was dedicated to a life of religion in the hope that her father's madness might thereby be alleviated. Royal daughters were all too frequently sacrificed to reasons of state, and Marie had been born in 1392, the year when her father's affliction had first manifested itself. At the time she entered the convent, it was the custom for the crown to provide dowries to the religious community for a certain number of other young women, or for well-born children to enter along with the royal child. It would appear that Christine's daughter was one of these, perhaps because she, too, was named Marie.[22]

The Abbey of Poissy had enjoyed many special privileges from its foundation because of the patronage of Saint Louis, who had been born nearby. In 1397, Charles VI's aunt Marie de Bourbon was the prioress, a woman distinguished by her wisdom as well as her royal birth. The abbey accommodated two hundred sisters who were expected to come from noble families and to bring with them rich dowries. In addition, a special authorization from the king himself was required in order to be admitted. Christine would have had every reason to be gratified to have such a haven provided for her daughter. In her *"Dit de Poissy"* ("Tale of Poissy") written three years later, she described with great charm a visit to her daughter in the venerable abbey, providing an interesting glimpse of what life in such a religious community must have been like.[23]

Little is known about Christine's third child, a son. He must have died around the same time the other two children left Christine's roof, for when Jean left for England she spoke of him as the older of her two sons, but when he returned home three years later, she said that death had left her only one son. Even after the departure of the children, Christine's mother continued to live with her, and her niece remained a member of her household until the duke of Burgundy provided money for her marriage dowry in 1406.

It was probably around 1394, four years after her husband's death, that Christine began to write poetry. The first of her ballades that can be dated with any certainty marks the fifth anniversary of her widowhood, although another early ballade refers to the duke of Bourbon's expedition to northern Africa in 1390. Christine herself speaks of 1399 as the date her literary career began, yet it is evident that she had started writing several years earlier and that she had also launched herself on the program of self-education that would provide her with inspiration for her later work. As she explained, "like the child that one puts at first to studying his ABCs," she took to the study of ancient history from the beginning of the world, the Hebrews, and the Assyrians, then descending to the history of the Romans, the French, the Britons, and various other nations. Next, she took up the sciences and, finally, the "books of the poets." When she arrived at the study of poetry, something responded in her inner being that led her to say to herself: "Child, be consoled, for you have found the thing that is your natural aspiration."[24]

It is clear that Christine did not take her early poetry very seriously. Writing verses in fixed forms—the ballade, the rondeau, the virelay—was an accomplishment much cultivated in the society of her day. In November 1392, Eustache Deschamps, perhaps the leading poet of the time, finished a treatise on writing poetry entitled *L'Art de Dicter et de Faire Chançons, Ballades, Virelais et Rondeaus (The Art of Versifying and of Composing Songs, Ballades, Virelays, and Rondeaux)*, so that anyone who wished could write verses, and Christine's efforts appear to date from soon after the appearance of this guide.[25] She explains that she began to write in order to distract her mind from her troubles and her sorrows, "regretting her good friends and past happiness." But presently she began to write love poetry, beginning with some virelays, to put a little pleasure into her heart, although she was "singing joyously with a sad heart," as she puts it in one of her rondeaux. By June 1402 she had written enough to assemble her poems into a collection, beginning with a series of a hundred ballades.

In order to survive the decade between her husband's death and her first literary success of any consequence, Christine must have had a source of income beyond whatever her husband left her. Even writers as relatively successful as Chaucer or Eustache Deschamps were unable to support themselves by their writings alone. Those who were not members of religious orders were usually employed in some sort of government service or attached to the court of a prince. Careers such as these, however, were simply not available to women at the beginning of the fifteenth century. There is also the question of how Christine obtained the books she speaks of reading in order to educate herself. Even if it is reasonable to suppose that through Gilles Malet she had access to the royal library, she speaks of working alone in her study, and it is there that she is portrayed in a number of miniatures that illustrate her writings, sometimes with several volumes on a reading stand before her and often with her little dog at her feet. Christine's father, and possibly her husband, might have owned a certain number of books, yet the libraries of well-educated men of that day were limited. In order to increase her supply of books Christine would have had to copy at least some of them for herself, the usual manner of acquiring books if one was not a wealthy person or a prince. It seems possible that she might also have copied manuscripts for others for a fee, thereby furthering her own education and improving her financial situation.

Interest in book collecting had brought into being a whole group of people involved in the book trade, not only writers, but also copyists, illustrators, parchment merchants, and entrepreneurs who organized the growing trade. Some bibliophiles, notably the royal princes, could afford to have books copied for them by direct order, making individual arrangements with copyists and artists; some had books copied for them by regular members of their households such as secretaries, if they did not copy them themselves; but booksellers also existed who bought the necessary materials and commissioned scribes and artists to create books for some specific clientele or for a general market that a given bookseller expected to be able to find. In fact, during these years, the sale of books to laypeople, even at the high price commanded by vellum and by both scribes and illustrators, presented an expanding market and would seem to have offered a promising opportunity for a literate person in need of money.

In her writings, Christine often refers to aspects of book production. In her biography of Charles V, for instance, she speaks of the scribes who were constantly at work copying manuscripts in the royal library. Although she is never referred to specifically as one of these scribes, that this is a sort of work that would have been available to women is confirmed by records of that time of women working as both copyists and illustrators. Such an apprenticeship would not only have given Christine a source of income and the range of knowledge that is evident in her writings but it also would have taught her how to organize and to operate a workshop of her own. There is ample evidence to suggest that Christine was in the habit of overseeing the manuscripts of the works that she presented to such princely patrons as the dukes of Burgundy or Berry, if she did not actually copy them herself.[26]

In *The Book of the City of Ladies,* Christine speaks of having paid a high price for the services of a certain woman artist:

> Regarding what you say about women expert in the art of painting, I know a woman today, named Anastasia, who is so learned and skilled in painting

manuscript borders and miniature backgrounds that one cannot find an
artisan in all the city of Paris—where the best in the world are found—who
can surpass her, nor who can paint flowers and details as delicately as she
does, nor whose work is more highly esteemed, no matter how rich or
precious the book is. People cannot stop talking about her. And I know
this from experience, for she has executed several things for me which
stand out among the ornamental borders of the great masters.[27]

Unfortunately, it has not been possible to identify Anastasia's work among
that of the several skillful artists who decorated Christine's manuscripts,
although there are certain borders that seem especially delicate.

Elsewhere Christine describes the lives of artists in such a way as to
suggest that their world was quite familiar to her. Her opinion of their
morals, however, is not high, and in *The Book of the Three Virtues,* she
advises their wives to try to encourage them in honorable habits and
especially to discourage them from accepting work from noblemen who
were known for not paying their debts. In *The Book of the Body Politic,*
she gives an even less flattering account of them:

Among these artisans there are some who are very skillful, more skillful
in Paris than those commonly found elsewhere, which is a fine and notable
thing . . . but as for their lives, to speak briefly of them, would it please
God, and especially these artisans themselves (which would surely please
God) that their lives were more given to moderation and not so free as
they are at the present time, for their excesses in the taverns, and the
indulgences they permit themselves can bring only ills and misfortunes
upon them. . . .[28]

The interview with the duke of Burgundy that Christine describes
at the beginning of *Le Livre des Les Fais et Bonnes Meurs du Sage Roy Charles*
(*The Deeds and Good Customs of the Wise King Charles V*) gives further
evidence of Christine's increasingly professional status as a writer. Invited
to the Louvre to discuss with the old duke the biography of his brother
he wished to commission, she says that she went there "accompanied by
my staff."[29] In an earlier day, she had been obliged to go frequently to
courts of law unaccompanied, suffering the many indignities from the
motley crowds that frequented such public places. One doubts that in
the winter of 1404 she was speaking of being accompanied by domestic
servants. Her choice of the word *staff* seems to indicate a professional
arrangement for producing manuscripts to order.

Furthermore, if Christine's handwriting in certain manuscripts has
been correctly identified, she wrote the cursive script that was used in

the correspondence of the royal chancellory, and not the *lettres de forme* that in the past had generally been favored for literary manuscripts and Books of Hours. At the chancellory, scribal assistants were in constant demand. They prepared official documents to be countersigned by one of the royal secretaries before being signed by the king or his chancellor and having the royal seal affixed. They frequently worked in their own homes, so it is possible that Christine had done some of this work for her husband and in that way learned the official handwriting. It is also conceivable that she had continued to copy documents after Etienne's death in order to maintain her household. This would explain a detail in a verse attached to a letter written in the fall of 1405 to the queen of France, in what is probably an autograph copy. There she noted that the letter, copied at one o'clock in the morning, was *"escript de ma main"* (written by my own hand), a legal formula that occurs in a variety of documents, meaning exactly what it says. She promised the lord who had commanded her to write the letter a better copy later, explaining that at such an hour no *other* clerk was available.[30]

This is merely one example of Christine's familiarity with the format of official letters. She used letters not only for persuading public figures to play a responsible role in public affairs, but also for purely literary purposes. The first and last of her longer works were cast in this form. The first, *L'Epistre au Dieu d'Amour (Cupid's Letter)*, is a takeoff on a royal letter, this one purporting to be presented by a royal secretary at the celestial court of the God of Love. The other, *L'Epistre de la Prison de Vie Humaine (A Letter concerning the Prison of Human Life)*, was written after the Battle of Agincourt (1415) to bring consolation to the suffering women of France, so many of whom had lost husbands and other relatives in the great military disaster.[31]

It has also been noted on various occasions that Christine was familiar with the official language of the chancellory, frequently making use of a formula such as "I, Christine" and taking care to mention definite dates and to give the people she mentions their exact official titles. These characteristics are especially noticeable in her most serious works, *The Deeds and Good Customs of the Wise King Charles V*, *Christine's Vision*, and *The Book of Peace*.[32]

An association with the royal secretaries goes far toward explaining her acquaintance with the men who later engaged her in the celebrated debate over the merits of *The Romance of the Rose*, and it throws important light on her evolving interest in humanism, which was enjoying its first flowering in France among certain royal secretaries who were in contact with Italian counterparts, notably Jean de Montreuil, who corresponded with Coluccio Salutati.[33] In that group she would also have encountered Ambrogio Migli, who had come to Paris in the entourage of Valentina Visconti, the young duchess of Orleans, after a period of service in the Visconti chancellory in Milan. This was a circle where Christine's Italian heritage, not to mention the association of both her father and grandfather with the University of Bologna, would have had considerable significance.

In *The Mutation of Fortune,* Christine explains how her change of fortune had obliged her to "become a man" and take on a man's responsibilities in the world. In *The Book of the Three Virtues* (III, iv), she further explains her meaning of this transformation when she admonishes widows to take on a man's heart and be constant, strong, and wise in pursuing their own advantage, rather than crouching in tears like a poor woman, or like a stray dog who retreats into a corner when other dogs attack him. By whatever means, Christine herself had the intelligence and the force of character to overcome her worst misfortunes and to establish herself in a new life. Most important of all, she recognized the fact that it was to circumstances of misfortune that she owed the life of study that she came to enjoy so much, as well as the discovery of her vocation for writing.

Louis of Orleans Receives a Manuscript from Christine

The Earl of Salisbury

3

The Beginnings of a New Life

Christine was fond of portraying herself in her writings as leading a solitary, hard-working life of study, yet once the most trying years of her widowhood had passed, she can be glimpsed enjoying a variety of social contacts resulting from the success of her early poetry. By 1399 or 1400, her poetry was beginning to be known beyond the limits of French court circles and even as far away as England and the Visconti court in Milan. She did not claim that this renown was entirely the reward of its merit; as she explained in *Christine's Vision,* it was because poetry written by a woman was such a novelty. Thus, she said, princes willingly received her poems and her reputation spread rapidly.[1]

As a woman's view on life and society were almost wholly without precedent, they did indeed offer a novelty. It has been claimed that Christine made too much of her condition as a woman, which is untrue of her later works in any case, and where her early lyric poetry is concerned, what other possibility would she have had for originality and authenticity? Her own experience was the best she had to offer, and another woman's voice would not be heard in France for more than a hundred years.

The court of Louis of Orleans was the setting for Christine's literary debut. With the royal court in disarray because of the king's insanity, the courts of the other princes—Orleans, Anjou, and Burgundy, in particular—provided centers for social, literary, and artistic life.[2] Of these, the most lively and attractive group was the Orleans entourage, centering around the king's handsome, if ambitious and willful, younger brother and his Italian duchess, Valentina Visconti. This court was also a bastion of aristocratic privilege and chivalric tradition, and so it attracted a group of lively, ambitious courtiers who were as ready to compose a ballade as to take off on a knightly adventure to Prussia or Constantinople.

Writing poetry in fixed forms was merely one aspect of the intense social life that centered around such a princely household. The prodigal habits of these princes who hastened to fill the void in patronage left by Charles V's death attracted artists to Paris from other parts of Europe— Flanders, Bohemia, Italy—to create the elegant and refined art forms that characterize the early years of the fifteenth century, those that constitute the so-called International Style. Because of his marriage, Louis of Orleans was particularly fascinated with Italy, and perhaps most of all by the possibility of claiming some territory there through Valentina's dowry. Italians, especially from the Visconti court in Milan, found places in his household, and it is not surprising that Christine should also have been attracted there. The influence of the duchess herself was far from negligible. She was a very literate princess with a library of her own, some of which she brought with her from Milan.[3]

Although Christine was scarcely inclined to take an active part in the frivolous social life, the tournaments, and the elaborate entertainments favored by this court, these form the background for some of her poems. The knights and ladies who populate her early poetry were undoubtedly to be found at the Orleans court, for some of them can be identified. In this milieu she would also have met others she had known in her earlier life, among them Gilles Malet, now the officer in charge of the duchess Valentina's household, Jean de Montaigu, and Bureau de la Rivière. The court was also composed of courtiers to whom she later addressed poems or mentioned in other ways: Guillaume de Tignonville, the provost of Paris; Jean de Garencières, a poet as well as a diplomat; and, most important of all, Eustache Deschamps.

The life of this court was divided among the duke's country estates and one or another of his large townhouses in Paris. At the time when Christine was most attached to this group, its activities often centered around the so-called House of the Porcupine, not far from the Hôtel St.-Paul. The house in question received its name from the duke's emblem, a porcupine, which was displayed over the main entrance. This mansion had formerly belonged to Charles V's ill-starred provost Hugues Aubriot, but the duke of Orleans had since acquired it. It was probably between 1399 and 1404 that Christine most frequented the Orleans court. After that, she was disenchanted because of the duke's unwillingness to find a place in his household for her son Jean, or otherwise to interest himself in the youth's future. There were also some doubts in her mind as to how seriously he regarded her poetry because he was as generous to popular entertainers as to poets. It was to Louis of Orleans, however, that her first important works were dedicated.

Society life was organized in a way that furnished a sort of poetic calendar for those who wanted to try their skill: New Year's Day, St. Valentine's Day, May Day—all occasions calling for poetry. Poetic contests, too, were popular. Along with the revival of chivalric customs, there was an interest in poetic traditions stemming from the early Provençal troubadours. Shortly after 1400, a Court of Love, on the Provençal model, was established in Paris under the patronage of the dukes of Burgundy and Bourbon.[4] Elsewhere, informal poetic debates and exchanges of ballades were also organized among poets and courtiers, including in the duke of Orleans' entourage. In spite of the international flavor of this court, it was the French poetic traditions that predominated there, and these are reflected in Christine's early poetry. Her first poems were short: the virelay, the rondeau, the ballade. Their success depends so largely on the fixed patterns of verses and rhyme scheme that much is lost in an attempt to translate them. Their charm is fragile, yet they reflect well the effete elegance of the society that enjoyed them.

More important than the social rewards that came from her poetry, writing verse gave Christine an outlet for her grief, her loneliness, and the pain caused by the financial burdens that were her lot. Most likely, she also began to take pleasure in the discovery of her considerable skill with words and to enjoy the challenge of fitting them into the intricate verse forms. The varied verse forms she attempted in this early poetry show a sort of zest for experimentation. As she gained experience, she began to collect her individual poems into cycles, sometimes telling a story. Usually the story was told from the point of view of a young woman in love, although in least one instance the point of view was that of the eager lover, and on still another occasion the story was a dialogue between a lover and his lady. But the most original of her poems are those expressing her own emotions as she continued to mourn the loss of her husband. This is the burden of her most famous ballade, "Seulette suy et seulette vueil estre":

> Alone am I, alone I wish to be,
> Alone my gentle love has left me,
> Alone am I, without friend or master,
> Alone am I, in sorrow and in anger,
> Alone am I, ill at ease, in languor,
> Alone am I, more lost than anyone,
> Alone am I, left without a lover.

Alone am I, standing at door or window,
Alone am I, in a corner creeping,
Alone am I, to feed myself with weeping,
Alone am I, suffering or at rest,
Alone am I, and this pleases me the best,
Alone am I, imprisoned in my chamber,
Alone am I, left without a lover.

Alone am I, everywhere, by every hearth.
Alone am I, wherever I go or be,
Alone am I, more than anything on earth,
Alone am I, by all men left alone,
Alone am I, most cruelly cast down,
Alone am I, often full of weeping,
Alone am I, left without a lover.

Princes, now has my pain begun,
Alone am I, to deepest mourning nigh,
Alone am I, gloomier than the darkest dye,
Alone am I, left without a lover.[5]

By 1402 Christine was turning her attention to more serious forms of writing, although she continued to compose love poetry for several more years. Around 1410, *Cent Ballades d'Amant et de Dame (One Hundred Ballades of a Lover and His Lady)*, her last lyrics, were copied into a luxurious manuscript of her collected poetry prepared for the queen.

Christine was writing just at the time when the forms she was practicing were separating themselves from the music that had long been a part of their tradition. Although dancing songs may have played their role in the origins of these forms, from the end of the eleventh century the Provençal troubadours and their northern imitators had usually composed both words and music.[6] This custom was brought to a high degree of perfection around the middle of the fourteenth century by Guillaume de Machaut, but the generation of poets that succeeded him was not able to imitate the musical complexity that was his particular talent. In any case, there is no evidence that Froissart, Eustache Deschamps, Christine, or their contemporaries ever attempted to set their poetry to music, although in certain cases musical settings were provided for them by others. The Burgundian musician Gilles Binchois, for instance, composed music for one of Christine's ballades beginning "Dueil angoissieux, rage demesuree" ("Anguished grief, unbounded rage"), which enjoyed a certain success, but this was quite separate from the composition of the poem.

As this poetry distinguished itself from a musical counterpart, it became more involved in rhetorical traditions. When Eustache Deschamps composed his treatise on writing poetry, he saw fit to differentiate between artificial music—that played on instruments—and natural music, which is produced by the human voice reciting words in various meters and in different patterns. Natural music, he claimed, cannot be cultivated by anyone who does not have a natural talent for it, although practice can improve one's skill in handling forms.[7] Thus a distinction continued to exist between true poets and court versifiers. Deschamps' definition suggests that importance was given to spoken poetry of the kind encouraged by the popular poetic competitions, although these poems might subsequently be circulated in written form. Several of Christine's poems, especially those celebrating St. Valentine's Day or May Day, suggest that they might have been composed originally for poetic contests, for which a theme was generally given out in advance. One example suffices to give an idea of the nature of all of these poems:

> Now has come the gracious month of May
> The gay, who brings such bountiful delights
> That these meadows, bushes and these woods
> Are laden all with greenery and flowers,
>   And each thing does rejoice.
> Among these fields all blossoms and turns green,
> And nothing there but does forget its grief,
> For delight in the lovely month of May.
>
> The little birds sing on their way for joy,
> With one heart all things do rejoice,
> Except for me, alas! My grief is great
> Because I am far distant from my love;
>   And I can feel no joy;
> With the season's mirth my sorrow grows;
> As you will know if ever you have loved,
> For delight in the lovely month of May.
>
> And so with frequent weeping I must mourn
> For him, from whom I have no help;
> The grievous hurts of love I now more deeply
> Feel: the stings, th'attacks, the tricks and turns,
>   In this sweet time than ever
> I have felt before; for all conspire to change
> The great desire I once too strongly felt,
> For delight in the lovely month of May.[8]

From various references to these poetic contests, it seems possible to conclude that women were often the judges who awarded the prizes, but there is no record of any other woman poet having taken part at this time. Nevertheless, Christine's relationships with other poets, insofar as they are known, seem to have been agreeable and often fruitful. In an exchange of poems with Eustache Deschamps, she claimed him as her master, and he insisted that she was unique in her talents.[9]

There is no reason to doubt that Christine was speaking the truth about her indebtedness to Deschamps, who had provided models for the beginner to follow, along with instructions for composing various verse forms. Christine's enthusiasm as a disciple led her to some rather extravagant experiments. In a group of "ballades of strange fashion," she followed Deschamps's instructions for composing a "ballade rétrograde," one that can be read equally well either forward or backward, and another with the rhyming word at the end of each verse being echoed at the beginning of the following. She also wrote two "ballades à réponses," one with the two parts of a dialogue presented in each verse, and another with the conversation carried on in alternating verses. These must, of course, be considered poetic games and not be taken seriously as poetry.

In a more serious vein, Christine tried her hand at virelays, short poems that may derive their name from *virer,* "to turn or twist," for the refrain, introduced in the first verse, is repeated at the end of the third and fifth stanzas.[10] There are only six of these in Christine's collected poetry, a small number in comparison with her ballades and rondeaux, although among them there is an especially charming Valentine poem that begins:

> My gentle friend, you surely know
> That on this day I've chosen you
> To be my friend, and vow anew
> To pledge my heart entire and true. . . .[11]

These lines refer, of course, to the medieval custom of choosing a "friend" for the year on February 14 the day on which birds were said to select their mates. St. Valentine's Day was the feast day of Valentina Visconti, which must have been a reason for its being especially celebrated at the Orleans court.

In another virelay, one of her first, Christine insists on the distance that exists between her poetry and her true sentiments:

This mask no grief reveals;
My eyes may overflow,
But none shall guess the woe
Which my poor heart conceals.

For I must mask the pain,
As nowhere is there pity;
Greater the cause to gain,
The less the amity.

So no plaint nor appeal
My aching heart can show
And mirth, not tears bestow;
Those my gay rhymes conceal.
May this mask no grief reveal.

So is it I conceal
The true source of my ditty,
Instead I must be witty
To hide the wound which does not heal.
Let this mask no grief reveal.[12]

In the complexities of the verse form, spontaneity can easily be inhibited to the point where the poem turns out to be little more than a tour de force. The rondeau, being a shorter and simpler form, offers the possibility of expressing sentiments more naturally. Like the virelay, it seems to have originated as a simple country dancing song called the *rondet,* or *rondet carolé,* no doubt devised to accompany a sort of circle dance.[13] The rondeau is characterized by a refrain that is announced at the beginning and returns in the middle of the poem and again at the end, the whole employing only two rhymes. In comparison with both her predecessors and her contemporaries, Christine excelled in this form. The variety of her poems is truly impressive, from examples where there are only two syllables to a line to others written in decasyllables. Sixty-three rondeaux appear among her poems, the majority having twelve lines arranged in stanzas of varying length. In the fourteenth century, such rondeaux were rarely employed to treat serious matters, yet Christine managed to achieve considerable skill and grace with the form. The first of these rondeaux expresses, like so many of her poems, the sorrows of widowhood:

I am a widow lone, in black arrayed,

With sorrowful countenance, simply clad.
In great distress and with an air so sad
I bear this sorrow now upon me laid.

It is not right that I should be dismayed,
Full of hot tears and with a tongue of lead,
I am a widow lone, in black arrayed.

Since I have lost my love, by Death betrayed,
Grief has set in, and to perdition led
All my good days, and thus all joy has fled.
In disarray have all my fortunes strayed—
I am a widow lone, in black arrayed.[14]

A somewhat less melancholy rondeau expresses the sentiments of a disappointed lover who complains about the moonlight that disturbs his clandestine meeting with his lady:

Oh moon, you shine too lengthily!
I lose those lovely gifts through you
Which Love prepares for lovers true.

Your brightness wounds so readily
My poor heart, where desire flames blue,
Oh moon, you shine too lengthily!

Because of you, quite drearily,
I lose, and my beloved too,
So we revile you thus, we two,
Oh moon! you shine too lengthily![15]

A rendezvous with a more fortunate outcome is suggested in another brief poem:

Friend, come to me again tonight
The hour I said the other day.

Then in our joy we can delight,
Friend come to me again tonight.

The one who makes our sorrowful plight
Will not be here; do not delay,
Friend, come to me again tonight.[16]

In spite of her success with the rondeau form, it was the ballade, the most popular form of her day, that attracted Christine the most. Guillaume de Machaut had popularized it around the middle of the fourteenth century, and his own ballades show a great versatility. The basic form consists of three stanzas with a refrain repeated at the end of each, but when the ballade was adopted by poets who were not musicians, an envoi of three or four verses was sometimes added after the third stanza for the purpose of directing the poem to some prince or other specific person in a sort of dedication.

Christine was evidently attracted by the possibilities for variation offered by this form, for she rarely composed two ballades according to the same pattern. By the time she wrote her final series, *One Hundred Ballades of a Lover and His Lady,* she had learned to vary the length of the verses to suggest the changing moods of the lovers whose joys and deceptions are set forth in a continuing dialogue between them.[17] On the whole, however, Christine seems to have favored the decasyllabic verse for her ballades.

Inevitably, she was also influenced by the poetry written by others, Machaut's 207 ballades in honor of ladies, or Deschamps's *Cent Ballades,* yet she was probably inspired even more by *Le Livre des Cent Ballades,* composed by a group of well-known courtiers around 1390 and inspired by a debate over the question of whether a knight should remain faithful to one lady or should be the lover of many. This collection enjoyed a great popularity and was undoubtedly known to Christine as she started to compose her own cycle of a hundred ballades.[18]

This first cycle of ballades is especially interesting in that it announces so many of the themes that were to recur throughout the greater part of her career as a writer: the trials of widowhood, of solitude; the dangers of "courtly love" for any woman, no matter how innocent the intention; the sorrows of lovers separated by circumstances beyond their control or by the tongues of gossips. Other poems indicate that she had already embarked upon the course of reading that would shape her later, more ambitious works, for there are references to Fortune's wheel, to the *Consolation* of Boethius, to the Trojan War, and to the sort of mythology elaborated in the *Ovide Moralisé,* the medieval version of Ovid's *Metamorphoses* that inspired, for instance, her Ballade LXXXVI:

The gods and goddesses, those great

Servants of Love, were diligent,
As Ovid tells, to celebrate
Love's rites—and suffered discontent
And woes of love. But true intent
And faith they kept, left none aggrieved,
If ancient fables be believed.

They left Olympus for some mate
Of lowly earth, in their descent
Impetuous to participate
In earthly joys, with quick consent
Embracing them, indifferent
To costs of all such zeal achieved
If ancient fables be believed.

Delights of love could subjugate
Enchantress and nymph; immortals spent
Time, strength and wealth immoderate
On maids and shepherds, earthward went
Bestowing boons munificent
On those whose favors they received
If ancient fables be believed.

So ladies, lords, submit, assent
To love, nor seek to be reprieved
From service proved so excellent
If ancient fables be believed.[19]

Whereas the greater part of the ballades were inspired by the conventions of courtly love, others are moralizing or reflective in nature, the most personal being those inspired by the anguish of widowhood. Christine also reveals her religious or moral convictions on various subjects, her attitude toward certain persons or events—her belief, for instance, in the superiority of spiritual values over material ones and their vulnerability to Fortune's whims, her ideas on the attributes of true chivalry, and, most exceptional for her day, the joys of a happy marriage as opposed to the dangers of extramarital affairs in the name of courtly love. Such expressions of individual rather than conventional emotions were not unknown, but at the end of the fourteenth century they were still rare and even unique in lyrics written by an intelligent and sensitive woman.

In common with later woman poets, Christine was more inclined to describe love's ending than its beginning, although she does provide a good description of the early stages of love in the first twenty-five poems of her *One Hundred Ballades of a Lover and His Lady,* where she examines the emotions of a lady who first resists and then succumbs to the advances of her lover. It was her conviction that society obliged a woman to pay far too high a price for any momentary pleasure experienced from love outside marriage; disillusionment was the only possible end to such an affair. This was a theme she treated repeatedly, developing it at particular length in this final ballade sequence, after giving it importance in *"Le Dit de la Pastoure"* ("The Shepherdess' Tale"), *Le Livre du Duc des Vrais Amants (The Book of the Duke of True Lovers),* and using it as the basis for several chapters in *The Book of the Three Virtues.* It led, logically enough, to the idea that the only possible love for a virtuous woman, certainly for a married woman, was the sort of platonic admiration she knew about through Dante's love for Beatrice and possibly through Petrarch's love for Laura. This point is made quite clear in *Le Débat de Deux Amants (The Debate of Two Lovers)* as well as at the end of *The Book of the Duke of True Lovers.* Such love might well have been the ideal expressed by certain early troubadours, but it had turned into something quite different at the court dominated by the lusty Isabeau of Bavaria and the all-too-charming Louis of Orleans. Christine's concept of love was, of course, the ideal popularized in France a century later by the Neo-Platonists, as well as through the translation of Baldassare Castiglione's *Book of the Courtier.* In the meantime, some of her ideas were taken up by Louis of Orleans' son, the poet Charles of Orleans, in poems where he describes his renunciation of love, his *Départie d'Amours (Farewell to Love),* and by Alain Chartier in his *Belle Dame sans Merci (Fair Lady without Mercy),* a lady whose ancestry is assuredly to be found in the pages of Christine's poetry.[20]

Between the two ballade cycles, there was a group of poems entitled *Autres Ballades (Ballades on Various Subjects),* fifty-three in all and generally poems of circumstance, such as the one in which in the spring of 1404 Christine mourns the death of the duke of Burgundy. Other poems were destined to accompany manuscripts of her various works, which she presented to patrons as New Year's gifts in keeping with a custom of the times. Through the revisions of this group of poems, it is possible to follow Christine's poetic progress during the early years of the fifteenth century. For example, an early ballade addressed to the French constable Louis de Sancerre is dropped in manuscripts copied after his death in 1403, whereas others, addressed to the young duke of Bourbon, can be dated after his succession to the title in 1410.[21] It was not unusual for poets to revise their works, and Christine and her contemporaries had above all the example of Petrarch, whose perpetual revisions of his writings ended only with his death.[22]

The period when she was putting together her first poetry collections also marked the beginning of a new stage in her development. She began to compose a series of longer poems, and this, in her own mind, represented the beginning of her real career as a writer. By the end of 1399 she was undoubtedly nearing the completion of her elaborate mythological commentary entitled *L'Epistre d'Othéa la Deesse, que Elle Envoya a Hector de Troye Quant Il Estoit en l'Age de Quinze Ans (The Letter of the Goddess Othéa, which She Sent to Hector of Troy When He Was Fifteen Years Old)*. But the gods and goddesses of Olympus had not only appeared in her early Ballade LVI, they had been present as well in a troop in the *Epistre au Dieu d'Amour (Cupid's Letter)* dated May 1, 1399, one of the poems that might have been composed for some sort of poetic contest.[23] Christine very amusingly presents herself here as a royal secretary at Cupid's court, developing the fiction that she had been requested to read an official letter from this sovereign in which he banishes from his presence all disloyal and deceitful lovers. The letter, she tells us, was a response to a complaint that he had received that some men at his court were heartlessly betraying women. The idea is elaborated that just such deceit as this had been the cause of many of the world's ills, beginning with the Trojan War. It is further pointed out that present-day lovers are neither as faithful nor as admirable as those of an earlier time.

This point gave Christine the opportunity to draw an amusing sketch of some vain young courtiers who, sparing no intimate detail, are given to boasting of their amorous exploits in Parisian taverns and even at the court. They are all too quick to slander women, whether with justification or not:

> There are women vilely named,
> And often without cause are blamed,
> And even those of noble race,
> However fair and full of grace.
> Lord, what company, what talk—
> Women's honor they freely mock.[24]

Christine was not alone in calling attention to such lack of gallantry. At Easter of the same year, thirteen knights had joined together to found a new chivalric order devoted to the defense of women's honor and to give special aid to poor widows and others in distress. This order, the *Escu*

Vert a la Dame Blanche (Green Shield with the White Lady), was founded on the initiative of the indomitable Boucicaut, marshal of France, who had just returned to Paris after a series of adventures in the Middle East. Evidently, Christine knew of this order, for one of her ballades (*Autres Ballades* XII) is devoted to praising it.[25]

Christine obviously agreed with Boucicaut and his companions in their opinion that far too many men were given to slandering women, and she was inclined to blame this tendency on the second part of *The Romance of the Rose,* written by Jean de Meun, as well as on Ovid's *Art of Love.* Her chief scorn, however, was reserved for Jean de Meun, of whom she wrote:

> Jean de Meun in his Romance of the Rose,
> What a long affair! What a tiresome pose!
> What sciences profound, both clear and obscure,
> Devised for many a great adventure—
> So many people either begged or bribed,
> Such far-fetched devices sought out and tried—
> All just to seduce an innocent maid,
> Such is the end of this silly charade:
> For frail defense, why such a great assault?[26]

Christine does not miss the opportunity to point out that if these books had been written by women, they would have had quite a different tone, and that indeed men would do well to cherish women, to whom they owe their existence and without whom their life in this world would be a dreary affair. Women are the source of many of men's pleasures.

> A woman brings joy to a normal man:
> As his mother, his sister, the one most dear—
> As his enemy she seldom gives cause for fear. . . .[27]

Therefore, Cupid determines to banish from his court all false lovers, and the gods of the forests and mountains are assembled there to bear witness to his proclamation. As Christine calls their roll, one can feel an early breath of the Renaissance blowing over the scene. There is also a glimpse of the new direction her writing would take, leading to the debate over *The Romance of the Rose* and works of a more didactic character.

Cupid's Letter must have enjoyed an immediate success, for it was soon translated into English, albeit in a slightly adapted form, by Chaucer's disciple Thomas Hoccleve.[28] It has often been assumed that the poem provided the opening volley in the debate over *The Romance of the Rose,* which before long would engage the interest of French intellectuals.

Three subsequent poems of this transitional period are devoted to the sort of psychological debate concerning problems of love that provided a form of social diversion from the days of the troubadours in the thirteenth century to the literary salons of the seventeenth and eighteenth. It is probable that Christine's inspiration for these poems came from the interests of the Orleans court, which she was frequenting at the time. The rules of the game had been codified long before by Andreas Capellanus in his treatise *De Amore (The Art of Courtly Love)* at the beginning of the thirteenth century.[29] Questions concerning the dilemmas in which lovers might find themselves were discussed and then presented to some person or some group of persons for arbitration. In the fourteenth century, it became stylish to appeal to a person of importance to give his opinion on some problem or another, suggesting that he was particularly competent to judge questions of love. Guillaume de Machaut set this precedent by appealing first to his patron the king of Bohemia and later to the king of Navarre, both of them giving judgments that formed part of the poems in question.[30] In the first of Christine's poems, *The Debate of Two Lovers,* the duke of Orleans is invited to decide the issues discussed, although there is no mention of what he decided. In *Le Livre des Trois Jugements (The Book of Three Judgments),* the appeal is made to Jean de Werchin, the seneschal of Hainaut, an amateur poet who was one of the ministers of the Parisian Court of Love. Christine had already praised him in *The Debate of Two Lovers* as worthy of being compared with Tristan, Lancelot, or Arthur of Brittany. One of her ballades, written in 1402, celebrates his prowess in arms.[31]

It has sometimes been assumed that the third poem of the group, the *"Dit de Poissy"* ("The Tale of Poissy") was also dedicated to Werchin because the knight to whom this poem (dated April 1400) is dedicated was absent from France at the time and it has been supposed that Werchin was on a pilgrimage to Santiago. That pilgrimage, however, did not take place until the end of the summer of 1402, and there is no evidence that he was away from France in 1400.[32] Either the marshal Boucicaut or his lieutenant Jean de Châteaumorand would seem a better candidate for this dedication. Christine knew both men, and in the spring of 1400 both were in Constantinople defending the city against the advancing armies of the Turkish sultan Bayazid. Either would have justified the description at the beginning of the poem: "Good knight, valiant, full of wisdom. . . ."

A particularly attractive aspect of these poems, quite aside from the love problems presented, is their settings, which reflect the life of Parisian society as Christine knew it. The poems' opening vignettes not only provide a framework for the debates, but also recall the illustrations of certain contemporary manuscripts, notably the Boccaccio translations made in 1402. Their realism is sufficient to make the discussions of love, in spite of their inherent artificiality, appear to be taking place spontaneously.

In *The Debate of Two Lovers,* the setting is a large Parisian house, not necessarily that of the duke of Orleans, as has sometimes been claimed, yet an elegant establishment where the guests, the music, and the decor have all been arranged for an enjoyable evening.[33] Christine is content to sit apart and watch others dance until she happens to fall into conversation with a knight who is also keeping to himself. Eventually, they are joined by a charming squire, seemingly the life of the party, and the three become involved in the inevitable discussion of the nature of love. In order to converse more at their ease, they decide to go into the garden, Christine prudently inviting another lady to join them. When all have seated themselves in a leafy bower, the charm of which Christine describes with relish, the conversation continues. The knight, a man of mature years, expresses his view that love is a snare, an emotion capable of turning the wisest of men into fools and almost inevitably leading to sorrow. He cites the examples of a series of ill-starred lovers, not only Paris, but also Pyramus, Leander, Achilles, and from more recent times, the Chatelain of Coucy. When Christine's companion is invited to give her opinion, she confesses that she is not moved by the knight's complaints, insisting that such tales of woe are more often than not invented and have little to do with reality. The first in a series of women from Christine's pen who are not in agreement with contemporary conventions concerning love, she elaborates the idea already expressed in *Cupid's Letter* that present-day lovers are not what lovers formerly were. They have been led astray by their reading of romances, especialy *The Romance of the Rose*. She agrees with the knight, however, about the blindness of love, thus reflecting a view point set forth in the *Moralized Ovid* and, more important, in Boccaccio's *De Genealogia Deorum (On the Genealogy of the Gods)*.

When it is the squire's turn to speak, he says that he finds love an agreeable and attractive emotion that enhances a man's valor. Loyalty and courtesy are its indispensable requisites, and he cannot imagine how true lovers could exist without these qualities. If men are sometimes driven to excesses in love, their own folly is to blame rather than the nature of love itself, just as it is not the fault of the wine if too much of it is drunk. In his turn, the squire cites examples of lovers who have been worthy of their ladies and whose lives have been enhanced by their love: Lancelot, Jason, Florimont, and Arthur of Brittany, among others. He, too, turns to more recent times, praising Bertrand DuGuesclin, Boucicaut's father, Othon de Grandson, and after them, Jean de Châteaumorand, who at that very moment is defending the city of Constantinople against the Turks. He concludes by mentioning the names, several of them contemporaries, some of them knights, to whom Christine has dedicated poems or mentioned in her other writings: Charles d'Albret, Jean de Werchin, and Clignet de Brabant. It is evident that he is not speaking merely of the subjective aspects of love, but rather of the sentiment that makes a brave knight able and willing to perform his duties well.

When the squire falls silent, the knight, considerably older and more experienced, is inclined to mock him, yet he ends by admitting that there is a certain novelty in the young man's attitude. Nevertheless, he continues to insist that love is impossible without jealousy, an attitude that irritates the squire, who interrupts to declare that even if they should continue to argue all night, he still believes that the true lover is joyful because of the pleasure that the experience of loving brings to him. Jealousy is to be shunned at all costs; one should be prepared to give one's heart freely and should certainly not bargain about its possession.

As there seems to be no reconciling their points of view, the knight and the squire agree to submit their differences to a third person. When they are unable even to agree on a judge, Christine proposes the duke of Orleans. Both assent to this and beg Christine to write a poem about their debate for presentation to the duke. Christine demurs with the humility expected of writers of her day, but in the end she naturally agrees to do what they ask. This leads to the conclusion of the poem, a graceful dedication to the duke of Orleans.

In *The Book of Three Judgments*, three problems are proposed for the seneschal of Hainaut's consideration. A lady who has been forsaken by her lover consoles herself by loving another man who proves more loyal. Is she false to the first through loving the second? A knight who has given up hope of seeing the lady he loves because she has been shut away by a jealous husband is in despair. Can he eventually permit himself a new love? A young woman is forsaken by a nobleman who aspires to the love of a lady of greater rank than she. When he is rejected by the haughty lady and seeks to return to her, should she forgive him? Christine concludes this poem by explaining that she has agreed to help these unhappy lovers find a judge for their cases because the wounded should always seek the services of a good doctor. She appeals therefore to the seneschal of Hainaut, Jean de Werchin, to give his opinion.

It is not entirely true, as has been contended, that there is no record of the seneschal's response, that is to say, his opinion on the subject of loyalty, the common theme of the three cases.[34] It was not until 1404, however, that Werchin found time to express his views. This he did in a poem entitled *"Le Songe de la Barge"* ("Dream of the Barge"), written while he was marooned for four months in the port of Brest, waiting to take part in an action intended to support the Welsh rebel Owen Glendower in his guerrilla warfare against Henry IV of England. This poem gives every evidence of being a reply to Christine, for it imitates the poetic form of Christine's *Book of Three Judgments* and makes use of the sort of framework she favored in her narrative poems.

In spite of the limitations of Werchin's poetic talent, "Dream of the Barge" reflects a realistic outlook and an element of common sense altogether appropriate to the personality of an extroverted knight, which a notable warrior like Werchin must surely have been. A similar spirit emanates from Werchin's advice to his squire Guillebert de Lannoy, with whom he exchanged a series of forty-six ballades on the same theme: one should not persist in loving another against the beloved's wishes. If a lady accepts a knight as her "servant," he should serve her loyally; if he is rejected, he should choose another object for his attention. His insistence on common sense and *courtoisie* throughout reveal a nobility of character that does him credit. His imitation of Christine's poem as well as his response to the problem she proposed are an indication of the regard in which she was held by her contemporaries, even during the early part of her career.

In the third poem of the group devoted to love questions, "The Tale of Poissy," Christine recounts a debate that arose between two traveling companions who accompanied her on an excursion to the Abbey of Poissy, where she went to visit her daughter one spring day.[35] The question posed is which of the two is to be more pitied, a lady whose lover has been a prisoner of the Turks since the French defeat at Nicopolis or a knight who has been rejected by a lady he cannot forget and whom he continues to love in spite of her disdain. The issue is discussed on the return voyage from Poissy, the first part of the poem being devoted to a description of

Christine's visit to the abbey, where her daughter has been a nun for several years. The poem dwells on the pleasures of the ride through the forest, the visitors' reception at the royal abbey, and Christine's own great joy at being reunited with her daughter for a few brief hours. The travelers spend a pleasant night at an inn near the convent where they dine well, drink wine sent for the occasion by the prioress, and pass the evening singing, dancing, and discussing examples of true valor as represented by the most celebrated knights they know. In the morning, they take leave of the hospitable nuns with regret and start on their journey back to Paris. At this point, the stories of the two unfortunate lovers unfold. The poem ends on a charmingly domestic note when Christine invites her two companions to dine with her at her home. In the meantime, she has agreed to write a poem requesting the judgment of a well-known knight, whose merits have been discussed the night before. A member of the group agrees to carry Christine's poem to the place where this knight is to be found, described as "overseas" and suggesting the possibility that the poem was to be sent to either Boucicaut or Châteaumorand in Constantinople.

Throughout the poem one is impressed by Christine's ability to observe and describe scenes of nature with sensitivity and relish, a trait that can be compared favorably with the miniaturists who, in the same period, were developing the ability to depict landscape. A fragile and highly stylized world is revealed, yet Christine has not failed to catch its essential charm.

A somewhat different aspect of nature forms the background for the last of Christine's narrative poems, which also departs from the pattern of the "judgments" and appears to be another sort of poetic experiment. This is *"Le Dit de la Pastour"* ("The Shepherdess' Tale"). Dated 1403, it could not have been a part of the first collection of Christine's poetry, which was made the year before. However, it was added on additional folios at the end of what appears to be the earliest manuscript.[36]

In the opening lines of the poem, Christine suggests that she is writing at the request of some personage whose desires she cannot refuse, but there is no clue to this patron's identity. She further says that the poem has a hidden meaning, which can be interpreted to imply that the characters would be recognizable to her readers, or perhaps the reference is merely to a definition of poetry as allegory, an idea she had already developed in *Othéa's Letter to Hector*.

The poem follows the pastoral tradition, which had already seen a

great flowering in the thirteenth century and whose popularity at the end
of the fourteenth was undoubtedly enhanced by Jean de Meun's association
of the shepherd world with the Golden Age, promising an eternal spring
to all who obeyed Nature's command to live freely and spontaneously.
Christine may have been protesting Jean de Meun's moral values in her
poem, or, possibly, calling attention to the growing artificiality, and even
falseness, of aristocratic society. Both concerns can be found elsewhere in
her writing. She may also have been attracted by the new enthusiasm for
Virgil's *Bucolics* and *Eclogues* in the Parisian circles she frequented. A
manuscript of these two poems, copied and illustrated in Paris the same
year she wrote her poem, is still in existence.[37] It belonged to an official
in the household of the duke of Berry, who subsequently had a volume
copied for his own library.

Christine had ample reason to think that a pastoral poem might find
a sympathetic audience, but she did not blindly follow her models. Instead
she made the form her own, giving it an original twist. Indeed, having
the tale told by a shepherdess rather than a shepherd was a novelty.
Particularly interesting, also, is the realism that pervades the conventional
framework of "The Shepherdess' Tale," especially where her description
of the life of the shepherds is concerned. She was well acquainted with
Jean de Brie's guide for sheep-raising, *Le Bon Berger*, which had been
commissioned by Charles V for the royal library in 1379.[38] It provided
a complete portrait of the medieval shepherd, prescribing his duties month
by month, and included information on weather prediction and the virtues
of herbs, as well as advice on necessary clothing, diet, and equipment.
Whereas Virgilian shepherds do little more than return their sheep to the
fold in the evening, Christine's milk the ewes, change the hay in the
manger, treat the animals for mange, and attend to other sorts of daily
tasks. To do this, they are equipped with the indispensable tools for their
work—crook and pouch, knife, shears, awl, needle and thread. They not
only spin and make cheese, they also picnic in the meadows, eating
flamiche, a tart made from leeks that is still a specialty of the Artois region
where the family of Christine's husband originated. They dance and sing
and play games in a way that recalls the more exuberant miniatures of
The Annunciation to the Shepherds in contemporary Books of Hours.
Although Christine's shepherds do not inhabit an earthly paradise, their
manner of life seems attractive and is enlivened by the birds and flowers
that are a natural part of their surroundings.

Equally realistic is the analysis of the emotions of the shepherdess

Marotile as she falls in love with a courtier who chances upon her in the forest. Although their love remains innocent for a long time and the young nobleman is basically kind and honorable, in the long run Marotile's sorrows far outweigh her joys. She suffers fears that he will abandon her, or that he will prefer a lady of his own social sphere. Her friendship with him separates her from her companions, who do not hesitate to suspect the worst of her relationship with the elegant stranger. When he finally asks to kiss her, she is quite incapable of concealing the strength of her love for him and inevitably gives in completely to his desires. For a time, they are happy in their love, and he continues to be faithful and compassionate, but she cannot avoid being jealous of the part of his life unknown to her. Eventually, when he must go away to fight in a distant land in pursuit of renown, as was expected of knights, Marotile can only suffer from his absence and is now quite incapable of enjoying the companionship of her old friends. A joyful reunion follows his return, but at the poem's end he has been gone again for a year, and Marotile doubts that he will ever return. Although she continues to love him and to cherish her memories of him, her sorrow is destroying her life. She concludes:

> Without him I've no care
> To live; the shepherd he
> Without whom there's no life for me.[39]

The young woman's sorrow is portrayed with delicacy and understanding: it is the intrusion of courtly values and ideas on her natural world that disturbs and eventually destroys it. To be sure, the young nobleman does not bring about this disaster intentionally. He is truly attracted to the shepherdess and her world, just as she is charmed by the appearance and courtly manners of the young man. Yet he cannot abandon his own world, and soon the normal life of the shepherdess is impoverished by her own emotional involvement. Although the best elements of the two worlds are fused momentarily, ultimately they prove incompatible. Christine does not choose to solve the problem by producing some noble antecedents for the shepherdess, and so the lover's departure marks the end of pastoral peace for her.

By the time Christine had finished "The Shepherdess' Tale," the last of her series of long poems dealing with the same courtly themes that characterize her shorter poetry, her interests had already turned to new forms of writing. She did not entirely give up writing society poetry, as can be seen from the *One Hundred Ballades of a Lover and His Lady,* written several years later. This cycle presents a story of love followed by disillusionment similar in many respects to her pastoral poem. But by 1403 she had already written, in quite a different vein, one of her most successful works, *Othéa's Letter to Hector,* and by the end of the year she completed a long allegorical poem entitled *Le Chemin de Long Estude (The Long Road of Learning).*

Reason Speaks to the Lover

Jean de Meun Instructed by Divine Grace

4

❦

The Quarrel of the Rose

No aspect of Christine's career has attracted more attention than her part in the first recorded literary quarrel in France. It has even been supposed that she instigated it with her *Cupid's Letter*, and that in this capacity she acted as the forerunner of all subsequent movements in behalf of women's rights. The truth of the matter is, however, somewhat less picturesque, although no less surprising when considered in the context of the times. Instead, it was Jean de Montreuil, one of the royal secretaries, who inspired the debate in the spring of 1401, which basically concerned the literary merits of Jean de Meun's part in *The Romance of the Rose*. The element of feminism was injected into the debate by Christine, who was prepared to admit some of the literary qualities of Jean de Meun's poem, but who had already deplored his attitude toward women and what she had called, in *Cupid's Letter*, written two years earlier, his bad influence on many contemporary men. It was this feministic aspect of the debate that caught popular attention, since to find a woman rising in defense of her sex against the sort of attack that was traditional throughout the Middle Ages was quite unheard of. Although other issues were involved in the quarrel, the attitude toward women continued to engender animus, not only in the fifteenth and sixteenth centuries, but right up to the present as well. Indeed, not long ago, a critic saw fit to attack Christine as an hysterical woman and a prude for her role in the affair.[1]

As far as Christine's literary development is concerned, it is more important to view her participation in the debate as marking a shift in her activities from purely courtly circles to broader contacts, notably with a group of intellectuals, some of them former colleagues of her husband's in the royal chancellery. In a certain sense, the debate over *The Romance of the Rose* was an outgrowth of the enthusiasm these Paris intellectuals were beginning to show for Italian humanism. At the end of the fourteenth century, a group of educated young men, primarily associated with the chancellery or the University of Paris, was filled with admiration for the writings of Petrarch and Boccaccio and also attempted to imitate their much-vaunted interest in the Latin classics. Some of these Frenchmen were in correspondence with such prominent Italians as Coluccio Salutati, their counterpart in the Florentine chancellery; or they were acquainted with the Italian merchants and bankers who had established themselves in Paris, in some cases seemingly purveying books as well as the silks frequently used for book bindings; or perhaps they had rubbed elbows with the duke of Milan's agents who arrived in Paris on diplomatic missions such as making arrangements for the marriage between the duke's daughter Valentina Visconti and Louis of Orleans in 1387. Among this last group was Ambrogio Migli, who remained in Paris to become the duke of Orleans's secretary and counselor.[2]

A number of manuscripts of the period bear witness to the interest of this group in what was going on in Italy. Frenchmen were inspired to translate Livy and Cicero and, eventually, Boccaccio, and also to write letters and verses in classical Latin. Jean de Montreuil was a prolific writer of Latin letters in which he, like his friends, aspired to cultivate a good classical style, despite the fact that Petrarch had already created a certain amount of bad feelings by referring to these French efforts as barbaric.[3]

One curious trait of the Italian humanists, who considered themselves talented orators as well as writers, was their enjoyment of debates on various subjects, such as comparisons of the moral qualities of Scipio and Caesar, the relative value of noble birth and personal merit in the conduct of life, or the virtues of law and medicine as professions.[4] In view of these Italian models, it is not surprising to find a literary debate attracting considerable attention in Paris shortly after 1400.

The Romance of the Rose was scarcely new. Written in the thirteenth century, it had enjoyed a success unmatched by any other work in the Middle Ages, and it continued to be read and to exercise an influence on its readers' minds and imaginations for nearly three centuries. The first 4,000 lines of the poem, written by Guillaume de Lorris around 1236, tells of a love affair conducted according to the best precepts of courtly love, but it is a psychological account, experienced in a dream world inhabited by allegorical characters. The poet, a young man of twenty, falls asleep on a May morning and dreams that he discovers a walled garden. The gate is opened to him by a young woman named Idleness, a friend of the garden's owner, Pleasure. Another lady, Courtoisie, invites the young man to join a dance that is in progress. He then discovers a magic fountain that catches his attention by the reflection of a rosebush, and he is attracted especially by one rose that he longs to pluck, although he is deterred by the thorns surrounding it. At that very moment, he is wounded by the golden arrows shot at him by the God of Love. He finds himself in Love's power and agrees to obey his commandments. These amount to a complete "Art of Love" as the poet has explained in the opening lines:

> And if a man or maid shall ever ask
> By what name I would christen the romance
> Which now I start, I will this answer make:
> "The Romance of the Rose it is, and it enfolds
> Within its compass all the Art of Love."
> The subject is both good and new. God grant
> That she for whom I write with favor look
> Upon my work, for she so worthy is
> Of love that well she may be called the Rose.[5]

The rest of the first part of the poem recounts the poet's efforts to pluck the rose, assisted by such allies as Fair Welcome, Hope, and Friend, but deterred by Danger, Slander, Shame, and Fear. Venus offers some additional help that allows him to kiss the Rose, but Jealousy immediately builds a castle around it, shutting up Fair Welcome in a tower where he can no longer help the poet. At this point, the first part breaks off, apparently unfinished.

Jean de Meun's continuation of more than 17,000 additional verses was written some forty years later. A philosopher more than a poet, he belonged to another generation as well as to another social world. He was less interested in the actions of the characters than in their ideas, and they therefore show themselves to be rather argumentative, transforming the simple allegory of courtly love into social satire. Similarly, the garden of love turns into a forum for debate on many subjects only loosely related to the subject of love. Indeed, they often stand in the way of love. Reason, for instance, makes a long speech intended to turn the Lover against love, insisting that friendship is a more important human relationship. In the course of his discourse, he makes remarks about the human reproductive organs that the Lover finds offensive. To Reasons's insistence that God created these bodily parts, he replies that God did not create the words, which he finds offensive in polite conversation. Friend then advises opportunism in relations with women, who are seldom virtuous, debauchery being the least of their crimes. The fine clothes of women do not really enhance them, for a dungheap covered with a silken cloth is still a dungheap.

Persisting in his quest in spite of such advice, the Lover decides to accept the help of Deceit in attacking Jealousy's castle. Deceit lectures him at length on the prevalence of hyprocrisy in society, especially in religious matters. When the Old Woman who has been guarding Fair Welcome is captured, she freely offers her advice on love. Men are deceivers and unworthy of trust, so a woman's main objective should be to amass as much money as she can manage from her admirers. She also tells how to deceive a jealous husband.

Finally, a plan is devised for storming the castle where the Rose is imprisoned. The God of Love appeals to his mother, Venus, and to Nature, who works unceasingly at her forge to preserve the human race from extinction. Nature is assisted in her work by Genius, who also has views to express on the deceitful nature of women. But Nature agrees to help Venus seize the castle, so Genius carries the message for her to the God of Love, taking the opportunity to deliver a long speech on the necessity of continuing the species by whatever means necessary. So in the final assault on the castle, Venus shoots an arrow that sets the interior on fire, and the Lover, disguised as a pilgrim, is able to enter and pluck the Rose. In the final scene, Jean de Meun is not troubled by the stylized delicacy that marked Guillaume de Lorris's beginning; his purpose is to call attention to the artificiality and falseness of the whole system of courtly love.

Perhaps the aspect of the long poem that particularly intrigued its readers was precisely that it represented so effectively the complex mentality of a society evolving from the idealistic, chivalric spirit to a different one dominated by realism and logic. The fact that the work belonged to the tradition of Arts of Love that went back to Ovid had the effect of attracting both those who were devoted to idealistic concepts of love and also others, more intellectual, who were impressed by the classical tradition it represented.[6]

Jean de Meun was a graduate of the University of Paris with a scholarly turn of mind, and a great passion for teaching. His culture was quite evidently the product of the encyclopedic spirit that dominated certain universities of his day. He was also a member of the rising middle class who saw a need for revising the increasingly decadent aristocratic ideals of chivalry, courtesy, and asceticism expressed in the part of the poem written by Guillaume de Lorris.

In this respect, Jean de Meun's part is more a refutation than a continuation of the first part, and it is evident that he intends for the Lover to have the Rose in the end, by fair means or foul. Following the original plot in a desultory way, he invents a series of new allegories and replaces narrative with discouse in the long speeches by Reason, Nature, and Genius, all of whom advise the Lover in his quest but at the same time delay his approach to the Rose. These allegorical characters also give Jean de Meun scope to develop his ideas on a range of subjects, with the result that his part of the poem becomes a *summa* of the sort so popular in his day. It was this aspect of the poem that appealed greatly to Jean de Montreuil and his friends.

Until recently, almost all knowledge of the discussion of Jean de Meun's merits that took place between 1401 and 1403 was based on Christine's account of it. At the beginning of 1402, apparently with the aim of giving publicity to what had until then been a more or less private discussion, she gathered together a group of documents intended to support her own point of view and presented it to the French queen. In an introductory letter, she begged Isabeau of Bavaria for her support in the defense of women against so-called learned men who had been belittling them, as she puts it, "in a manner which it scarcely seems praiseworthy to permit or support."[7] She also addressed a second letter and copy of the documents to Guillaume de Tignonville, provost of Paris and one of the ministers of the Court of Love, which pretended to be devoted to honoring women. Tignonville was also known as the translator of the *Dicta Philosophorum* compiled a century earlier by John of Procida, a Sicilian doctor and statesman.[8] This *Dits Moraulx des Philosophes,* as Tignonville's translation was called, enjoyed considerable popularity. Christine herself had already used it as a source for her writings and obviously thought Tignonville's judgment was worth having. It is interesting to observe, furthermore, that she was appealing for support to both literary and official circles through Tignonville and the queen.

According to her account, the debate grew out of a conversation she had had with Jean de Montreuil, at which an unidentified third person was also present. When Jean de Montreuil lauded the exceptional merits of Jean de Meun's part in *The Romance of the Rose,* Christine had replied that, saving his grace, she did not agree that the poem was worthy of such extravagant praise. The tone of Christine's account is polite and moderate, and the scene described recalls the beginning of *The Debate of Two Lovers.*[9]

More recently, further light has been thrown on the background of the debate by the publication of Jean de Montreuil's letters, including several referring to his part in the controversy.[10] It becomes evident that it was in April 1401 that Gontier Col, another royal secretary known for his humanistic interests, had persuaded his colleague to read *The Romance of the Rose.* (It is known that Gontier Col had been interested several years earlier in Jean de Meun's translation of the love letters exchanged by Abelard and Heloise, which could have led quite naturally to his interest in *The Romance of the Rose.*) Around the time that Col introduced his friend Montreuil to the poem, he was one of the diplomats involved in negotiations for the return of Isabelle of France to her father's court after the death of her husband, Richard II. During the same period, Christine was trying to arrange her own son's return from England, where the new king, Henry IV, would have been glad to retain him at his court. This combination of circumstances suggests that Christine and Gontier Col might have had some contact with each other with regard to the return of Christine's son to Paris.

In any case, the conversation between Christine and Jean de Montreuil, in the presence of someone who is referred to only as a "notable cleric" and who seems to have shared Christine's view of Jean de Meun, must have taken place in the late spring of 1401 because by the end of May Jean de Montreuil had sent both Christine and Gontier Col copies of his treatise, written in French, on the merits of Jean de Meun's poem. He also sent a copy of the treatise, with an accompanying letter in Latin, to his friend Pierre d'Ailly, the bishop of Cambrai, who may indeed have been the "notable cleric" in question.

Apparently, Christine replied to Jean de Montreuil before the middle of the summer. Her response was primarily concerned with expressing her support for the other person who had taken part in the original conversation, and she did this in a calm tone. Her tone changed only after others had entered the debate.

The most important of these other participants, from Christine's standpoint, was the chancellor of the University of Paris, Jean Gerson, another of the early French humanists. On August 25 he preached a sermon in which he seemed to be taking Jean de Montreuil to task for his views.[11] It was a custom for professors and students of the College of Navarre to meet together to celebrate the feast of Saint Louis and to hear a sermon delivered by one of their members. In 1401 it was Gerson who spoke, taking as a text "Consider the lilies of the field. . . ." In discussing the attributes necessary to a good teacher, he spoke of the matter of suitable language for such a person, making reference to his opinion about Jean de Meun's freedom of language in referring to physical and sexual matters. Perhaps this served as a warning to Jean de Montreuil, for he had nothing further to say to Christine on the subject, although he did continue the polemic with a lawyer of his acquaintance. It was Gontier Col who took up the discussion of Jean de Meun with Christine.

On his return to Paris in August, Col had learned of the affair from Jean de Montreuil, who wrote him a letter urging his support in the debate. So it was that Col wrote a letter to Christine on September 13, asking for a copy of her reply to Jean de Montreuil, which he had not been able to lay his hands on, and proposing an exchange of letters on the subject.[12] He expressed his astonishment that she should wish to detract from the reputation of such a learned man as Jean de Meun and suggested that she was merely the mouthpiece for others who did not dare to speak openly, adding that he was enclosing a copy of a short poem by Jean de Meun and promising to reply to whatever she wrote, no matter how busy he might be. The tone of Col's letter is noticeably arch, and there is a distinct suggestion that he is taking part in a literary game. It is true that the royal secretary was a great admirer of Jean de Meun, perhaps rather more because of the latter's translation of Boethius and his *Testament* than his part in *The Romance of the Rose,* for Col valued Jean de Meun as a link between French literature and the classical past, but, quite evidently, Col was also tempted by the idea of an exhange of letters, a debate in the style so favored by Italian humanists. His letter was signed in the presence of three other disciples of Jean de Meun, two counselors of Parliament and another royal secretary.

In Christine's first letter to Gontier Col, she enclosed a copy of her letter to Jean de Montreuil, which explains in detail her views on the poem. She insisted that her opinion of *The Romance of the Rose* was firm: she objected only to certain aspects of the poem and freely admitted certain merits.[13]

In common with Gerson, Christine had grave reservations about the propriety of some of the language of the poem, especially the naming in a literary work of private parts of the body, and through words put in the mouth of Reason, of all people. This point has led Christine's critics, both early and modern, to accuse her of attempting to exercise moral censorship.[14] A realistic consideration of her situation in life, however, makes it difficult to substantiate such an attack. She was a doctor's daughter and the mother of three children, neither of which circumstance is especially conducive to prudery; she was undoubtedly as well acquainted with the facts of life as the ordinary person of her day, and her references elsewhere to the accepted adulterous nature of so-called courtly love do not suggest any shrinking from reality. What she actually said was that words are neither good nor bad in themselves, but that the intention with which they are used makes them so. Jean de Meun had written, by way of an excuse:

> Sir lovers, I beseech, by Love's sweet game,
> That, if you find here words that seem unwise
> Or bawdy, whereof scandalmongering tongues
> Might make occasion to say slanderous things
> Of us because of what we have to tell,
> You'll courteously gainsay their criticism.
> And when you shall have stopped their calumny,
> Denied their charges, and reproved their speech,
> If still there shall remain some words of mine
> For which I rightfully should pardon beg,
> I pray that you will make excuse for them
> And make response to critics, as for me,
> That they are necessary to the tale,
> Which leads me to the words by its own traits.
> This is the reason why I use such words.[15]

Nevertheless, Christine suspected the motives of Jean de Meun, a sufficiently learned man to know that he was encouraging free love. Furthermore, she did not see why it was necessary to go to so much trouble to explain what comes all too naturally to most people, as she said:

If you wish to excuse him by saying that it pleases him to make a pretty story of the culmination of love using such images, I reply that by doing so he neither tells nor explains anything new. Doesn't everyone know how men and women copulate naturally? If he were to tell us how bears or lions or birds or some other strange creatures mate, this might make amusing material for a fable, but would not tell us anything new.[16]

She suspected even more the motives of some of Jean de Meun's disciples, who appeared to her to be devising elaborate intellectual excuses for licentious behavior. Jean de Meun's poem had long been recognized as belonging to the Ovidian tradition of erotic literature in spite of its great show of erudition. Christine was not interested in discussing his use of allegory to reveal obvious truths; she was concerned about the influence of his ideas in contributing to the low estate of public morality that was evident around her—greed, slander, and promiscuity, of which the handsome duke of Orleans's multiple love affairs were perhaps the most notorious example. The festivals at the court were frequently accompanied by licentious pleasures, giving an Augustinian monk, Jacques Legrand, occasion to admonish the queen: "Venus alone reigns at your court; drunkenness and debauchery follow in her train."[17] Froissart's account of the marriage festivities of Charles VI and Isabeau of Bavaria had already included references to the barely concealed innuendo that marked the lascivious attitude of the courtiers present. Eustache Deschamps's poem in celebration of the marriage of one of the duke of Burgundy's younger sons is even less restrained.[18] Yet these were the same circles that professed to honor the ideals of courtly love. Thus it is scarcely surprising that Jean de Meun's combination of the erotic central theme of the quest for the Rose with abstruse discussions of the fine points of lovemaking should have had a great appeal to them.

Christine had already called attention to the courtiers' hypocrisy in *Cupid's Letter* and denounced the deceit and insolence that characterized the attitude they displayed in real life. Later, in her reply to Jean de Montreuil's treatise, she also objected to Reason's advice that in the war of love it is better to deceive than to be deceived; she was horrified by the advice of the Old Woman; she saw no excuse for the meanderings of Jealousy; and, recalling examples of virtuous women, past and present, she found the unpleasant things Deceit had to say about feminine virtue especially distasteful. (In this last objection, it is possible to note the germ of a later work, *The Book of the City of Ladies.*) She concludes by asserting that she sees no need to remind the human race of its shortcomings, the "leg on which it hobbles," and that there is no reason to attribute her attitude to the fact that she is a woman, for it is but a small matter for her to object to what a single man says, when he has felt free to blame, without exception, an entire sex.[19]

One may insist that Christine worked herself into considerable frenzy over this debate, yet the fact that Jean de Montreuil, a public official, was not eager to have his treatise read outside a select circle suggests that he may have spoken rather freely of his enjoyment of the poem. He seems to have feared that his words would make him appear frivolous and lascivious, although it is of course impossible to know what he really did say.

Gontier Col's second letter to Christine provided little to soothe her feelings. He said that although she was in error in her interpretation of such a learned doctor as Jean de Meun, if she would repent and confess her error, she would be forgiven and her opponents would take pity on her. Col's obviously patronizing tone infuriated Christine, who insisted stoutly that she would stick to her views. She retorted again that her position had nothing to do with her female nature, which he had seen fit to slander. At the end of her letter, she made reference once more to "the noble memory and continuing experiences of many valiant women who are worthy of praise and entirely virtuous," adding that she would rather resemble this company than be blessed by all of Fortune's riches.[20]

This is the end of the collection of documents that Christine publicized by sending it at the beginning of 1402 to the queen and to the provost of Paris. In her mind, at least, the principal issue had now become the unjust slander of women, more than the merits of Jean de Meun's poem. It is this insistence on respect for women who deserve it that identifies Christine most directly with feminists of later generations, and it was on this issue that she made her appeal to the queen.

Her gesture of publicizing the letters by circulating them in official circles brought to a close the second round of the debate. Christine, for her part, was busy with other matters. In February 1402, she wrote *Le Dit de la Rose (The Tale of the Rose),* which she dedicated to the duke of Orleans, and she was also gathering together her poetry for presentation in its first "edition" toward the end of June.[21] In the meantime, Jean de Montreuil continued to circulate his treatise among a group of humanist friends, soliciting their support in his defense of Jean de Meun.

Within a few months, the tone of the whole affair was modified once more. On May 18, 1402, Jean Gerson released a treatise against *The Romance of the Rose* on which he had very possibly been reflecting for some time. Making use, in his turn, of a dream, he imagines the High Court of Christianity, where the case of Chastity versus the Fool of Love is being tried.[22] Seven charges have been presented against this misguided lover, of which the first two are of particular interest here. Chastity's first complaint is that the Fool of Love tried to drive her from the land along with her bodyguards, Shame, Fear, and Danger. This was attempted with the assistance of the foolish Old Woman, worse than the devil himself, who has admonished young girls to sell their bodies as fast as they can and to the highest bidder, adding that they should not mind lying or deceiving in the process but should give themselves in haste while still young and beautiful to anyone who will have them, whoever he might be.

Chastity's second accusation is that the Fool of Love has made a jealous old man complain about the institution of marriage, saying that it is better to hang or drown oneself than to become involved in wedlock. The Fool of Love intends to make all men despise all women so that men will not want to marry.

The trial continues on other counts of a religious nature, but the high point occurs when the Fool of Love is called to account for a long series of misdeeds, including the fall of Troy, the exile of Tarquin from Rome, and civil disorders of all varieties. (It is interesting to note that in *Cupid's Letter,* Christine had already blamed human deceit for a good many of these same misfortunes.) And the prosecutor in Gerson's treatise continues:

> Who deceives by fraud and perjury honest girls?
> The Fool of Love.
> Who forgets God and the saints and paradise and his own end?
> The Fool of Love.
>
> Whence come robberies to maintain extravagances,
> bastardry or the suffocation of infants . . .
> the death of husbands, in short, all wickedness and all folly?
> The Fool of Love.
>
> But I can see that because of his name you will
> wish to excuse his follies, because one cannot
> cure folly in a fool.[23]

Gerson also makes reference to the obscenity of some of the numerous manuscripts that were in circulation. An idea of what he was talking about can be gleaned from one particularly handsome copy illustrated in Paris around this time. A highly suggestive portrayal of Venus in connection with the Fall of Man, which marked the end of the Golden Age, and the erotic overtones of an illustration of the final assault on the castle to take the Rose leave very little to the imagination.[24]

Gerson does not always do exact justice to what Jean de Meun had actually said, yet there is no question of the force of his eloquence. Although Christine and Gerson were not defending precisely the same things—Gerson was more concerned with the virtue of women than with their reputation in the world—together they formed a powerful opposition to the supporters of Jean de Meun.

The third and final round in the quarrel took on a sharper, more personal tone. It was opened by Gontier Col's brother Pierre, a canon in the chapter of Notre Dame of which Gerson was the presiding official. In a letter directed to Christine, he saw fit to expose his disagreements with Gerson as well as with her. His references to Gerson's treatise were unmistakable, although neither he nor Christine mention the chancellor by name.[25] Point by point, Col took up the charges both had made against Jean de Meun, quoting extensively from *The Romance of the Rose* itself and demonstrating a tiresome tendency to quibble.

He took Gerson to task for his accusations of the Fool of Love, insisting that he could scarcely have any knowledge of such love himself yet suggesting that he might still be its victim in the future. It is scarcely to be wondered that Gerson took offense at such an implication about his private life.

It is amusing, however, to find Col following the custom dear to his contemporaries of citing a list of heroes of antiquity to prove his point. His list of those who were educated yet fools of love included Pompey, Caesar, Scipio, and Cicero, among others. Then he added: "But I think that the author of that appeal is a cleric, a philosopher, and a theologian without being love's fool, so he thinks it must be so with others."[26]

With regard to Christine, his tone was patronizing and seemingly calculated to offend when, for instance, he said:

> O most foolish presumption! O word too soon issued and lightly spoken from the mouth of a woman to condemn a man of such high understanding [and] profound study who, after such great labor and mature deliberation, has written such a noble book as *The Romance of the Rose,* which surpasses all others ever written in the language in which he wrote his book. . . .[27]

Such extravagant claims are nonsense and can scarcely be taken as an objective reflection upon Christine's judgment, but he continued in a playful, but still more offensive, tone:

> So I beg of you, woman of great ingenuity, that you preserve the honor you have acquired for the extent of your understanding and your well-chosen language, and that if you have been praised because you have shot a bullet over the towers of Notre Dame, don't try to hit the moon for that reason with an oversized arrow; take care not to resemble the crow who, when

his singing was praised, began to sing louder than usual and let the morsel he was holding fall from his mouth.[28]

Christine's reply to Pierre Col, dated October 2, 1402, shows increasing exasperation. She reproved him for his disrespectful remarks about Gerson, then replied to his points individually. Quite obviously, she felt that the affair had gone far enough, and she had ceased to be interested in going over the same ground again. In this second letter, she wrote:

I beg you and those of your persuasion that you do not hold against me my writings and the present debate about the *Book of the Rose,* for the beginning of it came about through chance and not because of any desire of mine, whatever opinion I might have held, as you can know from a little treatise where I described the first theme and the final position of our debate. It would be most distressing to me to be subject to such servitude that I dared not speak the truth to someone else without its being held against me; for even a wiser person than I may be well advised to think about what he may not have considered for a long time because, as a common proverb says: It can happen that a fool can give counsel to a sage.[29]

Only a fragment of Pierre Col's second reply to Christine has survived, if indeed it was ever finished, for Gerson lost no time in writing him a letter in Latin giving full expression to his disapproval. Not only did Gerson reprove Col for the indiscreet implications about his own private life, but he also called attention to the fact that in his remarks about unrestrained language in children and their sinless state Col was skirting the religious heresy of certain groups like the Adamites who were condemned by the Catholic Church. He also reminded Col rather strongly that he, Gerson, defended virtue first of all because it was his professional duty to do so, and he recommended that the canon turn his thoughts to more serious and useful matters, for instance, to a reading of Saint Augustine's *Christian Doctrine.* Gerson ended with the pious admonition "Let us pray for our mutual salvation."[30]

In the face of such a pointed rebuke, Pierre Col could not continue to take issue with either Gerson or Christine. One final echo of the quarrel is to be found, however, in a series of sermons that Gerson preached during the month of December in the Church of St.-Germain-l'Auxerrois, not far from the Louvre. The general subject of this series was penitence, notably for two sins of the flesh, gluttony and lechery, and more especially the latter. In the sermon for December 24, Gerson undertook once more to reply to those fools of love who had tried to defend this sin. His allusion to the Quarrel of the Rose was unmistakable.[31]

By this time, however, the chancellor appears to have realized that his thundering against Jean de Meun's poem might be having exactly the opposite of the desired effect by calling too much attention to *The Romance of the Rose* and keeping public interest aroused. The discussion was finally closed.

From a careful examination of all the documents generated by the debate, several points become clear. The principal quarrel was not really between Christine and the two Col brothers, as their exchange of letters might suggest, but rather between Jean de Montreuil and Jean Gerson, who was supported by all those who felt that *The Romance of the Rose* was having a corrupting influence on public morality. The injection of the antifeminist issue was perhaps accidental, but it gave the discussion an unusual turn that would have important repercussions. This was also the aspect of the affair that caught popular attention, especially because a woman had dared to rise to the defense of her sex against traditional clerical attacks.

Christine's position has been frequently misinterpreted, yet the fact remains that throughout the exchange of letters with the Col brothers she insisted that she was not bent on attacking Jean de Meun's poem as a whole, but merely the excessive claims for its merits that she considered unfounded. Few of Christine's critics have called attention to the discourtesy of her opponents, nor have they wondered that she should have objected to being compared by Jean de Montreuil to "the Greek whore who dared to write against Theophrastus."[32] It was only after Pierre Col's thoroughly ungenerous attack that she began to sound, not hysterical, but exasperated. She continued to insist, however, that she spoke only *"de vrai science,"* which should be interpreted in this context as meaning out of her own personal experience of the world.

The basic issues of the debate may have remained unsettled, but Christine's role was of lasting importance: she removed theoretical discussions on women from intellectual circles and made it possible for a layperson, and a woman at that, to take part. Perhaps even more important for Christine herself was the encouragement she felt to continue writing in prose about one of her major concerns, the defense of women against what she considered unjust slander and against some of the hypocrisies of contemporary society. Finally, she had achieved a sort of fame that she could scarcely have gained so quickly in less dramatic circumstances.

Christine's interest in the situation of women in the society to which she belonged had been reflected in her early poetry and in *Cupid's Letter*. It also provided the principal theme for the *One Hundred Ballades of a Lover and His Lady*. What troubled her particularly, on practical as well as on moral grounds, was the veneer of nobility that served to disguise illicit love, all too frequently providing a snare for unsuspecting or inexperienced women. As for condemning all women for the sins of a few, Christine found the idea unjust as well as ridiculous. Her common-sense approach can be seen in a passage from one of her letters:

> As I said once before in a poem of mine called Cupid's Letter: Where are the countries or the realms from which women are exiled for their great iniquities? Without prejudice, we would ask of what crimes even the worst of them, the most deceitful, can be accused? What can they do to you, how deceive you? If they beg you for money from your purse, if indeed they don't take it, you don't have to give it to them if you don't want to. And if you say that they make fools of you . . . do they go to your house to seek you out or take you by force? It would be interesting to know just how they deceive you.[33]

Christine would continue to develop this theme in two of her major works, *The Book of the City of Ladies* and *The Book of the Three Virtues*. The first grew directly out of the concern she expressed in one of her letters to Gontier Col. She returned to the praise of virtuous women, drawing examples from Boccaccio's *De Mulieribus Claris (Concerning Famous Women)* and citing parallel examples from French history. Thus she elaborated her earlier argument, undertaking to demonstrate that the achievements of certain women rendered them, as individuals if not as a whole sex, equal or superior to men. Special praise is reserved for the group of women who, inspired by conjugal love, risked or even sacrificed their lives for their husbands. Throughout her career, Christine consistently defended the institution of marriage and, as it has already been pointed out, this stand represented a more modern point of view than the ones held by her opponents in the debate, for while Jean de Montreuil and his friends were disparaging women, their Italian contemporary and admired friend Coluccio Salutati was composing a letter in praise of matrimony in terms that foreshadowed what Erasmus would have to say on the subject a century later.

It was, however, in *The Book of the Three Virtues*, which followed *The*

Book of the City of Ladies and was sometimes called *Le Trésor de la Cité des Dames,* its "Treasury," that Christine gave her most definitive view of woman's vulnerability, dwelling on the bitter price that must almost inevitably be paid by a woman for any sort of illicit love. Her ideas are summarized in a long letter that she had already made use of in *The Book of the Duke of True Lovers,* but it would appear that Christine considered the points she had made there sufficiently important to bear repetition. The letter is no theoretical discussion of love but instead offers extremely practical advice for a young woman who is ready to throw away her good name for momentary happiness:

> And further, my very dear lady, it remains to speak of the perils and difficulties which accompany such love, which are without number. The first and greatest is that it angers God, and then, if the husband or kinfolk find out about it, the woman is ruined, or falls under such reproach that she never again has any happiness. But even if this should not come to pass, let us consider the disposition of the lovers, for though all were loyal (which they by no means are, since it is known that they are generally faithless, and in order to deceive say what they neither think nor would be willing to do), nevertheless it is certain that the heat of such love does not long endure, even with the most loyal. Ah, dear lady, be warned that you cannot possibly conceive of the trouble which dwells in her breast when this love comes to an end, and the lady, who has been blinded by the environment of foolish delight repents, as she thinks of the distractions and perils to which she has exposed herself, wishing that whatever the cost, this experience had never happened to her and that she would not be subject to reproach because of it.[34]

The letter, which continues at some length in this vein, is penned by an astute and rather bold woman who has had occasion to observe, with all illusions spent, the cruelty of the society around her.

It has been said that the results of this somewhat laughable debate were inconclusive or even insignificant, and it has been suggested more than once that Christine had the worst of it. But such a point of view overlooks the secondary results, which in the long run were far more important than the debate itself. Some of the same issues were evoked in a second debate, around 1424, by Alain Chartier's *La Belle Dame sans Merci (The Fair Lady without Mercy).*[35] The lady in question, who turned aside her lover's pleas, puts into practice just the sort of behavior Christine recommended. Her ideas were also echoed in Martin LeFranc's *Champion des Dames (The Champion of Ladies)* and in a whole series of rather artificial treatises for and against feminine honor that made up the debate in the sixteenth century known as the *"querelle des femmes."* Some of the questions raised were argued around the middle of the sixteenth century in Marguerite de Navarre's *Heptameron,* making it evident that she was among Christine's readers.[36] Indeed, Christine can be considered a forerunner of certain ideas that became popular more than a century later when Baldissare Castiglione's *Book of the Courtier* became a model for social behavior throughout a good part of Europe.

Christine's letters in the debate over *The Romance of the Rose* represent only a small part of what she had to say about the position of women in society. But if these letters were relatively insignificant in her long effort to turn her contemporaries away from outworn concepts and traditions, they did have a certain value in publicizing her ideas and in bringing to public attention the issue of the right of half the human race to more consideration, a better chance for education, and a role beyond the domestic sphere.

Othéa Presents Her Letter to Hector

The Fountain of the Muses

5

The Long Road of Learning

Christine's involvement in the debate over *The Romance of the Rose* marked the turning point in her career toward a more serious form of writing than the society verse for which she had become known. It is curious to find that her new series of experiments was inspired to a considerable extent by the very poem about which she had been expressing her disapproval. It was, however, the dream vision and the allegorical characters that she chose to imitate. She may also have become acquainted with Boccaccio's ideas on poetry expressed in his treatise *De Genealogia Deorum (On the Genealogy of the Gods),* which was undoubtedly in circulation in Paris at the end of the fourteenth century and was beginning to influence poets even though it was not translated into French until the latter part of the fifteenth century.[1] Boccaccio saw poetry as inspired truth veiled in fictions or fables. For Christine, poetry had at least two levels of meaning, one apparent and another, or perhaps even several others, hidden under the ornamentation of language. She thus made it evident that she considered allegory a more worthy form of writing than the society verse she had composed earlier, for she wrote in *Christine's Vision:*

> I began by forging pretty things, rather light at first, but like the craftsman who progressively acquires greater skill through experimentation with various materials, my sense became imbued with novelties, directing my style toward more subtlety and more lofty inspiration, from 1399 until this year of 1405, when I have not yet ceased my efforts. . . .[2]

Although 1399 is the known date of her first long poem, *Cupid's Letter,* it is possible that she was speaking here of her most ambitious work to date, *Othéa's Letter to Hector.*[3] The inspiration of Ovid's *Metamorphoses* is evident in both of these works, although his *Heroïdes* may have suggested their epistolary form. Writing letters of various sorts was a favorite diversion of early humanists and, of course, had been practiced by Christine in the debate over *The Romance of the Rose*. In writing letters, either in verse or in prose, one had not only an opportunity to polish one's literary style but also the possibility of presenting personal views, so that in a certain sense such letters were the forerunners of the modern essay.[4] *Othéa's Letter to Hector* is the most complex of Christine's allegories, and though inspired by Ovid, it nonetheless gives an original twist to the material borrowed.

Christine's sources, and her use of them, have given rise to lengthy commentaries by scholars. She has been praised for her astonishing erudition as well as dismissed as a mere compiler of popular anthologies. Recent studies have shown that Christine knew a number of the writers of antiquity through the translations made either at the court of Charles V or at the beginning of the fifteenth century. Many of these had commentaries provided by the translator, and Christine was inclined to use these without always discriminating between the original text and the commentary. For instance, it would appear that she knew several letters from the *Heroïdes* because of their inclusion in a compilation of ancient history known variously as the *Ancient History since the Creation*, or *The Book of Orosius*, a series of texts that had undergone revision during the reign of Charles V and circulated in several slightly different versions at the beginning of the fifteenth century. It was from this history that she learned about the Trojan War and found other material she used from time to time.[5]

This history was the earliest of its sort available in French, and its purpose was to correlate the chronology of the Old Testament with secular history, the Greek section being based on the Troy romances and the Latin section on Virgil's *Aeneid*.[6] Christine's knowledge of Ovid's *Metamorphoses* came primarily from an equally popular medieval text, the *Ovide Moralisé*, as it was usually called, which was less a translation than an adaptation designed to make Ovid suitable reading matter for the Christian Middle Ages; that is to say, historical, moral, and theological interpretations of the original stories had been added to the text. The considerable number of copies still in existence, some of them delightfully illustrated, attests to this version's popularity. Christine might have known the manuscript illustrated for the duke of Berry around 1390 or possibly read a second copy prepared for his library around 1400, which has a format remarkably similar to the duke's copy of her own poetry.[7]

Christine had already shown her familiarity with the *Ovide Moralisé* in her Ballade LII, which begins "By all the Gods of whom Ovid speaks . . . May all false lovers be cursed."[8] This source is also reflected in the roll call of the Olympian gods in the last lines of *Cupid's Letter*, naming the gods who were present at the marriage of Peleus and Thetis as described in the *Ovide Moralisé* (Book IX). The marriage itself is mentioned in *Othéa's Letter to Hector,* and a miniature in the duke of Berry's copy shows Discord arriving to disrupt the feast, a good example of the way in which Christine, though seemingly repeating herself, reuses the same material to achieve different effects.[9]

Boccaccio's vast compilation of Greek and Roman mythology, *On the Genealogy of the Gods,* undertook to give a Christian interpretation to ancient myths, and the taste for "moralized" literature was also responsible for the *Moralized Bible.* This Bible was made up of passages from the Vulgate, "moralizations" from Biblical commentaries, and, usually, abundant illustrations.[10]

At the time of writing *Othéa's Letter to Hector,* then, Christine was well aware of the tastes of her contemporaries and her potential patrons, yet there is no reason to doubt her genuine enthusiasm for learning for its own sake. By 1399 she had reached the age of thirty-five, and like Dante in the opening lines of the *Divine Comedy,* she considered herself at the midpoint of life. One seems to hear an echo of her Italian model as she writes:

> Thus at the time when my age had brought me in due course to a certain stage of knowledge, considering past adventures and the ultimate end of everything before me, just as a man who has passed along a dangerous road turns back in wonder, vowing that he will never again attempt such a thing, but will try to do better in the future, and likewise considering the world so filled with dangerous illusions, where there is only one good road, the path of Truth, I turned toward this road, to which both Nature and my stars inclined me, which is to say the love of study.[11]

This path led Christine to a new consideration of poetry and the discovery of the new style that pleased her most, as she went on to explain: "Subtle coverings and fine matter modified by delightful and moral fictions, verse and prose inspired by fine and polished rhetoric ornamented with subtle language and singular proverbs. . . ." A new concept of poetry replaced the facile versification she had formerly practiced. She defined it in these terms:

> The word poetry is taken to mean either some fiction used for the narration as a whole, or the introduction of something which signifies one thing on the surface, but has one or more hidden meanings, or, one might better say, poetry's object is truth and its technique is doctrine clothed in ornamental words and suitable nuances.[12]

In *Othéa's Letter to Hector,* Christine was engaged neither in a popularization of Ovid nor in the development of allegory for its own sake but instead was developing a system of instruction for a young man of fifteen, the accepted age to begin training for knighthood. The problem would have been of particular interest to her at the moment because her son Jean had just reached that age, and so she undertook to compile precepts that she considered essential to his moral well-being, along with some useful lessons in worldly wisdom. She therefore includes commentaries on such standard doctrines as the Four Cardinal Virtues and the Seven Deadly Sins, together with the usual list of opposing virtues and vices, standard educational fare at the end of the Middle Ages.

The allegory Christine develops is more unusual. The goddess Othéa, whose intent is to educate the youthful Hector of Troy, is completely original with Christine and does not figure in any source. She can best be understood as the goddess of Prudence and the personification of Feminine Wisdom. Hector was clearly one of Christine's favorite heroes. In the course of the Middle Ages, he had come to exemplify the ideal knight and as such he was included among the Nine Worthies introduced to literature in the early years of the fourteenth century by Jacques de Longuyon's *Les Voeux du Paon (Vows of the Peacock).*[13] Along with Alexander the Great and Julius Caesar, Hector was one of the three pagan heroes portrayed repeatedly—carved on the Rathaus in Cologne; painted on the walls of Manta Castle in northern Italy; woven into tapestries created for the duke of Berry. Charles V and another brother, the duke of Anjou, also had sets of these Nine Worthies tapestries and there was another series woven to depict the history of Hector alone. Thus, Christine had chosen a hero of great popularity for her new literary venture.[14]

The organization of the material selected for *Othéa's Letter to Hector* is another unusual aspect of the work. There are a hundred sections, or short chapters, each beginning with a quatrain (the text) referring to an episode drawn, for the most part though not invariably, from Ovid. Christine then proceeds to interpret her text in two different manners. First there is a Glose pointing to a useful lesson for the young knight's prowess in worldly society. This is generally supported by a quotation from a philosopher of antiquity. Second, following the Glose is an Allegory that calls attention to the spiritual significance of the Text, for the benefit of the young knight's soul. Usually, the Allegory is reinforced by a quotation from one of the Church Fathers or by a passage from the Scriptures. Thus, the work as a whole represents a sort of amalgamation of the *Moralized Ovid* with the *Moralized Bible.* For all of its seeming complexity, the work is relatively brief. It fits into a slender edition of fifty folio pages, or even as few as twenty pages in unillustrated copies. Such a volume could be carried around easily and held in the hand, in contrast with the large, heavy tomes of the Ovid or the Bible that inspired it.

The manuscript that appears to be the earliest copy of the text (B. N. Ms. fr. 848) contains only *Othéa's Letter to Hector,* with just four illustrations. These are handsome black-and-white drawings, although they can scarcely be compared in splendor with the hundred colored illustrations to be found in three later copies. The Text is placed in the center of the page with the Glose in the margin on the left and the Allegory on the right, a format recalling legal texts and their commentaries from the University of Bologna, or Diogini da Borgo San Sepulcro's commentary on Valerius Maximus, or, indeed, Benvenuto da Imola's gloses on Dante's *Divine Comedy.* Such texts were undoubtedly familiar to Christine, and her use of a similar format suggests that she had in mind some sort of commentary on Ovid.

Of the four drawings that illustrate this early manuscript, one shows Othéa presenting her letter of advice to Hector and the others illustrate the Four Cardinal Virtues. The most interesting of these, which depicts the virtue of Temperance, shows Othéa pointing to a clock drawn in remarkable detail, even though it is nowhere mentioned in the accompanying text. Only in a revised version was an explanation of the drawing added:

> Temperance was also called a goddess, and because our human body is composed of various elements and should be tempered by reason, it can be represented as a clock where there are various wheels and measures, and yet a clock is worth nothing if it isn't tempered; such is the case with our body if it isn't governed by Temperance.[15]

Apparently, Christine saw in the recently perfected escapement wheel of the clock the sort of restraint exercised by Temperance. This was a distinct iconographical innovation because in Italy the virtue of Temperance was traditionally represented by a depiction of the mixing of water and wine. The clock of Temperance could also have been inspired in part by the popularity of Heinrich Suso's *Horlogium Sapientiae (The Clock of Wisdom),* first translated into French in 1389, or by Charles V's clock on a tower of the old palace on the Ile de la Cité, which must have been a familiar sight to Christine from childhood. Whatever its source in the artist's imagination, this clock came to be accepted in Northern Europe as an attribute of Temperance, and as such it appears on Louis XII's tomb at St.-Denis and in Jan Bruegel's engraving *The Allegory of Temperance.*

The story of Andromeda's rescue by Perseus, who represents Good Repute, shows another interesting iconographical association. The rescue mission exemplifies both the protection of women as a knightly duty and the need of Good Repute for the soul's salvation. Perseus is shown flying through the air on the winged horse Pegasus, and the Glose explains:

> The poets said that he rode the horse that flew through the air, whom they called Pegasus, which is to be understood to mean a Good Name, which likewise flies through the air.

And the Allegory adds:

> The horse that carries him will be his good angel, who will give a good report of him on Judgment Day. Andromeda, who will be delivered, is his soul, which he will deliver from the Devil by overcoming sin. [16]

Christine wants to show that the knight should prefer to seek Good Repute in virtuous ways, rather than through egotism and vainglory. However, the most interesting aspect of the episode is that in the *Moralized Ovid* Perseus ties two wings to his feet in order to fly through the air on his way to do battle with a menacing sea monster, whereas Pegasus is mentioned only in another adaptation of Ovid made by Petrarch's French friend Pierre Bersuire. Christine could have known this version, although it is more likely that she found the detail in Boccaccio's *Genealogy of the Gods,* where Perseus is also described as riding on the back of Pegasus. Christine, like Boccaccio, attributes to Perseus the naming of Persia. [17]

Another interesting departure from medieval tradition is Christine's choice of Atropos to remind the young knight of death, which is, of course, to be followed by resurrection and life everlasting. But Christine points out to the young man:

> The poets called death Atropos, wherefore this means that a good knight should reflect that he will not live forever in this world, but must soon depart from it.

In the copies where there is an accompanying miniature, a dark woman brandishing a sword is to be seen soaring on a dark cloud above a bishop and a king who are quite obviously dying, while two other noblemen and a foe seem to be faltering. [18] Although the representation of Death coming to men of all estates is far from rare in late medieval art or literature, it is usually represented by a skeleton. Notable exceptions to this tradition are the old woman who wields a scythe in Traini's *Triumph of Death* in the Campo Santo at Pisa, and a comparable old woman in certain illustrations of Guillaume Deguilleville's *Pèlerinage de la Vie Humaine (The Pilgrimage of Human Life)*. Christine could have known of Atropos from a passage in the *Divine Comedy*, although Boccaccio also speaks of her as the Daughter of Night in *On the Genealogy of the Gods*, and in Petrarch's *Triumph of Death* the mighty are described as being victims of a furious old woman wrapped in a black dress.[19]

The story of Narcissus serves to admonish the young knight to avoid self-esteem and, for his soul's sake, to shun pride. Pygmalion's fate is a warning against allowing frivolous interests to detract from prowess at arms, a message that is also conveyed by Leander's excessive love for Hero, already the inspiration for the refrain of Ballade III:

> But great love has the wisest fooled,
> See how lovers by love are ruled.[20]

The same idea is associated with Venus, who is shown surrounded by her "children," the lovers who offer up their hearts to her in a particularly appealing scene of the illustrated copies. Othéa is there, however, to admonish lovers to shun excessive love and, by extension, to avoid vanity and vain love:

> Of Venus never make thy goddess
> Nor set great store by any promise.
> To follow her is ruinous,
> Dishonorable and perilous.[21]

Venus also appears as one of the planetary gods, for *Othéa's Letter to Hector* presents the first literary development of the planetary gods and their children in Northern Europe, where they would continue to be popular for the next century or more.

These planetary gods are a picturesque aspect of the revival of interest in astrology that was widespread at the time. The planets are an essential factor in all astrological calculations and so were inevitably depicted in astrological manuscripts. In Italy they appeared on public monuments as well: the capitals of the Doge's palace in Venice, the grisaille frescoes by Guariento in the Ermitani Chapel in Padua, and on the Campanile of the Church of Santa Maria del Fiore in Florence, to mention only a few.[22]

The illustrations of *Othéa's Letter to Hector*, being a considerable novelty in France, contributed substantially to the work's popularity, but at first

Christine apparently felt the need to explain what she had in mind, for she added to her original Prologue:

> So that those who are not learned poets may understand readily the significance of the stories in this book, especially wherever the images are shown in clouds, that means that they are gods or goddesses of whom the following passage in the book speaks in the manner of ancient poets. Because deity is a spiritual thing, above the level of the earth, the images are shown surrounded by clouds, and the first of these is Wisdom.[23]

In speaking of Mercury, she follows the example of Dante's *Il Convivio,* which relates eloquence to this god's sphere of influence:

> Mercury is the planet that gives the gift of fine language, and so he was called the god of language. He holds a flower because, just as the flower pleases by its appearance, so well-turned language is pleasing to hear. He has his mouth full, for great richness often comes from fine language. Thus he has beneath him wise men who are speaking together.[24]

This passage also exemplifies Christine's close cooperation with her illustrators, particularly, the talented artist known as the Epître d'Othéa Master.[25] His contribution to her success is not to be underestimated. His illustrations have continued to generate interest and to serve as a prime example of iconography as an auxiliary to the history of ideas.

Christine also made reference, both here and elsewhere, to nonplanetary gods in their role as pioneers and leaders in the development of civilization, especially as founders of cities and discoverers or inventors of arts and crafts, a theme she would develop to a far greater extent in *The Book of the City of Ladies.* It is interesting to observe that in the *Othéa* the goddesses already outnumber the gods in their contribution to humanity.[26] Thus Minerva is shown to have been not only the discoverer of the art of weaving, but also as the inventor of armor, which replaced with metal the primitive warrior's protection made of boiled leather. Ceres discovered the art of tilling the soil, and she is shown in the *Othéa* hovering over a recently ploughed field, sowing seeds while she leans from the frame of her cloud. Isis was especially skilled in the art of making the plants grow, and it was she who taught the Egyptians the art of grafting. Among the men, Aesculapius is praised for writing medical books, and Bacchus is mentioned as having planted the first grapevines in Greece.[27]

Particularly noteworthy is Io, who stands for the love of learning. The Epître d'Othéa Master shows her writing in the kind of study in which Christine herself is frequently portrayed. There she is surrounded by four assistants, three of whom are busily writing while the fourth is presenting a text to the goddess for her approval. The accompanying Glose ends with a quotation attributed to Hermes: "Who makes the effort to acquire learning and good habits will find it pleasing in both this world and the next."[28] This theme runs through all of Christine's subsequent writings and, indeed, sums up her philosophy as a writer.

The final chapter of *Othéa's Letter to Hector* is devoted to the Cumean sibyl's prediction to Caesar Augustus of Christ's coming. Although Christine's basic source was probably the *Moralized Ovid,* she may also have shared a common inspiration with an artist who painted one of the initials in the duke of Burgundy's manuscript known as The Brussels Hours. The Limbourg brothers were later inspired to use this same theme in the illustrations of two manuscripts they prepared for the duke of Berry. In each instance, the sibyl stands beside the kneeling emperor, pointing to the Madonna and Child who are revealed encircled by the sun's rays. Christine lends her own particular emphasis to the episode by calling attention to the fact that it was a woman who announced Christ's coming to the Roman emperor, about which she comments: "Good words and good teachings are praiseworthy from any person who utters them."[29] Christine would develop this idea on subsequent occasions, and the Cumean sibyl would soon appear in her writings again.

Aside from the obvious attraction of the well-known illustrated manuscripts, the text of *Othéa's Letter to Hector* was copied in an impressive series of manuscripts throughout the fifteenth century and was printed in at least six editions continuing well into the sixteenth century. It was also translated into English no fewer than three times, the third an imprint of 1540. Perhaps its value to the modern reader is the insight that it permits into the mentality of Christine's contemporaries, who were evidently fascinated by the myths and legends of antiquity and by their application to issues of their own day. The late Rosemund Tuve suggested that it was because Christine was able to explain successfully to her readers a method of reading the allegorical material she presented that she continued to be read for so long.[30] As far as Christine herself was concerned, the book's success undoubtedly gave her additional confidence in her powers as a writer. Furthermore, she had sown the seeds of a number of ideas she would develop later, in *The Book of the City of Ladies, The Book of the Three Virtues,* and eventually in the treatises she devoted to the education of the French dauphin.

Having successfully launched *Othéa's Letter to Hector,* Christine set to work on another long allegory, this one aimed, for one thing, at explaining the circumstances that led her to become a bluestocking, as she put it, a *"fille d'étude."* This poem also shows for the first time a preoccupation with the misfortunes of France and a concern for the sorry state of Christendom as a whole.

The frame for this poem, entitled *Le Chemin de Long Estude (The Long Road of Learning)*, is a dream Christine claims to have had on October 5, 1402, shortly after she had written her reply to Pierre Col's stinging letter about her views on *The Romance of the Rose*. The first copy of the poem was ready for presentation to the duke of Berry in his Paris residence, the Hôtel de Nesle, on March 30, 1403. Thus the actual writing of the poem must have occupied Christine for less than five months. Although dedicated to the king of France, it made a special appeal to the royal dukes who held the destinies of the country in their hands and whose seeming lack of serious concern for their responsibilities was already becoming a cause for preoccupation among some of their subjects. Along with the copy prepared for the duke of Berry, there were others for the duke of Burgundy and the duke of Orleans. These, like the earliest copy of *Othéa's Letter to Hector,* have finely drawn grisaille illustrations in a style that has long been related to the artist who decorated the striking copy of *The Romance of the Rose* now at the University of Valencia.[31] Apparently, Christine could not yet afford the services of the two artists who would make her manuscripts famous.

Christine's economical habit of repeating material that had particular appeal is already evident in this poem, but she also added new material from other sources to each succeeding undertaking, continuing to experiment, always searching to find better modes of expression for her ideas. In *The Long Road of Learning*, she makes use of the dream vision for the first time. Although *The Romance of the Rose* was obviously on her mind during the fall of 1402, she was also inspired by her enthusiasm for Boethius's *De Consolatione Philosophiae (The Consolation of Philosophy)*, of which she speaks at the beginning of the poem.[32] (She had already expressed her admiration for the book in Ballade XCVII.) Indeed, Boethius provides her point of departure; her persona in the poem claims to have sought distraction that autumn evening by reading his book. Having taken refuge in her little study, as she explains (no doubt the one where her illustrators sometimes showed her working with her little dog at her feet), she picked over one volume after another until her hand fell on a copy of Boethius. After reading for a while, Christine goes to bed, still reflecting on the lesson to be learned from his philosophy:

So one should not have any care
For great possessions rich and rare
By Fortune given; she gives and takes,
And at her whim also forsakes.
Only in virtue is there good,
Fortune can often be withstood
By virtue, which can't be taken away.[33]

Once in bed, Christine is unable to sleep, continuing to dwell on the world's troubles: war everywhere, even in the animal kingdom; all nature seemingly bent on pursuing selfish ends. Finally, of course, she does fall asleep and her dream begins.

The apparition who comes to escort her on a journey bears a striking resemblance to Dame Philosophy, who consoled Boethius in his prison cell. She reminds Christine of Pallas, "the goddess of Wisdom of whom Ovid writes," but she eventually reveals herself as the Cumean sibyl, who has already figured at the end of *Othéa's Letter to Hector*. The sibyl's first words to Christine are an encouragement in her aspirations for a life of study, assuring her that the greatest reward will inevitably be the renown that will outlive her.

Through this love you have for learning,
To which by nature you're inclined,
Ere your life shall have declined
Such great knowledge will be your gain
That through it will your fame remain
After you in long remembrance. . . .[34]

The sibyl then proceeds to recount the story of all ten sibyls, dwelling especially on her own life. It was she who had offered to Tarquin in Rome the nine books of prophecies recorded by all the sibyls, as recalled by Virgil in the *Aeneid*. She ends by assuring Christine that under her guidance she will find the source of the world's troubles.

So it was that the two of them embarked on an imaginary voyage which undoubtedly owed its inspiration to Dante's. As Dante had chosen Virgil to be his guide, Christine was to be accompanied by Virgil's own guide to the Underworld. It has been supposed that Christine could not have known the *Aeneid* directly, even though she quotes some verses from it in *The Book of Peace,* but she could have known some copies of this text which were produced in Paris workshops during the early years of the fifteenth century.[35]

At the sibyl's bidding, Christine gets out of bed and makes preparations for her voyage, forgetting neither a girdle to bind up her skirt so she can walk easily nor a scarf in case the October weather should prove chilly. They start out by traveling for a time through a pleasant field, but eventually they come to a plain near a mountain, the Mountain of Wisdom, as it turns out, from which flows the Fountain of Knowledge known to the Ancients as Hippocrene. This fountain is seen in the illustrations of the poem, showing the nine Muses bathing there as the winged horse Pegasus flies overhead. The scene recalls the myth of the spring's creation according to which it was formed by a blow from Pegasus's hoof as he prepared to take off from the slope of Mount Helion. The drawing seems inspired by an illustration from a slightly earlier copy of the *Moralized Ovid* that shows Pallas watching the Muses as they bathe in the pool formed by this spring. In *The Long Road of Learning,* it is, of course, Christine and the sibyl who watch the Muses disporting themselves.

When Christine complains that she does not recognize the road they have been following, as befits a sibyl, her companion gives a somewhat cryptic explanation;

> Know that its name is Long Study
> And no rude person may enter therein. . . .[36]

Those who have sufficient courage to climb the mountain can quench their thirst at the fountain itself, but others must content themselves with drinking from the stream lower down the mountainside. Christine then admits that she has heard of both the road and the fountain:

> Dante of Florence both recalls
> In the poem that he composed,
> Where in fine style is all exposed:
> For when he to the dark woods came
> Congealed by fright would he remain
> Until great Virgil should appear
> To succor him from his great fear. . . .[37]

Dante wrote of the Mountain of Grace, but Christine chooses to alter the figures slightly, as was often her habit. It has been suggested that her thirst for knowledge was more reminiscent of Petrarch than of Dante, but there is no question here of the inspiration of the *Divine Comedy.*

Christine and the sibyl next embark upon a terrestrial voyage of considerable proportions, passing Constantinople then going rapidly through the Holy Land, where they pause for a look at Jerusalem, the

Holy Sepulcher, and other well-known pilgrimage sites. Christine shows a particular interest in the Monastery of Saint Catherine on the slopes of Mount Sinai and mentions especially the site of Troy and the Island of Rhodes, both of which they pass on their way to Egypt. In Egypt they stop long enough to admire Babylon and the Nile River, noting the rise and fall of the river's tidal waters. There is also reference to Bayazid's realm in Turkey, which was all too well known in France because of the captivity there of the duke of Burgundy's heir and a few of his companions following the French defeat at Nicopolis in 1396, and Christine is pleased to speak of the Turk's recent defeat by Tamerlane. The battle that brought this about had taken place only the July before, but news of it had reached Paris in September with the return of Jean de Châteaumorand from Constantinople, where he had been defending the city against the Turkish sultan Bayazid's threats. The travelers then cross the Arabian desert, where, as it is noted, supplies for the journey must usually be transported by camel, although these travelers are spared that material consideration. At this point, Christine confesses that she has skipped over many details of what they saw because she does not want to write a whole book about them. They cross the country of the Great Caan, where they see all sorts of exotic beasts—crocodiles and dragons, as well as elephants and unicorns—on their way to Tartary and Cathay. In India they see pepper being cultivated and encounter strange people, both giants and pygmies. They see the four Rivers of Paradise, the lands of Prester John, the tomb of St. Thomas, all favorite geographical lore reported by medieval travelers and often illustrated in copies of a popular book known as *The Flower of Stories of the Orient.*[38]

It has long been supposed that all of this exotic information came from the imaginary travels of Jean de Mandeville, and there is little doubt that Christine knew his book.[39] But some of what she has to say reflects an acquaintance with the reports of actual travelers to the Orient, not only by Marco Polo but also by Oderic of Podernone and William of Boldenseele, whose writings were also available to her. Christine would undoubtedly have known something of the recent adventures of Boucicaut and his companions in the Middle East, and there is no doubt that she was acquainted with Philippe de Mézières, who had spent a good part of his life in the region. During the first half of the fifteenth century, the Orient was still much less mysterious than it became after the Ottoman Empire had succeeded in establishing a barrier between the East and West by the capture of Constantinople in 1453. When Christine was writing, French interest in the Middle East was intensified by the presence of the

Byzantine emperor, Manuel Palaeologus, who had come to Europe seeking allies to help him save Constantinople from the encroaching Turks. On his arrival in Paris in June 1400, he had been magnificently received by Charles VI, who made lavish promises of help, all of which came to very little in the end. The emperor was still in Paris in the fall of 1402, although he left, virtually empty-handed, at the beginning of November, escorted by Jean de Châteaumorand and two hundred men-at-arms. Christine could scarcely have failed to know of his plight.[40]

The terrestrial voyage was by no means the end of Christine's adventure, for she next climbs a high mountain (possibly the Mountain of Wisdom referred to earlier, although Christine leaves the reader in doubt), and from its heights she and the sibyl take off into the celestial sphere. The sibyl calls out some words in Greek, and a ladder is let down to them from the firmament, a ladder that Christine refers to as the Scale of Speculation, another idea borrowed from Dante. The excursion through the skies provides Christine with an opportunity to explain her ideas on cosmology. As the sibyl points out to her the planets, naming their properties and describing eclipses of the sun and moon, she admires the stars in their courses. She also describes the "houses" of the planets while they observe the sun making its rounds to light the sky and to govern time. The concepts expressed here are basically Ptolemaic and undoubtedly reflect knowledge Christine had gleaned from her father. His ideas are further reflected when, in the fourth sky they traverse, she encounters the servants who carry out the astrological destinies of human beings, fixed according to the conditions of the skies at the hour of their birth.[41]

Finally, Christine and her companion arrive at the source of the problems that had been distressing her as she fell asleep—wars, famines, rebellions, earthquakes—and for good measure, she learns the cause of the comet that had been observed over France the year before. She has reached the realm of Dame Fortune, who is surrounded by her court of allegorical personages. But above this crowd can be perceived, at the four cardinal points of the compass, four thrones upon which are seated the four queens who govern the world: Wealth, Wisdom, Chivalry, and Nobility. In the center of the four sits Queen Reason accompanied by her household of Virtues.

As Christine gazes at the scene, a delegation can be observed arriving from Earth to complain of the kidnapping of Proserpina. There is also talk of the folly of Phaeton, who tried to drive the chariot of the sun, for Earth is complaining that the Phaetons have multiplied to the point of creating general havoc. Earth is appealing to Queen Reason to put an end to the anarchy that has resulted. Before expressing any view of her own, Reason calls upon the four ruling Powers to account for the existing situation, especially reproaching Wealth for making men covetous. Wealth accuses Nobility of thinking only of feats of arms, and Nobility in turn blames Chivalry for this alarming state of affairs. Wisdom concludes, however, that Wealth is indeed the primary source of the trouble. The Powers therefore agree that one man should be chosen to restore order and rule the world, but the problem, naturally, is how to find a suitable ruler. Each queen then proposes a candidate, presenting her portrait of the ideal prince. Nobility proposes a prince related to all the reigning houses of Europe. Chivalry recommends a perfect exemplar of the chivalric ideal, unsurpassed in his personal qualities. Wealth insists that the world should be ruled by the man who has the most wealth, because without it no other qualities are respected. Wisdom, not unexpectedly, counters that what is really called for is a philosopher-king, and she is ultimately the winner of the contest. This discussion inspires Christine to recall, citing many examples, that in antiquity power, knowledge, and wisdom were often united to conquer the world, first in Greece and then in Rome. But what nation shall follow Rome? The answer, of course, is France, with Paris as the new Athens, and it is there they should look for a prince to rule the world.

> Then all by communal accord
> Agreed they straightaway would record
> That at the French court he'd be found.
> It is throughout the world renowned
> For eloquence and sense profound;
> There candor, noble hearts abound.[42]

The problem remains as to how to send this message to the French princes, and Christine is commissioned to carry it from Wisdom's court back to the earthly planet. Nothing remains but for Christine and her guide to descend the Scale of Speculation, make their way back to Paris, and return to Christine's house. There she is awakened in her own bed by her mother knocking at her bedroom door.

So ends Christine's long allegorical poem. Making use of octosyllabic couplets and a variety of recognizable sources, she develops the principal themes with considerable invention. The success of Christine's quest for knowledge and her journey away from earthly realms encouraged her to suggest quite boldly to the French princes where she thought their path of duty lay. The poem therefore marks the first occasion on which Christine saw fit to write of the deteriorating political situation in France, although it is not entirely clear what at this particular moment moved her to do so. One possible factor could have been her dismay at the failure of the princes to support Manuel Palaeologus's quest for help in the struggle of Christendom against the encroaching Muslims, the cause to which Boucicaut and Châteaumorand were so ardently devoting their energies. Her admiration for these two knights and their efforts may well have extended beyond the praise she recorded for their championship of women.[43]

Moreover, Christine was clever enough to turn the tables here on Jean de Meun and his admirers. If *The Romance of the Rose* celebrated a revolt against Reason, she undertook to demonstrate the advantages of following Reason's advice, in this case with regard to the public life of France and of the whole Christian world. She could scarcely have been so naive as to expect the actual triumph of reason in these matters, yet the scene at Reason's court gave her an opportunity to demonstrate a grasp of the political troubles around her that would in fact ultimately lead to France's ruin. This knowledge pointed the way to a new stage in her career, during which she would devote the major part of her attention to her concern for her country's welfare.

Inspired by Dante, Boethius, and her other sources, Christine produced a remarkably original work. From the perspective of modern times, it is perhaps not difficult to grasp the singularity of a woman who claimed Boethius as her favorite bedtime reading, yearned to drink at the Fountain of Wisdom, and discoursed on the qualities of the perfect prince, a theme much favored by later Renaissance writers, but in the autumn of 1402 these qualities were quite extraordinary, scarcely to be believed. The discovery that she was able to write on serious questions undoubtedly increased Christine's growing self-assurance and encouraged her to undertake even more ambitious projects.

The goddess Fortune had inspired writers from antiquity onward; her turning wheel was a familiar symbol in both art and literature.[44] It is not surprising that Christine, who had just described a visit to Fortune's seat and who had long considered herself one of Fortune's victims, should have wanted to write a long poem on the subject. Early in 1403, she set out to write *The Mutation of Fortune*.

New popularity was given to the theme by the first French translation of Boccaccio's *De Casibus Virorum Illustrium (On the Fates of Illustrious Men)*, which Laurent de Premierfait had finished in November 1400. Boccaccio's work had been influenced by Petrarch's treatise on Fortune, *De Remediis*

Utriusque Fortunae (On the Remedies for All Fortunes), already known in France through Jean Daudin's translation of 1378.

Christine was early attracted to the theme, for her Ballade VII begins:

> Ha! Fortune ever perilous
> How you have brought me from high to low.
> Your dreadful sting so venomous
> Has dealt my heart a mighty blow.
> You could not harm me more, you know,
> Than to take from my heart the glow
> Which made my life so joyous.[45]

In Ballade X she complained that Fortune had sworn out a death warrant for her, and in Ballade XII she warned:

> Who dares confide in Fortune's boon
> He is, in truth, deceived.
> Less constant she is than the moon,
> As many have perceived.
> Those who have greater heights achieved
> Are oft knocked down, as is well known,
> All joys, like empty winds, soon flown.[46]

Fortune had likewise figured in *Othéa's Letter to Hector* (LXXIV), where Christine explained:

> Fortune, according to the poets, may well be called a great goddess, for by her we see how worldly things are governed. And because she promises prosperity to many, and indeed gives it to some, though in a little while, whenever it pleases her, she also takes it away, the good knight should not trust her promises, nor be discomfited by his own adversities. For Socrates says: The course of Fortune runs like a snare.[47]

Thus, it is apparent that Christine had been reflecting for some time on the material that formed the basis of *The Mutation of Fortune,* which she finished on November 18, 1403. One copy was presented to the duke of Burgundy on January 4, 1404, and another was presented to the duke of Berry. Two other manuscripts were copied and illustrated at the same time. It is not certain for whom they were intended, although one must surely have been prepared for the king of France.[48]

It is difficult to believe that such a long work could have been entirely written in one year and, indeed, references to the fall of Richard II of England and to the deposition of Wenceslas, king of the Romans, suggest that it might have been started as early as 1400, perhaps soon after the conclusion of *Othéa's Letter to Hector*. The poem's 24,000 lines (again in octosyllabic rhyming couplets) are divided into seven parts, the first of which is devoted to an allegorical account of Christine's own life to date or, as she puts it, of "the person who compiled this book and her adventures." She especially wanted to recount one experience that "seemed scarcely believable": how she was changed from a woman into a man in order to deal with the problems that confronted her after her husband's death. Although it is tempting to take this change of sex in modern psychological terms, it seems probable Christine was simply explaining her need to change her role in life and, as she herself said, to guide her ship across stormy seas, meaning that she had to provide for her family.

Speaking of her childhood, she describes her father as a philosopher and her mother as Dame Nature. Her father's wealth consisted of some stones he had gathered from the Fountain of the Muses on Mount Parnassus, already described in *The Long Road of Learning*.[49] Two of these stones were of particular value, one because it gave him the power to foretell the future and to interpret the revolutions of the planets and the movements of the stars, the other because it gave him the skill to cure all human ills. Having been born a girl, Christine is unable to inherit her father's treasures, she tells us, and is obliged to content herself with the scraps and fragments of his knowledge she was able to gather up.[50] As she cannot have her father's learning, her mother puts her into the service of Dame Fortune, giving her her own chaplet of precious stones (virtues), although these are not as valuable as the stones possessed by her father. When she reaches a certain age, Fortune decides to send Christine off with a message to Hymen, the god of Marriage. So it is that Christine embarks on another imaginary voyage, this time in a ship specially prepared for her and on a journey that will last ten years. At the beginning of her travels, the god of Marriage receives her in his palace, places a ring on her finger, and presents her to a young man who pledges himself to her. As the voyage continues, the ship, now skillfully piloted by her husband, encounters a storm so violent that the young man is hurled into the sea and the ship all but founders. Christine is tempted to follow her husband into the stormy waves but is restrained by Fortune from leaping overboard. Fortune then takes pity on her plight, transforming her into a man so that she can undertake to guide the ship herself.[51]

Christine accounts for her transformation, which she says has already lasted thirteen years, by recounting other metamorphoses that have taken place in the past. Inspired once more by Ovid, she tells how the companions of Ulyssus were turned into swine by the enchantress Circe and how the sex of Tiresias was changed. Because of her own transformation, she has been able to rescue the ship from menacing reefs and to sail it to Fortune's dwelling.

The symbol of the ship tossed on Fortune's seas had already provided the inspiration for Ballade XIII. It had been used by Boethius (*The Consolation of Philosophy* 2.1), by Dante (*Paradiso* 27), and by Petrarch; in the future it would be used by others, but the idea of combining the voyage in the ship with a metamorphosis from woman to man was entirely Christine's.

The second book of *The Mutation of Fortune* describes Fortune's dwelling place. Medieval descriptions of her palace all stem more or less directly from Alain de Lille's *Anticlaudianus,* written in the latter part of the twelfth century. Often, this work was known by way of Jean de Meun, who, in *The Romance of the Rose,* had given a similar description of this dwelling as situated on a rugged island cliff, buffeted by the winds. To this traditional account, Christine added a few details of her own.[52] In her poem, the castle stands on a rock in the midst of the Sea of Great Peril. As it turns ceaselessly and sways from side to side, blown by the winds, it is held in place by four heavy chains. The castle itself has four façades. The first of these, guarded by Fortune's sister Wealth, is imposing, but the walls are not as solid as they appear to be. The second side is less imposing and even less solid than the first, but the entrance is considerably wider. This gate is guarded by Dame Hope, who graciously welcomes the large crowd of people trying to make their way through this gate into the castle. The third façade, guarded by Poverty, is not only ugly, but the door is also black and malodorous. People naturally fear the sight of Poverty and try to avoid this entrance, yet there are long lines of those who have no alternative. The fourth façade, even darker and more menacing, tilts precipitously, and parts of the wall are crumbling. The gate is low and narrow, and its frightful guardian is Atropos, Death. Nobody wants to enter through this door, but all are obliged to leave by it, paying their own passage and taking with them only their good deeds.

Wealth's gate leads to a large inner court paved with bright tiles. Here are to be found the lodgings of those who serve Fortune's court, but this part of the castle is vastly inferior to the donjon perched high in the clouds, which is Wealth's own residence. Four roads lead up to it: Great Pride, with golden steps; Great Malice, arranged so that Fortune's other sister, Envy, can spy on those who mount this way. To climb by way of the third road, Great Science, one must overcome the serpent that Cadmus once vanquished. The road is secure yet little used. The fourth road is Saint Peter's way to Paradise, which is also called Just Life. It is the steepest of the four and also the most narrow. Wealth's donjon is inhabited by the world's princes, but loose planks make the floor there treacherous, and those who fall through them drop into the depths of the tower.

Within the palace dwells Fortune, too. According to tradition, she has two faces, one laughing and the other black and ugly. As in *The Romance of the Rose,* she looks like a queen, wearing a golden crown on her smiling side, although on the other side the crown is made of pointed knives. Her right hand holds a sceptre and her left one a sword; her right foot rests in water, her left in fire.[53]

Fortune's two brothers, Eure and Meseure, are the governors of the palace. They exercise their functions without any semblance of justice. Eure is a rather unattractive little man dressed in green who never harmed anyone and is liked by all, although his friendship, often gained with difficulty, is readily lost. A laurel crown in his hand, he precedes Wealth everywhere. Meseure, on the other hand, is tall and ugly, with a disagreeable face mostly covered by a beard. He whistles as he speaks. In spite of his size, he is agile, running here and there with a big stick with which he frequently injures those from whom he removes Fortune's favors. The two brothers take turns operating Fortune's wheel. Meseure, standing at Fortune's side, is ready to inflict injuries at her slightest word. Christine pauses in her description to recall that she has suffered more ill fortune from him than favors from Eure.

The manuscript illustrations usually show the House of Fortune with Wealth standing at the gate and Eure receiving newcomers. In another miniature, the two-faced Fortune is accompanied by her brothers as she stands at her wheel. A third illustration shows the pope and the antipope seated at the top of the donjon. As this is the safest part of the castle, there is a great struggle to reach it, and the climbers try to throw the mighty from their seats there. Some inevitably rise while others fall, not necessarily according to merit, and the air is filled with the cries and lamentations of the unlucky.[54]

Book III of *The Mutation of Fortune* is devoted to the other inhabitants of Fortune's castle. This provides Christine with the opportunity to discourse on the misfortunes of contemporary society, beginning with the schism in the papacy and the throne without any true occupant. She expresses concern, too, for the lack of leadership in world affairs and about the civil wars in Italy, where the tranquility and prosperity of Venice is exceptional amid widespread conflict. Speaking of England's situation, it seems little better; she cites especially the decline of chivalry there since King Arthur's day. Finally, she dwells on the troubles of France, where she analyzes the shortcomings of society, class by class, speaking particularly of the nobles who are so dissipated and given to luxury that one wonders if they would be capable of sustaining serious warfare. Christine shows here her awareness of the very weaknesses that would lead these noblemen to defeat at Agincourt some ten years later. She does not fail to mention the public officials who are more eager to enrich themselves than to perform their duties, or the governors of the royal children who flatter and humor them rather than educate them, or the educated who are full of pretensions while really disdaining learning. Merchants are depicted as sometimes kind, but more often not. Common people possess certain virtues yet are often lacking in sobriety. In the end, only the villagers are blameless. Their industry in the face of multiple hardships makes them often more admirable than their "betters." This is the first of several occasions when Christine devoted passages in her writings to a critique of the shortcomings of the various "estates" in society, and her testimony is valuable because it is based on firsthand experience. It is interesting to note that she makes a particular point of explaining that she does not speak about the vices of women because they are not involved in public affairs, and, in any case, they are more likely than men to be virtuous.

Returning to the theme of Fortune, Christine explains how all lands and people are subject to the movements of the stars, but if God permits Fortune to have power over worldly affairs, it is because he does not consider them of any great importance. Thus Christine makes clear her views on the relationship between the pagan goddess Fortune and Christian theology, a sensitive issue in the medieval world that troubled many writers, Petrarch and Boccaccio among them. Christine's intention was quite obviously to avoid any accusation of heresy on her own account.

At the beginning of Book IV, there is a description of the marvelous Hall of Fame at the top of Fortune's donjon. Although placed high and subject to the buffeting winds, it is spacious and richly decorated by mural paintings of the best and worst episodes in the lives of personages whom Fortune has wished to commemorate. Christine insists that she is unable to describe them all because they are so numerous, and before describing any of them she discourses on the qualities of the soul, which are the only human attributes not subject to Fortune's whims. This leads her to a discussion of the liberal arts—the "sciences," as she calls them—first the theoretical ones (theology, physics, mathematics) and then the practical (ethics, economics, politics), those that instruct not only in "works" but also in "words" through Grammar, Dialectic, and Rhetoric. All of these branches of knowledge are born of Philosophy:

> Their nursemaid she and their mother,
> None there is that comes not from her;
> She is the fountain and the source
> From which the others take their course.[55]

The descriptions of the paintings in the great Hall of Fame to which Christine then returns recall the miniatures of a copy of the *Moralized Bible* illustrated by the Cité des Dames Master and his collaborators.[56] If Christine did not actually work in close collaboration with her illustrators, she was herself endowed with a remarkably graphic imagination and was capable of transmitting scenes in great detail to her readers, a quality that must have appealed greatly to her contemporaries.

As she was in the midst of writing a part of the poem that is a sort of universal history, while discussing the early history of the Jews, Christine unexpectedly turned to writing in prose, excusing herself by saying that she had been overcome by "a sudden fever" (although she also claimed that she was repeating what she found written on a wall she was examining). But having recovered from her illness, she continues the next part (Book V) in verse, again with an explanation of the extent to which greed has given men a taste for worldly honors that makes them especially vulnerable to Fortune's whims. She then gives an account of ancient history from the Assyrians to the Greeks, recalling especially the story of Theseus's triumph over the Minotaur. If her command of history seems astonishing, it must be remembered that she was undoubtedly making use of the *Ancient History since the Creation,* which had already served her as a source for *Othéa's Letter to Hector.*

The sixth part includes a history of the Amazons and the conquest of the Golden Fleece and dwells on the Trojans, with a vivid description of the destruction of Troy. Part VII is largely devoted to Roman history—the foundation of Rome, the adventures of Aeneas, and the wars between Rome and Carthage. Like Petrarch, Christine was attracted by Scipio's career, but she also describes the exploits of Julius Caesar. She ends her account of universal history by naming what she considered the four greatest ages of the world: the Assyrian, Carthaginian, Macedonian, and Roman, all of which have revealed themselves as subject to Fortune's whims.

Only in the final pages of the poem does she consider the age in which she herself is living, recounting the lives and misfortunes of some outstanding people about whom she knew: Peter of Cyprus, Pedro the Cruel of Spain, Johanna of Naples. She also speaks of Richard II of England and, finally, of John II and Charles V of France, whose deeds are depicted on the walls of the great Hall of Fame. She concludes by wishing that Fortune's continuing favor be granted to the French princes who are still living, notably those to whom she would offer copies of her poem. In fact, the year 1404 was almost the last moment when these nobles could be considered in Fortune's good graces at all. Soon the duke of Burgundy would be dead and within a few more months his heir would embark on a deadly rivalry with the duke of Orleans. All the while, Charles VI would continue to sink ever more completely into insanity.

In the final lines of the poem, Christine makes it clear that she herself puts no trust in the machinations of Fortune. She has chosen a peaceful, solitary life as the greatest protection against the turning of her implacable wheel:

> For never, nowhere are things sure
> Because that ubiquitous Meseure
> Takes his way. So to find repose—
> Even though everywhere he goes—
> I've chosen now for all my joy
> My life in study to employ.
> With peace and chosen solitude,
> A studious world makes my life good.[57]

In a certain sense, Christine had reached the end of her intellectual apprenticeship, if not the end of the long road of learning. In her review of universal history, she was able to relate her own troubles to the natural order of the universe. Her study of history would dominate much of the rest of her literary career, which was about to move into a new phase, one that would produce several of her best works.

Whatever her motivation for writing *The Mutation of Fortune,* this was the work that brought her to the attention of the duke of Burgundy, who was to play an important role in the shaping of her future. Christine's sense of history impressed him so greatly that he commissioned her to write an official biography of his brother, the late king Charles V.

Charles V Consults Sages of Antiquity

Philip the Bold, Duke of Burgundy

6

The Lessons of History

The events that led from the presentation of *The Mutation of Fortune* to Philip the Bold, duke of Burgundy, to his commissioning a biography of his brother are described in the opening pages of *Le Livre des Fais et Bonnes Meurs du Sage Roy Charles V* (*The Book of the Deeds and Good Customs of the Wise King Charles V*):

> The truth of the matter is that in this present year of grace, 1404, after a volume of mine entitled *The Mutation of Fortune* was presented to the said prince, my Lord of Burgundy, as a gift on the first day of January, which we call New Year's Day, which he received most graciously and pleasantly, I was informed by his treasurer Montbertaut that it would please him if I were to compile a treatise concerning a certain matter, which he would explain to me fully, if I should be willing to carry out the wishes of this prince; and so, moved by the desire to comply with his bidding to the best of my small ability, I betook myself with my assistants to the place where he was to be found in Paris, the Louvre, and there, when he was informed of my arrival, he had me brought into his presence most courteously by two of his courtiers, John of Chalons and Toppin of Chantemerle.[1]

The plan for the biography of Charles V was discussed, and Christine was provided with a manuscript containing some useful material, a manuscript that has been identified subsequently as a collection of several chronicles, one of them Bernard Gui's translation of a *Flores Chronicorum* (*Flowers from the Chronicles*), which had been made at the late king's order.[2] The manuscript also contains the chapters from the more or less official *Chroniques de France* (*Chronicles of France*) that have to do with his region. Undoubtedly, Christine was also given an idea of the kind of biography she was expected to write.

115

In preparing her life of Charles V, Christine not only made use of these texts, but also drew on other sources, such as a popular translation of *De Regimine Principum (On the Regiment of Princes)*, by Egidio Colonna (Gilles de Rome), which had also been prepared especially for the Charles V's library; a commentary on Aristotle's *Metaphysics* from the pen of St. Thomas Aquinas; as well as other books she had already used for *The Long Road of Learning* and *The Mutation of Fortune*.

Although Christine attributed the duke's commission to the success of her treatise on the role of Fortune in human affairs, with its long discourse on universal history, it seems equally possible that he was impressed by her encomium of Charles V in *The Long Road of Learning*. Philip of Burgundy had every reason to remember his brother with gratitude because he owed him nearly everything he possessed. Even though his father had originally promised him the Duchy of Burgundy, without the concurrence of Charles V the gift would have come to little. Also important was his extraordinarily advantageous marriage to Margaret of Flanders, one of the most desirable heiresses in Europe at the time. Her hand had been promised to Edward III's son, the count of Cambridge, and the English alliance had much to offer Flanders, but Charles V's skillful diplomacy had been sufficient to win her, with all her territories, for his youngest brother.

If gratitude does not seem an adequate explanation for Philip's desire to honor his brother's memory, one might estimate his political ambitions at the beginning of 1404. During the preceding year, he had been preoccupied with promoting a series of marriages between his own grandchildren and the children of Charles VI. He had already succeeded in arranging advantageous marriages for his children and counted on his grandchildren to continue adding to his territories and strengthening his political alliances. In July 1394, only seven months after the birth of his first granddaughter Marguerite of Nevers, he arranged an alliance for her with the French dauphin Charles, who was born on February 6, 1392. The betrothal was celebrated at the beginning of 1396, and the little princess was known thereafter as "Madame la Dauphine," even though she never left her own nursery. When Charles died in February 1401, Philip lost no time in arranging another match with his successor, Louis of Guyenne. At the same time, his grandson Philip was betrothed to Michelle of France, and one of the younger Burgundian princesses was promised to Prince John, duke of Touraine. A new prince Charles, then only three months old, was to be the husband of Jacqueline of Bavaria, the two-year-old daughter of the duke of Holland and Margaret of Burgundy.

Although the duke of Burgundy was determined to have a role in the future of the French monarchy, Fortune turned her back on him. The first two marriages took place according to plan, but Louis of Guyenne died in 1415 and John of Touraine, by then Jacqueline's husband, outlived his brother by only a few months. It was the infant Charles who finally succeeded to the French throne as Charles VII and at a moment when Burgundy had become one of France's principal enemies.

Because Philip was so preoccupied with the future of France, it is understandable that he should want certain traditions of the monarchy to be known and preserved. The poor mad king Charles VI was incapable of transmitting such information to his children, and the queen and the king's brother, Louis of Orleans, were already being criticized for their frivolity. It was therefore to the duke of Burgundy's political advantage to show himself as the member of the family most concerned with ensuring the welfare of the dynasty, who took seriously Aristotle's admonition that one must see to the education of the children for the future well-being of the state.[3]

There was also the more immediate concern of the regency. In 1393, shortly after the onset of Charles VI's insanity, the dauphin Charles was only a year old. It was decided that, should the king die before the prince reached the age of fourteen, Louis of Orleans would exercise the regency and the queen, together with the dukes of Berry and Burgundy, would be the guardian of the royal children. This arrangement did not please the duke of Burgundy and was undoubtedly a factor in his attempt to try once more in the spring of 1403 to modify the situation in his own favor. During a period of the king's active insanity, when Louis of Orleans was away from Paris, he tried, with the collaboration of the duke of Berry, to change the decrees governing the majority of the dauphin and the establishment of a regency. It was his idea to promote another ordinance proclaiming that in the case of the king's death there would be no regency; the dauphin would be crowned at once, whatever his age; and the government would be carried on by the queen, the dukes, and the royal council. Since the intent of this act was to limit Louis of Orleans's role in the government, Louis could scarcely have been expected to agree with such a procedure, especially in view of the announcement soon afterward of the series of Franco-Burgundian marriages. Louis was powerless to change the marriage agreements, but he was able to nullify effectively the duke of Burgundy's other maneuvers and continued to be considered the potential regent and the member of the royal family closest to the crown.[4] These circumstances made it all the more advantageous for the duke of

Burgundy to present himself as the person most concerned with preserving his brother's memory and preparing the reign of a new king who would almost certainly have a connection through marriage with his own immediate family.

His choice of Christine as the person to write the biography is a matter of considerable interest. Up to that time, she had been known primarily as a poet and had been associated with the duke of Orleans's household. In both *The Long Road of Learning* and *The Mutation of Fortune,* however, she had been generous in her praise of all French princes. She knew Charles V during her childhood and was still in touch with others who remembered him. Moreover, her talent for popularization was probably more in keeping with Philip of Burgundy's purposes than the services of a more learned historian. Perhaps, most of all, the duke was aware of Christine's contacts with the humanistic currents that were sympathetically received in his own entourage. She would be capable of understanding the value of a biography conceived to ensure the late king's reputation.

The difficulty of Christine's task becomes apparent when one considers the lack of models in France for such a biography. There was Joinville's biography of Saint Louis, as well as another written by Guillaume de Saint Pathus, both of them available in the royal library in the Louvre. Secular biographies were beginning to attract the attention of humanists in Italy, but none had yet been written in France, with the possible exception of *La Vie de Bertrand DuGuesclin (The Life of Bertrand DuGuesclin),* a poem by Jean Cuvelier of which a prose version was made toward the end of the fourteenth century.[5] It is probable that neither Christine nor Philip the Bold had in mind any of these, but rather the sort of biography favored by the early humanists, Petrarch above all others, which was intended to preserve worldly fame in the face of the triumph of death.[6]

Christine's primary undertaking would be therefore to show that Charles V was a "wise" king and that his manner of ruling was worthy of emulation. As for the details of his exploits, she would refer her readers to *The Chronicles of France,* where they were fully recounted. She was more concerned with drawing parallels between his qualities and those represented in episodes from ancient history, clearly a humanistic technique that reflected Petrarch's concept of using the past to inform the present. More recently, the Florentine chancellor Coluccio Salutati had written that he "cherished the historian whose duty it is to hand down to posterity the memory of things accomplished, so that the examples of kings, nations, and illustrious men can be equaled or surpassed by imitating them" and that "the knowledge of things done warns princes, teaches people, and instructs individuals, and is thus the most certain basis for the conduct of affairs."[7] The role of historian under such circumstances was to arrange material in such a manner as to save individuals and events from the ravages of time, and to call attention to the lessons to be learned.

As this was Christine's first attempt at writing a long book entirely in prose, she was understandably uncertain about how to approach the task. In the end, she adopted a plan she would repeat in several other works, which was to divide her material into three parts. Possibly she was inspired by Egidio Colonna, who had used such a plan in his *On the Regiment of Princes,* the treatise on the education of a prince written at the request of Philip III in the second half of the thirteenth century. It had enjoyed renewed popularity through the translation made at Charles V's request by Henri de Gauchi.[8]

The first part of her own text on kingship is devoted to a discussion of how the man should rule himself according to high moral standards; the second deals with the king's government of his family; the third, about the king's rule of his subjects, is a treatise on politics that discusses the best way to govern a kingdom or a state. It is in the opening part that Christine follows Egidio Colonna most closely, setting forth the moral character of the former king as "nobility of heart," which she considered the proper basis for *"renommé"* or worldly renown, a concept including both fame and good repute, with the additional idea that a king should give thought to the image he will leave behind him in the world. The second part of the book describes Charles V's relationship with other members of his family, and also discusses the nature and purpose of chivalry; the final part is devoted to the former king's wisdom. Throughout, Christine adds to her written sources the testimony of people who had known the king personally, along with her own recollections of his reign. These elements are reminiscent of the sort of reportage for which Froissart was famous, yet, curiously, there is no evidence that Christine was influenced by his *Chronicles.*

The first part of the biography, which concentrates on the king's "virtues," is less interesting than the other two. Certain pages are important, however, for what they reveal about Christine's concept of writing history. There is first of all a genealogy of the kings of France, showing their descent from Franco, the son of Hector of Troy. She had already discussed this Trojan lineage in both *The Long Road to Learning* and *The Mutation of Fortune,* and it is probable that she had gleaned her information from Bernard Gui's *Flowers from the Chronicles*.[9] (This legend continued to flourish into the sixteenth century to inspire Pierre Ronsard's ill-starred epic *The Franciade*.) Christine was undoubtedly wise in restricting her use of it to one short chapter entitled "Preamble to Glory," where she notes in passing the "variation in Fortune" that brought it all about.[10]

She proceeds to an account of Charles V's birth in the Château de Vincennes, yet for some curious reason gives the date incorrectly. Although he was born on January 21, 1338, Christine was under the impression that the event had occurred a year earlier.[11] Apparently, she found little in his early years worthy of comment, launching instead into a discussion of a suitable education for a young prince based on the ideas found in Egidio Colonna, and adding the suggestion that there were shortcomings in this particular prince's early training for which he later paid a heavy price: For example, when he was unexpectedly forced into a position of leadership because of his father's capture by the English at the Battle of Poitiers. It is true that Charles had been accused of cowardice by certain historians unfavorable to him, including Froissart, and of having abandoned the field of battle during that French disaster, but another, more reasonable, interpretation of events is that he had been removed more or less forcibly from the action by his advisers in order to prevent his being captured by the English along with his father and younger brother.[12]

Christine also passes rapidly over the dauphin's painful experiences when trying to reign in his father's place between 1358 and 1361 without the real authority of kingship, a time when he had been obliged to deal with the perfidy of his brother-in-law Charles (the Bad) of Navarre and the highhandedness of his uncle, Emperor Charles IV, not to mention the popular uprising in Paris led by Etienne Marcel, and the Jacquerie, the series of peasant's revolts to the north of Paris that first broke out in 1358. It was a tribute to the quality of the dauphin's intelligence that he learned so much about ruling from these trying experiences and that many of his later ideas of government were based on this knowledge, but it is equally true that recalling this period added little to his ultimate glory. Noting that these events were recorded in the chronicles of the reign, Christine passes on rapidly to the coronation.

In the chapter entitled "The Coronation of King Charles and How Soon Afterward He Undertook to Follow the Rule of Virtue," Christine may be understood to be saying that the king applied his intelligence to the numerous problems created by the wars and the shortcomings of his predecessors. Several further chapters devoted to the problems of a youthful ruler are inspired once more by Egidio Colonna and buttressed by examples drawn from antiquity. Throughout the biography, there is a basically humanistic insistence on the importance of good instruction and the usefulness of acquired knowledge. Christine thus arrives at a concept of the age of maturity as the time when one "knows the truth and the proper application of all that one has learned in childhood and youth; then, when one is knowledgeable enough to know how to demonstrate the truth, one is able to give advice as an expert, based either on what one has learned in theory or seen in practice and continued. . . ."[13] She makes a particular point of the fact that Charles, even at an early age, wished to know the effects of virtue, and in this manner she introduces the concept of the "wise" king, the same concept Charles had undoubtedly formulated for himself.[14]

There follows a description of the way in which Charles organized his official life, how he chose to be guided by well-qualified counselors, and especially of the way in which "according to the custom of noble, ancient emperors" he sought out competent advisers, even from other countries, including, of course, Christine's own father who had been sought out by royal messengers in Bologna.[15]

Thereafter Christine begins a description of the king's daily life. If, as it has been pointed out by a modern biographer, her account leaves the king little time for the serious business of governing a kingdom, it nonetheless gives a glimpse of the domestic life of a monarch as it is seldom recorded in the chronicles.[16] One is given the opportunity to observe the king's good spirits as he talks to his chamberlains and his servants on arising in the morning, his conscientious observance of religious devotions, his desire to receive all sorts of individual petitions on coming out from hearing mass at one of the royal chapels. On certain days he then met with the royal council, and all of this he accomplished before he took his first meal, which was strikingly simple, at ten o'clock in the morning. While he breakfasted, like King David he listened to the music of stringed instruments. When he rose from this meal, it was his custom to receive ambassadors or knights from foreign lands, each according to the honor due him, and to hear their reports of matters of particular interest to him. After disposing of any problems that might result from these reports, he spent about two hours signing letters or disposing of vacant offices to which appointments needed to be made, after which he retired to his private apartments for an hour of rest. This rest period was followed by some time set aside for recreation, necessitated, as Christine pointed out, by the perpetually delicate state of the king's health. During this interval, he sometimes went to his treasury in the Louvre, for instance, to admire the extensive collection of jewels and gold plate he had been gathering there since his youth. After attending vespers, he strolled in the palace gardens if weather permitted, or if he was in residence at the Hôtel St.-Paul, he spent some time with the queen and their children, or, on other occasions, he received merchants who brought luxurious textiles, jewelry, or unusual objects about which he was in the habit of consulting the connoisseurs of the royal family, the duke of Berry in particular. In the winter, he often had someone read aloud to him until supper, which was also a frugal meal. Before retiring, he conversed with his knights and barons and so, Christine informs us, he "used the course of his life."[17]

Even if this cannot be regarded as an absolutely exact account of the way in which Charles V conducted all of his days, it gives a vivid impression of the king moving through his daily tasks much like any head of government. This impression of reality is reinforced by the description of the king himself that follows, a verbal portrait corresponding with admirable accuracy to many of the sculptures and miniatures preserving his likeness. Christine mentions the king's pallor, the outward sign of his constantly poor health, and his calm manner and disciplined behavior, which had early been apparent when he had shown that he could keep his temper in the face of the taunts of Etienne Marcel and his collaborators. Finally, she mentions the attractive masculine quality of his voice and his eloquence in speaking.[18]

Christine next describes the king's stately progress across Paris, or beyond to one of his country residences, concluding with the observation that for him the purpose of all royal ceremonies was to "maintain and give examples to his successors that the noble crown of France should be upheld and maintained by solemn order, for all sovereign magnificence was due it,"[19] a principle echoed by later monarchs and by none more than Louis XIV.

The portrait of the king is accompanied by another, somewhat less lifelike, of the queen, Jeanne de Bourbon, whom Charles married in 1350 when she was twelve years old. Her virtuous, though far from beautiful, face has been preserved by two statues and several miniatures depicting the royal family, but perhaps best of all by the Parement de Narbonne, the silken altar cloth that shows the king and queen kneeling in devotion. Christine mentions the queen's rich, though modest, garments, which she changed several times in the course of a day, according to royal custom, and also the elegant decor of her apartments in the Hôtel St.-Paul. But a truer image of this queen seems to emerge later from the pages of *The Book of the Three Virtues,* where she is undoubtedly the model for the virtuous queen whose daily life is described there.[20]

Christine makes a particular point of the king's devotion to his queen and her willingness to support him in all his undertakings. She passes over in silence, no doubt accepting it as an inevitable misfortune of life, the fact that of the nine children born to the marriage only three outlived their parents and that the birth of the ninth child cost the queen her life. There were also several anxious years when there was no heir to the throne, and during two periods of the queen's life she suffered from a serious nervous affliction, which may well have been a form of mental instability. Whether this was temporary insanity or merely deep depression is not entirely clear, but the unfortunate fact remains that Jeanne de Bourbon passed on to her first son, the future Charles VI, this mental instability, and it would later reappear in her great-grandson, Henry VI of England.

Christine ends the first part of her biography by discussing a series of personal qualities necessary for a good king, based primarily on Egidio Colonna's recommendations, although she does not arrange them in the same order as in her model. She also continues to compare Charles V's actions with those of the heroes of antiquity. She admits that there is even more to be said about the king's virtues then she has included in the book, which she nevertheless finished writing on April 28, 1404.

Before starting to write the second part, Christine had heard a most distressing piece of news: Philip the Bold had died suddenly in the city of Halle, near Brussels. She decided to continue with the undertaking in spite of her patron's death and devoted the first chapter of the second part to deploring his loss. She also composed a ballade in which she attributed the misfortune to the malevolence of Fortune as well as to the unfortunate confluence of constellations that had brought about a spell of damp and foggy spring weather in the county of Hainaut.[21]

The second part of the biography is given the general title "Chivalry." In setting forth Charles V's qualities of kingship, Christine was faced with the problem of showing how it was possible for a man not noted for physical courage and plagued with deteriorating health to be considered a model of chivalry. Charles suffered from the additional disadvantage of an unfavorable comparison with his younger brother Philip, who had remained at his father's side throughout the Battle of Poitiers and had accompanied him to captivity in England, even though Charles had done a great deal more to preserve his country by acting as its regent during his father's absence.

Christine was therefore at pains to show that intelligence in directing a battle is superior to sheer force at arms, pointing out that Charles had four qualities that represent the very essence of true chivalry: good fortune, common sense, diligence, and strength. This standard, she writes, was established long ago by Romulus in Rome. Christine's ideas about the origins of chivalry were derived in large measure from Honoré Bouvet's *The Tree of Battles,* which had been dedicated to Charles VI in 1387. She would also make extensive use of this work in further writings.[22] Then Christine describes the benefits that France has enjoyed because of the efforts of the late king. It was quite true that Bertrand DuGuesclin's victory over Charles the Bad at the Battle of Cocherel, at the moment of Charles V's coronation, had marked a significant change in the direction of France's fortunes. It is scarcely surprising in this context, moreover, that the account of the king's abrogation of the Treaty of Brétigny, which the Franch had signed after their defeat at Poitiers, should have been presented as the king's desire to carry out the will of his subjects. Undoubtedly, this is how he intended it to appear, even though in reality it represented a triumph of French diplomacy not entirely free from duplicity. The accord actually signed by the French ambassadors was a revision of the original treaty presented by the English at Calais at the moment John II was about to regain his provisional freedom. The revised text, which Edward III ratified, did not include the article, which was a part of the original dealing with the renunciation by the two kings to certain territorial rights. Although the consequences of this omission may not have been apparent to the English at the time, the French were probably quite aware of the possibilities it presented, for it gave the French king and his jurists the basis for abrogating the treaty in 1368. A further justification of Charles V's policies appears in *Le Songe du Verger (The Dream of the Orchard),* where there is a lengthy discussion of his own point of view as opposed to the English stand on the renewal of warfare.[23] It is not surprising to find the king's decision to defy the English and his plan to reconquer Gascony presented by Christine as examples of his good judgment. Especially when judged from the perspective of thirty-five years, his actions could scarcely have been seen as anything less.

Having concluded her discussion of the king's chivalric virtues, Christine proceeds to a curious series of portraits of other members of the royal family that can only recall the dynastic sculptures on the Louvre staircase. The qualities Christine attributes to the French princes have often been criticized as unduly flattering. She herself seems to have been aware of this problem, and she devotes a chapter to justifying these laudatory descriptions of living princes. She assures her readers that she has not included the portraits merely to flatter the originals nor to ingratiate herself with them. She is abundantly aware that all human beings have faults, yet she insists that nobody has the right to pass final judgment on them until their lives have ended. Her purpose in this case is merely to carry out the task that has been assigned to her, and it has seemed pertinent to recall the late king's family. As for their virtues and shortcomings, she explains: "I reply that the text of my book is intended to praise virtues and not to blame vice. . . . I know nothing of this matter, nor have I made inquiries."[24] A somewhat ambiguous observation to be sure, yet at the time of writing Christine apparently believed that it was unseemly to reprove the princes in public for their shortcomings. It could also be dangerous to court their displeasure, although only a few years later Christine would join her contemporaries in taking a considerably different view of the failings of certain members of the royal family.

Christine next turned her attention to other important figures of the royal court, particularly Charles V's great military leader Bertrand DuGuesclin, to whose exploits she devotes several chapters.[25] It is evident that she has at last come upon some excellent material for her discussion of chivalry, and she dwells on DuGuesclin's exploits against a background of tactical theory drawn from Egidio Colonna and from accounts of Roman military prowess gleaned from the *De Re Militari (On Military Affairs)* by Vegetius, with considerable material drawn from Bernard Gui. Although her numerous comparisons between the recent past and antiquity provide an important insight into a concept of history that was advanced for her time, Christine frequently seems overwhelmed by the bulk of the material she is trying to deal with. She is all too aware that her competence in military matters could easily be called into question, and so she devotes a chapter to explaining how she, like the architect or craftsman, merely puts together materials available to her:

for as the architect or mason has not made the stones from which he builds and constructs the castle or house which he attempts to perfect and on which he labors, although he assembles the materials, putting each object where it belongs according to the plan he is trying to carry out; likewise the embroiderers, who create various designs according to the subtlety of their imaginations, but do not create the silk, the gold, or the other materials they use. . . . It is sufficient for me merely to know how to apply all of this to my purposes, so that it may serve the inspiration which I am trying to fulfill.[26]

An especially interesting chapter near the end of the second part is devoted to Charles V's concern for developing a navy, a contribution for which he is still honored. He was aided by the support of Henry of Trastamara and the flourishing Spanish fleet until, by 1377, there was a French navy capable of dominating the English Channel and even raiding the English coast. Christine makes a great point of the French capture of the coastal town of Rye. She also quotes advice from Vegetius on the construction and provisioning of battlecraft, and it is amusing to find her recommending a large supply of soft soap to be thrown onto the adversary's decks in a sea battle. (Should the ship break up, the enemy would inevitably slide into the water.) It is perhaps not surprising to find a native of Venice dwelling on the importance of naval power, but it is a fact that Charles V was almost unique among early French kings in perceiving the value of a navy. There would not be his equal until Francis I.[27]

At the end of the second part of the biography, Christine concludes, not unexpectedly, that Charles V met satisfactorily the qualifications required for chivalry:

Wherefore, all things considered, if my reasons may be accepted as true proof, our very wise king was also truly chivalrous, possessing the conditions already mentioned as necessary to the lofty title of chivalry, which is to say good fortune, sense, diligence, and force.[28]

In certain respects, the third part of the biography is the most interesting. Here Christine discusses Charles V's intellectual accomplishments, comments on several of the most significant events of his reign, and describes his building program in Paris as well as his development of the royal library in the Louvre. She insists on the qualities expected of a wise king, pointing out to her readers that the term "wise" should be understood to combine learning and prudence with inherent wisdom. She explains further, on the basis of Aristotle's *Ethics,* that wisdom has to do with a knowledge of first principles, the quality of mind that makes the expert superior to the amateur, the artist superior to the artisan, and the speculative scientist superior to the applied scientist. This observation offers an important clue to the mentality of the late Middle Ages, and it is on the basis of this concept that Christine demonstrates that Charles V was a philosopher, a true lover of knowledge. It was because of his desire to understand first causes that he commissioned translations of books on theology (Saint Augustine's *City of God,* for instance) as well as works of pagan philosophy (Aristotle's *Ethics, Politics,* and *Economics*). She also describes the king as an *astrologien,* which, in this case, means that he was concerned with understanding the first causes of the natural universe.[29]

In speaking of Charles V's interest in scientific speculation, Christine was undoubtedly recalling her father's role in his service, but she also mentions Nicole Oresme's *Book of the Sky and the World,* a translation and commentary based on Aristotle's treatise on cosmology prepared for the royal library in 1377. This text provided the most detailed and accurate analysis of terrestrial dynamics from the Greek astronomers to Copernicus. As bishop of Lisieux, Oresme was obliged to harmonize theology and philosophy with science. He dared to raise the question of the constant motion of the spheres before Copernicus. He could not prove positively the motion of the earth, but he did prove it was possible that the earth did not stand still. This treatise was never published, so it is not known whether Copernicus was aware of its existence. Nevertheless, it serves as a reminder of the importance of Charles V's patronage of scientific speculation.[30]

Turning to the king's building program in Paris, Christine explains that here he showed himself to be a great artist. Certainly, this was one of his major contributions to his country. Not only did he modernize and beautify Paris, but he also encouraged the talents of architects, stonecutters, and masons, setting in motion a flowering of talent that outlasted his reign.

The same might be said of the translations and other books he commissioned for the royal library where, as Christine observes, he kept scribes occupied in copying manuscripts. By the end of his life, Charles V's collection included some nine hundred volumes, the major portion being divided between the Louvre and Vincennes. Although many of these books reflected the king's personal interests, others were intended for his successors, to encourage them in the pursuit of knowledge and virtue and perhaps to mold their political thought. But most important of all, by his devotion to learning, Charles V initiated a period in which manuscript production flourished in Paris, resulting in one of the outstanding artistic achievements of the later Middle Ages.[31]

A new trend toward naturalism is observable in the style of manuscript illumination from this period onward. One may wonder to what extent it was related to the scientific interests encouraged by the king. Especially important were the contributions of certain court painters, such as Jean Bondol of Bruges, who painted the dedication miniature in the Bible presented to the king by his courtier Jean de Vaudetar, or the Master of the Parement de Narbonne, who was, next to Jean Bondol, the best artist of Charles V's time, and who, toward the end of the period, illustrated a part of Jean de Berry's *Les Très Belles Heures* and pointed the way to the great flowering of manuscript painting in Christine's own day.[32]

Next, Christine compares the king's excellent relationship with the University of Paris to Charlemagne's admiration for Alcuin, the founder of the celebrated school at Tours, to whom she attributes the shifting of the traditional center of learning from Rome to Paris. She thereby lends her support to the French side of the controversy on this subject between Petrarch and the early French humanists. At the same time, she mentions Charlemagne's knowledge of several languages, an observation that would have been less surprising at the beginning of the sixteenth century than in 1404.[33]

In the course of several more chapters, Christine accumulates examples of the wise king's deeds and sayings, always with a parallel drawn from ancient history. A point is made here of the king's preference for a wise poor man over a foolish rich one. Other illustrations are drawn from the testimony of people who had known Charles V personally, with special mention accorded to the royal librarian, Gilles Malet, and to the royal chancellor, Bureau de la Rivière, both of whom Christine knew.

She recalls Charles V's felicitous relationships with contemporary monarchs, noting the presence in France of Pierre I of Lusignan, king of Cyprus and Jerusalem, whose brief capture of Alexandria had been celebrated by the poet Guillaume de Machaut. Christine is also led to recall having seen with her own eyes the ambassador of the sultan of Egypt Shaaban II (1363–1377)—whom she refers to as sultan of Babylon—when he appeared at the French court richly and exotically dressed.[34] The king's gracious reception of such visitors serves as the introduction to one of the most important passages in the third part, the visit to Paris in 1378 of the Holy Roman Emperor Charles IV of Luxembourg and Bohemia, who was also Charles V's uncle. This event, which marked one of the high points of Charles V's reign, is described with lavish detail. The king himself had been at pains to have a special account of it inserted into *The Chronicles of France,* and this is undoubtedly Christine's source for much of what she relates. She might well have seen in the Louvre the king's own copy of these *Chronicles* illustrated in such an exceptional fashion as to make the miniatures alone an outstanding record of the event.[35]

Recalling that his interview with his uncle at Metz in 1358 was one of the lowest points in his fortunes, Charles V took understandable pride in receiving the emperor this time with great ceremony. Christine's account provides a remarkable glimpse of official court life at its most magnificent. She emphasizes that everything was so well arranged that, in spite of the enormous crowds everywhere, the official guests were neither overwhelmed nor hemmed in by the spectators at the pageant. She speaks with evident relish of the banqueting tables:

> the arrangement, the noble draperies of gold and silver worked in raised patterns that were hung on those walls and in those rich chambers, velours embroidered with large pearls, gold and silver in a variety of patterns, ornaments everywhere, hanging golden draperies and canopies on high rods and curtained chairs, vessels of all descriptions in gold and silver, large and heavy, for table service, great dressers covered with golden flasks, cups and goblets, along with other vessels of gold studded with jewels, finely prepared dishes and desserts, wines, delicious meats, all in great abundance. . . .[36]

Charles IV, though not really old, was badly crippled by gout, and he may have sensed the end of his life approaching. Not only did he want to make a pilgrimage to the Abbey of St.-Maure-des-Fosses, near Paris, but he also longed to see once more the French capital and the court where he had spent a good part of his youth. In spite of his infirmities, his enjoyment of the visit is everywhere evident. He reached the Abbey of St.-Denis, to the north of Paris, during the first days of January, having already been welcomed by the king's brothers. At St.-Denis, he took the opportunity to admire the relics in the treasury and the funerary sculpture that Charles V had commissioned there for his ancestors as well as for himself and his queen. Unable to travel long distances on horseback, the emperor continued his journey in one of the queen's litters. But at the gates of Paris he mounted a horse for his official entrance into the city.

When the two monarchs met at the city gates, it was arranged that the king would be riding on a white horse, which would make him stand out in the crowd of dignitaries, whereas a more inconspicuous black one would be provided for his guest. This detail is carefully recorded not only by Christine, but also by the illustrator of the king's copy of the official chronicle of the reign. The difference in color symbolized the fact that the king was playing host in his own territories, whereas the emperor was merely a foreign visitor, however distinguished. Throughout the visit, the king took pleasure in showing off the marvels of his refurbished city, while the emperor recalled with emotion the scenes of his youth. Although Charles IV was lodged in the old royal palace on the Ile de la Cité, he was taken to visit both the Louvre and the royal residence of St.-Paul. At the latter, the queen received him, and he was especially moved to greet again, after many years, the queen's mother, the duchess of Bourbon, whose sister, Blanche of Valois, had been his first wife. The two of them enjoyed a long conversation together in private. Eventually, the king took the emperor to his favorite country retreat, his château Beauté-sur-Marne, where they had a few days of leisure in which to talk at length and to exchange magnificent gifts. Outstanding among these gifts was a golden cup studded with precious stones and engraved inside with the signs of the zodiac, the planets, and the fixed stars. It was presented to the emperor by the duke of Berry.[37]

The leave-taking was prolonged and emotional; afterward, a group of courtiers escorted the royal guest to the frontiers of the country. But aside from the king's great personal satisfaction, little of substance had been accomplished. No alliance was formed against England, and the following year, during the religious crises brought on by the dual papacy, the emperor and his son chose to support the Roman pope, to the grave disappointment of Charles V. This visit marked the high point of Charles V's reign. Almost immediately thereafter a series of misfortunes befell the king, saddening and darkening the two remaining years of his life.

The first of these was the queen's unexpected death early in February. On the fourth day of the month, a daughter, christened Catherine, was born in the Hôtel St.-Paul; the queen died two days later. At the age of forty she was bearing her ninth child and, according to Christine, the birth had been difficult. It was characteristic of the king, Christine notes, that although overwhelmed with grief, he immediately concerned himself with the salvation of his queen's soul and the necessity of providing her with a funeral worthy of her status in life. Her body was conveyed to St.-Denis, where the funerary effigy already awaited it. Her heart was given to the Friars Minor for burial and her entrails were interred in the chapel of the Celestine monastery near the royal residence where she had spent so many days of her life.[38]

After describing the queen's burial, Christine turns to the other major event of these final years, the schism in the Church after the death of Pope Gregory IX in 1378. She treats the matter with the greatest discretion because by the time she was writing these pages the problems that resulted from the king's decision to recognize Robert of Geneva rather than the Italian candidate for the papacy Urban VI were all too apparent. Charles V himself had begun to see that he had committed a serious error in judgment and on his deathbed went so far as to declare that he was prepared to revise his position if the Church showed him to be in error. Christine nowhere mentions the deposition he signed to this effect, too late to have any bearing on subsequent events, yet her treatment of the subject gives the impression that she was aware of it and regarded it as representing the king's official attitude.[39]

It is certain that when Urban VI was first elected, he was recognized as pope even in France. But soon afterward a dissident assembly of French cardinals elected Robert of Geneva as Clement VII. When Clement decided to remain in Avignon instead of attempting to establish himself in Rome, a royal ordinance from Paris declared him the true pope. Moreover, this act was followed by letters from Paris to other princes urging them to follow France's example. Although Charles V insisted to the last that he had acted for the good of France, the suspicion remains that one reason for favoring Clement was that he was willing to further the Italian territorial ambitions of Charles's brother, the duke of Anjou. Christine, in common with other contemporaries, presents the king as having acted on the counsel of his most respected advisers, but she says that his conscience began to trouble him when other European princes, notably his uncle the emperor, decided to support the Roman pope.

The stress of these problems and the death of the constable Bertrand DuGuesclin undoubtedly played a part in undermining the king's already delicate health. (Perhaps his physical state had been undermined in the first place by the trials to which he was subjected by the crisis in Paris following his father's capture at Poitiers. Until that time his health had apparently been normal.) As he grew older, he was subject to gout, as Christine's reference to his constantly swollen right arm makes clear, and he suffered from an abscess on this arm that resisted healing. However, the account of his death suggests that Charles V died from heart disease.[40]

As the summer of 1380 drew to a close, the king's health was so precarious that he retired to Beauté-sur-Marne where he had always enjoyed the tranquility and the country air. He died on September 16. The details of his last days were recorded soon afterward in an anonymous Latin account that was certainly written by one of the people present at the time.[41]

Christine made use of this account, and it is also possible that she had heard about it from her father, one of the king's physicians. Her account includes one curious detail not recorded anywhere else. As the end of his life approached, Charles V had the abbot of St.-Denis bring to his side the crown that had been used for the coronation ceremony and that was kept in the treasury of the royal abbey. This fact is mentioned by all chroniclers. According to Christine, however, he also had the bishop of Paris bring to him the Crown of Thorns, the precious relic preserved in the Sainte Chapelle since Saint Louis had brought it back from the Holy Land. The symbol of the king's spiritual life thus formed an antithesis to his official life, represented by the royal crown, an image that is striking and laden with significance.[42]

All the members of the royal household and the counselors wept bitterly, which was no wonder, according to Christine, for they had lost so good a master. This loss may have been enhanced in her memory by a knowledge of the years of tribulation following his death. The unfortunate truth was that Charles V's ordinary French subjects were somewhat less affected by his death, habitually complaining as they did of the burden of taxes he had imposed. On his deathbed, Charles did abolish the *fouage*, or hearth tax, one of the most unpopular of them, and his heirs were left to cope with the disastrous economic consequences of his benevolent gesture.[43]

Christine finished the biography on November 30, 1404, nearly a quarter of a century after Charles V's death. Although the duke of Burgundy was no longer alive to read it, she presented a copy to the one remaining brother, the duke of Berry, on the following New Year's Day. To judge from the relatively few manuscripts that still exist, the work does not seem to have enjoyed any great popularity in its day, although its influence in later times was considerable. It stands as one of the few eye-witness accounts of the reign.

Christine has been accused of writing a panegyric rather than a true biography, but on the whole her information has been repeatedly demonstrated to be exact, far more so than Froissart's, whose knowledge of the French court was less direct than hers. Her portrait of the king and other details of his personality have been repeated by all who have written about him, whether or not they have given Christine credit for the information. Charles V was the only Valois king who had a genuine political sense and a true aptitude for ruling. If Christine recalled with enthusiasm, and a certain amount of nostalgia, the years of his reign, it was not merely because of the personal gratitude she freely expressed, but because France was a good deal better governed then than at the time she was writing.

Critics have also frequently failed to understand the sort of biography Christine intended to write. It stressed a new attention to the recent past and to a portrayal of personal, human detail, conceived to honor and preserve the fame of a great man as an example to those who followed. This concept of biography had spread from Italy to France, encouraged, it would seem, by the translations of Valerius Maximus and Boccaccio that were becoming known in the early years of the fifteenth century. Charles V had already played a part in the preservation of his reputation by the commissioning of his tomb at St.-Denis and by his supervision of the official record of his reign in *The Chronicles of France.* It was Christine's task to preserve the memory of his personality and his life-style.[44]

Rectitude Welcomes Christine and Her Companions to the City

Christine Greets the Three Virtues

7

A Feminine Utopia

For about two years after she had concluded her part in the debate over *The Romance of the Rose* at the beginning of 1403, Christine was preoccupied by other matters, yet she had not renounced her desire to speak her mind in women's behalf. Therefore, having completed her biography of Charles V, she turned once more to the subject that was particularly near to her heart, and in the course of 1405 finished two of her most significant works, *The Book of the City of Ladies* and *The Book of the Three Virtues*, which has sometimes been called *The Treasury of the City of Ladies*. The first of these undertakes to show the importance of women's contributions to society in the past, whereas the second attempts to teach women of all estates how to cultivate useful qualities in the society in which they live and thus become worthy inhabitants of the City of Ladies described in the first book.

The title of this first volume was inspired by Saint Augustine's *City of God*, which had been translated into French for the royal library. The artist who would illustrate several copies of Christine's new work had probably already illustrated at least two copies of this translation. Even more important to Christine, however, was Boccaccio's *De Mulieribus Claris (Concerning Famous Women)*, a compendium of brief lives of notable women from mythology and antiquity that was translated into French in 1401. The copies prepared for the dukes of Berry and Burgundy were finished about the time Christine was embarking on her new project, and she has even been suggested as a possible translator of Boccaccio's Latin text, albeit without convincing evidence.[1]

Christine made extensive use of Boccaccio's examples of famous women, to the point that the work has sometimes been considered a translation, although this is not at all the case.[2] In common with her contemporaries, Christine borrowed freely from her sources; Boccaccio himself had done the same in gathering together material for his work.

Christine's original contribution is the way in which she uses her material, and none of her writings shows her method better.

Boccaccio's treatment of feminine history was chronological, starting with a sketch about Eve ånd ending with an account of the misfortunes of his contemporary Johanna of Naples, queen of Sicily. Moreover, he had no discernible didactic intention, as had been the case with his *De Casibus Virorum Illustrium (The Fates of Illustrious Men)*, where he had undertaken to show the devastating action of Fortune in the lives of certain historic figures. This work also enjoyed a considerable success in France, having been translated in 1400. In contrast, Christine did not pursue her subject chronologically, and her purpose was clearly didactic, to illustrate certain feminine traits to which she wanted to call her readers' attention. In addition, Christine tailored her examples to her purposes, a process not always understood by those who have seen her work as a translation.[3]

The framework that Christine invented for her examples of famous women adds originality and interest to her undertaking. She proceeds on three levels, beginning with the symbolic construction of a city devoted exclusively to the needs of women, where the most worthy among them would be invited to dwell, free from the demands and the preoccupations of the world. Then there is a detailed discussion of the causes of anti-feminism and the outlining of women's special contributions to society with further reference to their potentialities, which they are not always able to realize because of the prejudices of society. Finally, there are historical examples to support these claims. It is evident, however, that this is primarily an allegorical city rather than a sort of feminine hall of fame. The city's construction is carried out by Christine under the guidance of three supernatural queens who appear before her in a vision, presenting themselves as Reason, Rectitude, and Justice. They are stylishly dressed and wear golden crowns on their heads. Reason carries a mirror in her hand, Rectitude a ruler, and Justice a measuring vessel.

These Virtues are quite different from the well-known theological Virtues, Faith, Hope, and Charity, and they bear only a slight resemblance to the traditional Cardinal Virtues, Prudence, Magnanimity, Fortitude, and Justice, although these last were the basis for Christine's *Book of Prudence* and appear elsewhere in her writings. Reason, Rectitude, and Justice are primarily secular Virtues come to offer lessons in *prudence mondaine* (worldly prudence), which they make clear in the course of *The Book of the Three Virtues*.

Dame Reason explains at once that the mirror she carries is intended to show people who look into it their true selves, so that if they are straying from the path prescribed by their basic natures they will be guided by this revelation back to the proper course. Christine was probably inspired here by Vincent of Beauvais's *Speculum Historiale (Historical Mirror)*, another important source for *The Book of the City of Ladies*, which recommended "holding the mirror up to nature." But one is inevitably astonished to find Christine making use of this idea so frequently associated with Molière more than two hundred years before him. She had already seen Dame Reason enthroned in the heavens during her allegorical journey in *The Long Road of Learning*.

The second Virtue, Dame Rectitude, explains that she dwells more frequently in heaven than on earth because she is the defender of the just, those faithful servants of God, and is their advocate in heaven. The ruler in her hand serves to separate right from wrong and to demonstrate the difference between good and evil. Dame Rectitude had made an earlier appearance in Philippe de Mézières's *Songe du Vieil Pèlerin (The Dream of the Old Pilgrim)*, written in 1387.[4]

Dame Justice is already familiar through representations of the Cardinal Virtues, where she is usually seen carrying a sword or a balance, or sometimes both. Christine's concept of Justice is somewhat different, although not entirely new here, for she has been shown in *Othéa's Letter to Hector* receiving her measuring vessel from God. It has been pointed out that this concept of Justice had already appeared in another of Christine's favorite sources, a medieval anthology known as *Les Fleurs de Toutes Vertues (The Flower of All Virtues)*, in which Aristotle is quoted as saying that "justice is a measure that God has established on earth to limit all things." Justice explains to Christine that she dwells in hell as well as in heaven and on earth because of her appointed duty to judge, separate, and provide retribution or reward according to each individual's deserts. This is the purpose of the measure she carries. It is perfect, whereas earthly measures are sometimes false, being too generous for some, but inadequate for others.[5]

It is Reason who suggests to Christine the idea of building the City of Ladies, promising to provide her with materials for its foundations. Rectitude will help build the high walls to surround it as well as the bastions and moats that will protect it. Rectitude then offers her ruler for laying out the plan of the streets and for constructing the houses, palaces and temples that will be built within the walls. Justice will add the finishing touches to the high towers and palaces, which will glitter with gold. It will also be her responsibility to select a queen as well as the other women who will be invited to dwell in the city. At first, Christine objects that she is not capable of such an undertaking, saying: "I am not Saint Thomas the Apostle, who through divine grace built a rich palace in Heaven for the king of India, and my feeble sense does not know the craft, or the measures, or the study, or the science, or the practice of construction."[6] But Reason assures her that all answers can be found in written texts and urges her to begin digging at once, following the lines that have already been traced for the foundations. Christine is then directed to take a trowel in hand and to start building the foundations, and it is thus that Christine is depicted in illustrations on the earliest manuscripts of the work.

Four of these first manuscripts, which show her holding a trowel, were illustrated by the artist known as the Cité des Dames Master, who with his associates formed one of the largest and most prolific groups of illustrators in Paris at that time. Their technique of painting is noticeably Italianate in inspiration, and in addition to Christine's works, the group illustrated early copies of the first French translations of Boccaccio.[7]

As the building of the city progresses, Christine discusses with her supernatural visitors the true nature of women, their contributions to society, and the reasons why they have so frequently been unappreciated and even scorned. Christine raises here the question of misogyny, of which she herself had felt the sting, not only in the debate over *The Romance of the Rose,* but even more unpleasantly during the first years of her widowhood.

As in *The Long Road of Learning,* she takes as her point of departure a book she has been reading, in this instance the *Lamentations* of a certain Mathéolus (known as The Bigamist), a Latin poem written at the end of the thirteenth century and translated into French by Jean Le Fèvre around 1370. The translation, more than the original, met with a success which lasted well into the sixteenth century. The combined efforts of Mathéolus and Jean Le Fèvre, both admirers of Jean de Meun, sum up all the traditional arguments against women and against marriage in a work attacking the illusion of love and making much of conjugal servitude from the masculine point of view. Together they represent everything Christine most resented.[8]

Allowing her readers another glimpse of her private life, Christine explains that she was starting to read the *Lamentations* when her mother called her to supper. When she takes the book up again the next morning, she finds herself profoundly depressed by the constant attacks on women. Recalling conversations she has had with other women, she wonders if women could possibly be as deceitful and undependable as they have been depicted, for she is not alone in finding the traditional opinions unjust. Finally, she asks herself if she would not have been better off if she had been created a man, the idea that had already had its part in *The Mutation of Fortune*. As she sits with her cheek resting on her hand in unhappy meditation, she falls asleep but is soon startled by the appearance of the three goddesses who stand before her in a ray of light.

Christine and Dame Reason open their discussion of misogyny by examining possible motives for all the slanderous remarks in literature about women. Christine considers such ideas against nature, for men and women are in reality capable of great love for each other, as she had already pointed out in *Cupid's Letter*. Dame Reason, for her part, undertakes to prove to Christine that she is mistaken in feeling so downcast about women's reputation in past ages, and on this basis she begins to give examples of women who have made important contributions to civilization. These, indeed, provide the cement to hold the city's foundations together.

Christine next proposes to Dame Reason a series of questions concerning various sorts of limitations placed on women by society, asking first why women should not be allowed to sit in seats of justice. Reason replies by citing the example of Nicaula, the empress of Ethiopia, and follows it with the story of Queen Fredegund of France, who governed after the death of her husband, King Chilperic. She also mentions in passing some more recent French queens who have served in a similar capacity, Charles IV's Queen Jeanne as well as Blanche, the wife of King Philip VI, both of whom served as administrators for their husbands. A pattern is established here that will be repeated in following chapters where parallels are drawn between classical models and more recent examples of comparable virtues, for Christine is clearly unwilling to have feminine virtue relegated to a mythological past. Special attention is devoted to Penthesilea who, according to one tradition, had gone to Troy in the hope of rescuing Hector from the Greeks. This warrior had already figured in *Othéa's Letter to Hector* and in *The Mutation of Fortune*. Christine repeatedly showed a fascination with the Amazons, those superwomen who would continue to be admired—and attacked—throughout the Renaissance.[9]

She also inquires of Dame Reason if there have ever been any women known for their scientific ability, which leads the goddess to admit that women are handicapped in this pursuit because they are generally expected to devote themselves to their families and households, but she insists that if it were the custom to send women to school with their brothers, their capability would undoubtedly be equal to men's. One has only to consider the differences between educated men and those without learning to see that women's accomplishments cannot be judged without allowing them fair opportunities for proving themselves. Nevertheless, she cites the example of a Roman maiden called Proba, who not only read Virgil's works but also conceived the idea of writing a summary of Old and New Testament history in Virgilian meters. There was also the case of Manto of Thebes, the soothsayer for whom Virgil's birthplace Mantua was said to have been named, a legend Christine could have known from her reading of Dante.[10]

Ceres, who had already figured in *Othéa's Letter to Hector,* is mentioned here for her patronage of agriculture and her invention of certain methods of tilling the fields. Circe is also mentioned here for her knowledge of herbs and for her unusual shrewdness in the conduct of her affairs rather than for her reputation as an enchantress.[11]

When Christine asks Reason for the names of women who have been inventors, there are accounts of Nicostrata, who civilized the Latins and provided them with the Italic alphabet, and of Minerva's invention of armor. (Minerva was one of Christine's favorite goddesss, appearing repeatedly in her writings.) References to Isis and Arachne are accompanied by Dame Reason's comment: "And let no one say that I am telling you these things just to be pleasant; they are Boccaccio's own words, and his credibility is well known and evident."[12]

Christine is finally moved to say to Dame Reason:

> My lady, I greatly admire what I have heard you say, that so much good has come into the world by virtue of the understanding of women. These men usually say that women's knowledge is worthless. . . . In brief, the typical opinions and comments of men claim that women have been and are useful in the world only for bearing children and sewing.[13]

She concludes that the practical gifts provided by women have been as valuable to humanity as Aristotle's philosophy.

As the foundations of the city have now been laid, Dame Reason allows Dame Rectitude to take charge of the construction. Rectitude, in her turn, calls attention to the handsome white stones she has collected for the lodgings to be built in the city, obviously symbolic stones representing such qualities as filial piety, represented among others by Julius Caesar's daughter Julia, the wife of Pompey; wifely devotion as seen in Alexander the Great's wife Antonia; and chastity, of which the cases of Lucretia as well as Sarah, Rebecca, and Penelope are cited. There is also constancy in the face of male fickleness represented by the case of Griselda; faithfulness in love as illustrated by such women as Dido, Hero, and two women cited from Boccaccio's *Decameron*, Ghismonda and Lisabetta.[14] Lucretia and Queen Blanche of France are examples of integrity, and generosity is represented by the Roman lady Busa and Christine's contemporary Marguerite de la Rivière, the wife of one of Charles V's most favored courtiers. Also included are tales of a number of other women, all outstanding for one virtue or another. As Rectitude explains, only the perfect stones have been retained, all others having been cast aside. Finally, Dame Rectitude announces that the city has been constructed, with its tall buildings and broad streets, its royal palaces with keeps and defense towers, which can be seen from a great distance, so the time has now come to invite those who will dwell in the city.

The question arises as to who is worthy to live in the city. The first to be invited are the ten sibyls, whose history is then detailed in greater length than in *The Long Road of Learning*. Christine regarded prophecy as a special divine gift or, as she explains, special sensitivity to God's thought. That she was so impressed by the power to predict the future is a reflection of her father's influence, although it also reveals a concern for what would later be known as psychology.

When it is decided almost immediately that no dissolute woman will be included among the inhabitants, this decision gives rise to a discussion of whether women really deserve all the ill that has been said of them and of the reasons why they have so often been criticized in books written by men. This subject is the context for citing examples of women who were devoted to their parents in old age, those who supported their husbands when they were faced by difficulties, even showing themselves capable of guarding their secrets. Dame Rectitude does not fail to praise Christine herself for her devotion to her own mother.

With regard to the devotion of wives to their husbands, Christine wants to know if it is true that marriage is really so painful for men to endure through the fault of their wives, as has so frequently been claimed, to the point where some writers admonish men not even to think of marriage.[15] To this question, Dame Rectitude replies tartly that far more women suffer from marriage than men, for they are sometimes really worse off than if they were slaves of the Saracens! What has been said in books has little to do with reality, for everyone knows that men are their wives' masters and would never permit it to be otherwise. Luckily, it is also true that happy marriages exist, but any woman who finds herself so blessed should indeed be grateful to Dame Fortune. As for the many good wives who serve their husbands with devotion in sickness and in health as if they were their gods, these will be among the first to be welcomed into the new city. It is here that the story of the patient Griselda is told.

A particularly interesting chapter in this part of the book, entitled "Against those men who claim that it is not good for women to be educated," introduces the question of the value of a liberal education for women.[16] Christine and Dame Rectitude agree that the evidence shows that women are improved by knowledge, and that it is indeed surprising that some men oppose the idea. Dame Rectitude insists that these could only be men whose opinions are not founded on reason. She then recalls the case of Hortense, the young Roman whose father was a rhetorician and orator. He allowed his daughter to be trained in these same skills to the point that she became his equal. She then used her talents to defend other Roman women against certain legal impositions. It is here, too, that the story of Novella is recounted: The daughter of a legist at the University of Bologna, who might well have been known to Christine's father, Novella was educated to the point that she was capable of giving her father's university lectures when he was not able to do it himself, although she made it a practice to stand modestly behind a curtain so that her beauty would not distract his students.[17]

With these daughters of learned fathers, it is inevitable that Christine's own case should be mentioned, and Dame Rectitude reminds her:

> Your father, who was a great scientist and philosopher, did not believe that women were worth less by knowing science; rather, as you know, he took great pleasure from seeing your inclination to learning. The feminine opinion of your mother, however, who wished to keep you busy with spinning and foolish girlishness, following the common custom of women, was the major obstacle to your being more involved in the sciences. But just as the proverb already mentioned above says, "No one can take away what Nature has given," your mother could not hinder in you the feeling for the sciences which you, through natural inclination, had nevertheless gathered together in little droplets. I am sure that, on account of these things, you do not think you are worth less but rather that you consider it a great treasure for yourself; and you doubtless have reason to.[18]

Understandably, this was a sentiment with which Christine could only agree.

Marguerite de la Rivière, whom Christine cites as an example of generosity, had also been praised in the biography of Charles V. Christine relates that at a gathering in the duke of Anjou's residence, this lady noticed that a certain well-known knight was absent. On inquiry, she learned that despite his long record of courageous service to the country he had been imprisoned because of debts incurred during his travels. Protesting that it was shameful for such a loyal defender of the country to suffer imprisonment even for an hour, she removed the golden tiara she was wearing on her blond hair, replaced it with a leafy circlet, and sent the ornament for the old knight's ransom with the message that he should be escorted at once to the gathering.[19] The incident is reassuring evidence of human kindness in a society that was noted for egotism and materialism, and it is also an excellent illustration of Christine's habit of adding modern examples to parallel those drawn from antiquity.

Inevitably, the ladies of the French royal family are invited to inhabit the city, beginning with the queen, Isabeau of Bavaria, about whose qualifications some question might well have been raised. It cannot be said that Christine speaks of the queen with great enthusiasm, for she merely says that there is no harm or meanness in her nature. (In a letter addressed to Isabeau later the same year, Christine would remind her in stronger terms of her duty to preserve the national peace and unity, and she would again cite to her the example of various queens of antiquity and those of more recent times.) Mention is also made in *The Book of the City of Ladies* of the young duchess of Berry and the duchess of Burgundy, and special praise is reserved for Marie de Bourbon, the duke of Berry's daughter, who seems to have been one of Christine's favorite patronesses. To her Christine dedicated not only some early poems, but also one of her last works, the *Epistre de la Prison de Vie Humaine (A Letter concerning the Prison of Human Life).*

Having issued a special invitation to these honored guests, Christine addresses herself to all virtuous women, inviting them all—from the past, present, and future—to draw benefit from the existence of the new city, the fruit of her great study and effort on their behalf.

It has been suggested that Christine should have ended her book at this point, but this is to misunderstand the nature of medieval thought, even in the case of a person as liberal and as little given to extreme piety as Christine.[20] In common with her contemporaries, she believed, at least theoretically, in the superiority of the contemplative life over the worldly, a point that is made quite clear at the beginning of *The Book of the Three Virtues.* Thus Dame Justice decides that the Virgin Mary should be called upon to reign over the new city, and at the beginning of the third part she leads her to the city gate, inviting all other women to come forward to receive her. The Virgin graciously accepts the invitation, expressing her willingness to dwell among the others as the leader of the feminine sex, as it has been God's will from the beginning. She comes accompanied by her sisters and Mary Magdalene and is followed by a host of martyr saints who were, after all, the first women in Christian history to be recognized for their achievements on the same basis as men. Prominent among them are Saint Catherine of Alexandria and Saint Margaret, whose stories Christine would have known not only from the *Historical Mirror* of Vincent of Beauvais, but also from Jacobus de Voragine's *Golden Legend.* It is scarcely surprising to find an account of the life of Saint Christine of the city of Tyre, whose father shut her up in a tower and tried to make her worship pagan idols although her spirit was imbued with Christianity. Christine describes at length her heroic martyrdom and concludes with a special prayer to her:

> O blessed Christine . . . pray for me, a sinner, named with your name, and be my kind and merciful guardian. Behold my joy at being able to make use of your holy legend and to include it in my writings, which I have recorded here at such length out of reverence for you. May this be ever pleasing to you! Pray for all women, for whom your holy life may serve as an example for ending their lives well. Amen.[21]

Dame Justice finally complains that it is impossible to go on speaking of the merits of such women because they have been so numerous. In all of them God has shown the power of virtue so that even many who are unnamed are worthy to dwell in the City of Ladies.

Christine then concludes with a discourse directed to the city's inhabitants, both present and future, where she points out that though it is natural to rejoice when a victory has been won and enemies have been confounded, they must use their newly found heritage wisely, avoiding arrogance but rather remembering the humility of the Virgin, who called herself God's handmaiden. Superior virtue should make one kind and humble. She commends to all women skill in defending themselves against those who would assault their honor or their virtue, adding:

> Make liars of them all by showing forth your virtue, and prove their attacks false by acting well. . . . Repel the deceptive flatterers who, using different charms, seek with various tricks to steal that which you must consummately guard, that is, your honor and the beauty of your praise. Oh my ladies, flee, flee the foolish love they urge on you! Flee it, for God's sake, flee! For no good can come to you from it. Rather, rest assured that however deceptive their lures, their end is always to your detriment. And do not believe the contrary, for it cannot be otherwise.

So she returns once more to the issues raised by *The Romance of the Rose* and other antifeminist literature:

> Remember, dear ladies, how these men call you frail, unserious, and easily influenced but yet try to catch you, just as one lays traps for wild animals. Flee, flee, my ladies, and avoid their company—under these smiles are hidden deadly and painful poisons.[22]

This is the theme that had preoccupied her from the beginning—women's vulnerability in the face of social structures that fail to protect them from harm.

The final chapter of *The Book of the City of Ladies* serves as an introduction to the second undertaking, *The Book of the Three Virtues,* which was designed to deal with certain problems of contemporary society and to prepare any woman who so desired to become a worthy inhabitant of the City of Ladies. (She seems to have begun to write it almost immediately after having finished the first book.) Although the three Virtues figure in it far less than they did in *The Book of the City of Ladies,* they do reappear in the opening pages to spur Christine on to continue writing and to organize a school for all women who wish to attend. Much of the instruction there will be given in the name of Worldly Prudence, who sometimes appears as a fourth figure in the miniatures that illustrate the manuscripts.

Worldly Prudence is related to the concept of the active life that is recommended to women at the beginning of the book. Although far from scorning the contemplative life, Christine did not believe that many women would be willing to give up family and all worldly desires in order to follow that path. She considered that in most cases it was more reasonable to attempt to cultivate the active life in this world to the best of one's possibilities. Previously, a great deal of moral literature had been devoted to discussions of achieving otherworldliness, but Christine was preparing to offer something new, in accordance with developing humanistic ideals. Furthermore, she was continuing to draw lessons for the present on the basis of the examples from the past already provided by *The Book of the City of Ladies.* Nothing of this sort had ever been attempted for women, yet the extraordinary originality of Christine's concept has not always been sufficiently recognized.

Mistaken conclusions about the nature of this book have sometimes arisen from the seemingly conventional framework, in which advice is offered to women from various segments of society, beginning with the queen and ending with the wife of a farm laborer. It has often been assumed that it is little different from other treatises written for women in the late Middle Ages, such as *Le Ménagier de Paris (The Goodman of Paris)* or *Le Livre du Chevalier de la Tour Landry pour l'Enseignement de ses Filles (The Knight of La Tour Landry's Book of Advice for His Daughters).*[23] The truth is, however, that Christine's book is quite different from these. She concerns herself with the problems of women of all social classes, rather than addressing a specific group of women, and furthermore she is concerned not only with prescribing for them a domestic and spiritual life (which she recognized as the assigned lot of most women) but also with encouraging them to stand on their own feet, to make some sort of contribution to society, to dominate the conditions of their lives that make or break them. In the course of achieving her ends, Christine includes scenes from contemporary life, which might best be called vignettes of Parisian society at the beginning of the fifteenth century. These are worthy to be compared with the miniatures decorating the manuscripts produced in Paris at the same period.

Christine had a further reason for wanting to write *The Book of the Three Virtues* during the summer of 1405. Recently, a marriage had taken place between the heir to the French throne Louis of Guyenne and the duke of Burgundy's oldest daughter Marguerite. It was to this princess, whom she naturally assumed would be the future queen of France, that Christine dedicated this work.

Marguerite of Nevers was eleven years old at the time of the marriage but, according to the custom of the day, she was expected to go at once to the French court, there to grow up with her husband and to learn to perform the role that fate had chosen for her. The new duke of Burgundy, John the Fearless, may have suggested to Christine that such a book would be welcome, for Marguerite's parents might well have felt some concern at sending their daughter to a court dominated by the frivolous Isabeau of Bavaria. The House of Burgundy generally showed concern for the welfare of its daughters, even if it did not hesitate to marry them off to gain political or territorial advantage.

Marguerite had been marked for an alliance with France almost from birth. On July 9, 1394, when she was barely seven months old, her grandfather had signed an agreement for a future marriage between her and an earlier dauphin, Charles of France, but the young prince died at the beginning of 1401. Undaunted by this setback in his plans, the old duke renewed and reinforced his alliance with the French crown in May 1403. Thus Philip the Bold hoped to ensure continuing Burgundian influence at the French court, even though he was not destined to live long enough to witness the fulfillment of his plans.

Although in the dedication Christine insists that Marguerite has no real need of instruction, it is apparent that the first part of the book was written with the young princess in mind. Several chapters are devoted to recommendations for the education of a young princess at her husband's court, where, Christine insists, she should be instructed by a wise and virtuous governess capable of guiding her toward virtue through kindness and good example. She explains:

> In such a manner this wise lady will be prepared for whatever needs to be done to bend the twig while it is young, as is desired, so she will undertake to form her mistress in such a mold that she will remain that way, accomplishing this gradually rather than all at once lest the twig break. She will find a way to begin so that she can attain the ends she desires, and so she will start out to the best of her ability in a pleasant and courteous manner by giving her mistress some trifles of the sort that please young people, thus trying to gain the confidence and affection of her young mistress. . . . So that when she has her confidence . . . she will begin to tell her stories . . . about ladies and maidens who have governed themselves well, how they have turned out and the honor they have gained thereby. . . .[24]

Regret has sometimes been expressed that Christine devotes fully half of her book to the needs of queens and princesses, but it must be remembered that they were generally the most literate women in society. They were also the most promising patrons for a writer, as Christine herself points out at the end of the book, where she expresses the hope that through the influence of such noblewomen her book will be disseminated to other sections of society. Moreover, the fact remains that she devotes the other half of the book to more ordinary women, speaking not only to the wives of merchants and artisans, but also to the poor and humble. Descending the social hierarchy from rank to rank, she also pauses to devote one chapter to the lives of nuns in religious communities and three others to the problems of the relationships between young women and old, providing evidence that the fifteenth century was not immune to the troubles of a generation gap. At the same time, she does not spare the shortcomings of one group more than another; she is no more indulgent to the lazy, self-seeking queen than to the prostitute, for she warns the queen:

So help me God, just as the log nourishes the fire, so lechery and gluttony and superfluity of meat and drink provide nourishment for sensuality, which inflames pride and makes the heart desire all that is most pleasing to the body. . . . Pride, which delights in this rich nourishment, also makes you covet a superabundance of clothes, jewels, ornaments until you can scarcely think of anything else, neither the cost nor where they will come from, as long as you have them when you want them.[25]

Although it had been agreed that women of doubtful reputation would not be admitted into the City of Ladies, Christine was inclined to show compassion for those victims of society. Medieval society had a profound confidence in the ability of a sinner to reform, recalling, for instance, the example of Marie the Egyptian who, although once a sinner, ended as a saint in Paradise. Therefore, Christine does not hesitate to offer practical advice to the prostitute who might fear that she has no better means of making her way in the world. Christine admonishes her that "if she had a body strong enough to do evil and suffer bad nights, to withstand blows and other misfortunes, she should be strong enough to earn her living honestly."[26] She should live simply and soberly in a little room on a respectable street and devote herself to helping with the laundry in the great houses, to spinning or to tending the sick. She should avoid being found drunk, ill-tempered, or quarrelsome, and she should avoid unseemly or dishonest language—a dull life, perhaps, but one guaranteed to assure her ultimate salvation.

Between these two extremes, Christine addresses herself to a variety of typical situations of life in her day. Like certain contemporary preachers and writers—the author of the satirical *The Fifteen Joys of Marriage,* for instance—she is dubious about the spiritual value of going on pilgrimages.[27] She warns the middle-class wife against "being seen in gatherings arranged in gardens, or elsewhere, by clerics, lords, or anyone else who on the pretext of entertaining a group of people conceals some other arrangement. . . ." and adding, "Nor should she seek out those pilgrimages away from town in order to have some place to frolic or kick up her heels in some gay company, for it is no less than sinful and very bad for those who do it, for it is using God for the pretext and cover, so such pilgrimages are without benefit. . . ."[28] Chaucer's Wife of Bath obviously had French counterparts not unknown to Christine as she wrote these lines.

As amusing as such scenes may be for permitting glimpses of everyday Parisian life, it must not be imagined that Christine limited herself to finding fault with the behavior of her contemporaries. Most of the book is devoted to constructive suggestions for improving the quality of their

lives, illustrated by accounts of women who have been able to deal successfully with the demands made on them by society. Thus, in contrast to
the selfish queen, there is the recollection of a virtuous one, presumably
Charles V's devoted Jeanne de Bourbon, whom Christine had seen as a
child.

Even more interesting is the advice offered to the woman who must
manage an estate in her husband's absence or as a widow take the sole
responsibility of her lands. She must deal with legal matters, supervise
the operation of the vineyards or the management of the flocks of sheep,
later seeing to the weaving of their wool into garments needed in the
household. If she is a widowed noblewoman who chooses to live in the
country, she must be mindful of her relationships with those who live on
her lands:

> This noble lady will not be above calling sometimes on women in childbed,
> both the rich and the poor. She will give alms to the poor and honor the
> rich. She will sponsor the christening of their children and, in short, will
> show herself so charitable and so kind in all things and so humane toward
> her subjects that they will speak only good of her, praying for her and
> holding her in great affection.[29]

On the other hand, if a lady is charged with the defense of a castle
during her husband's absence, she must demonstrate more forceful qualities:

> We have also said that she should have a man's heart, which means that
> she should know the laws of warfare and all things pertaining to them so
> that she will be prepared to command her men if there is need of it,
> knowing how to assault and defend, if the situation requires it. . . . She
> should try out her defenders and ascertain the quality of their courage and
> determination before putting too much trust in them, to see what strength
> and help she can count on in case of need; she should make sure of this
> and not put her trust in vain or feeble promises. She must give special
> attention to what resources she would have until her husband could get
> there. . . .[30]

Perhaps women brought up to expect such demands to be made on them
were less surprised than has generally been supposed by the appearance
of Joan of Arc at the head of French armies less than twenty-five years later.

Her advice to women living at court has particular interest because
of a scandal that occurred at the French royal court during the summer
of 1405. In the middle of August, according to the Chronicler of St.-Denis,
several of the queen's ladies-in-waiting were either dismissed or imprisoned

for calumny, although the queen absolutely refused to permit any investigation of the validity of the charges.[31] In the end, some of the ladies were permanently exiled from court, whether justly or not it is impossible to know. In the chapters Christine devotes to court life, there seems to be a veiled reference to this affair because she recommends to women living there that they make every effort to avoid envy, falsehood, and disloyalty to their mistress, all of which can easily result in scandal. The summer of 1405 was the time when gossip began to circulate in Paris about the relations between the queen and the duke of Orleans, a liaison that lasted until the duke's assassination in a Paris street near the queen's residence in November 1407.

The permissive behavior at court probably also accounts for what Christine has to say on the dangers of illicit love affairs, although she had already given her views on this subject in her early poetry as well as in the final chapter of *The Book of the City of Ladies*. This had also been the principal theme of another of her earlier works, *Le Livre du Duc des Vrais Amants (The Book of the Duke of True Lovers)*, a sort of forerunner of the psychological novel, written in a combination of prose and poetry some time between 1403 and 1405.[32]

In *The Book of the Duke of True Lovers*, as in the pastoral poem Christine wrote around 1403, *"Le Dit de la Pastoure"* ("The Shepherdess' Tale"), a love affair turns out unhappily because marriage is out of the question.[33] (The shepherdess falls in love with a courtier who happens to pass her way, and the young duke falls in love with a married cousin. In both cases, frustration is the inevitable result.) The ultimate point is that no matter how pure and honorable a love may be, it is corrupted by the force of circumstances, inevitable separations, and the gossip and menacing attitude of society. The idealism that exists in both of these relationships during the early stages of their love has no chance of resulting in lasting happiness for the lovers, because, in the case of the shepherdess, of the social distance that separates them, and because the duchess, however much she may love the young duke, is irrevocably married to another man.

To make the same point in *The Book of the Three Virtues*, Christine invents the case of a governess who sees her mistress giving in to the pressing attentions of an admirer. After a vivid description of the early symptoms of the young woman's infatuation and her efforts to elude the vigilance of the older woman, to whom she has previously been devoted, the governess decides to retire to private life on the best pretext she can find. Once withdrawn from official responsibility in the delicate situation, she sends her former mistress a letter reminding her of her duties to her husband and warning her of the consequences of the course on which she has embarked. This was the same letter that was included in *The Book of the Duke of True Lovers*.

Christine has been accused of prudishness for upholding a high standard of virtue, yet the realism of her analysis demonstrates her awareness of the penalty society is capable of exacting from a young woman if she allows herself to be compromised, beginning with the possibility that she may be repudiated by her husband. The cruelty of society is remarkably similar toward such women, not only in the fifteenth century, but also in the seventeenth, as shown by Madame de Lafayette in *The Princess of Cleves,* and in the nineteenth, as demonstrated by some heroines of Balzac's novels. Above all, Christine did not want to see women the victims of their own lack of experience in a society that showed them so little mercy.

A similar attitude governs her advice to widows, not only to a queen faced with the dangers of being left with a young heir and a regency but also to the ordinary woman, who can easily be led into disastrous lawsuits, a misfortune Christine could speak of from personal experience. Of such widows as this she says:

> If she wants to bring her case to a successful conclusion, she must take on the heart of a man, which is to say that she must be constant, strong, and wise in judging and pursuing her advantage, not crouching in tears like a simple woman, or like a poor dog who retreats into a corner when other dogs jump on him. By acting thus, you women, you will find some people so lacking in pity that they would take bread from your hand because they consider you either ignorant or simple-minded, nor would you find pity elsewhere because they did. . . .[35]

Her repeated admonition to women to take on a man's heart illuminates her own transformation, which she describes at the beginning of *The Mutation of Fortune*.

The advice she has to offer to the wives of artisans, whom she apparently considered a rowdy bunch, is equally realistic and practical. Along with knowing his business well enough to oversee it when her husband is absent, protecting it against lazy and dishonest employees, such a woman should try to protect her spouse from worldly temptations:

> She should keep her husband attached to her through love, as best she can, so that he will stay home the more willingly and not be tempted to consort with those foolish bands of young men in taverns or to become involved in other superfluous and outrageous expenses, like other young artisans, especially in Paris. But by treating him with tenderness, she should keep

him at home as much as possible, for it is commonly said that three things drive a man from his house: a quarrelsome wife, a smoking hearth, and a leaking roof.[36]

Christine shows herself more kindly disposed to the poor, who live close to nature and are therefore less prone to worldly vices. Her description of the peasant's wife brings to mind the scenes of country life in the duke of Berry's *Les Très Riches Heures* with which it is contemporary, recalling, perhaps, most of all the February miniature with its group of country folk huddled before the fire in a humble cottage; or the June miniature showing haying going on outside the walls of Paris, with the men cutting while the women rake the hay into rows to be stacked. Christine's compassion for the problems of the poor foreshadows the attitude of Jean de la Bruyère in the seventeenth century, but it is significant that she does not hold out to these less fortunate members of society any hope of change, nor does she expect them to be anything other than subservient to their masters, when she says to them:

Now we must draw to the end of our exposition . . . by speaking of the simple wives of workers in the villages, to whom it is scarcely necessary to forbid expensive ornaments and extravagant clothes, for they are well protected from all that. Nevertheless, though they are commonly nourished with black bread, bacon, and soup, and their thirst is quenched with water, and they have trials enough to bear, still their lives are often more secure and even more abundant than the lives of those who are seated in the high places. But because all creatures, to whatever estate they belong, have need of instruction in living well, it pleases us to have these women participate in our lessons.[37]

Her inclusion of the poor here recalls her pleas in their behalf in *The Mutation of Fortune,* in her long description of Poverty's Gate to the Castle of Fortune, where she concludes:

You may be bored by reading here
All the sad tales I'm telling you.
Some may refuse to read them, too,
Unmoved by pity at their plight
Because they feel they hold by right
All their silver, riches and gold
So toward the poor their hearts are cold;
But pity all should feel for them
And, for God's sake, should be their friend,

For they are creatures such as we,
Men and women similarly.[38]

So Christine offers advice to all women on a great variety of subjects, and in so doing summons up many scenes of the daily life with which she was familiar. In common with contemporary preachers and early humanists alike, she taught by the use of example that virtuous living would help to achieve, if not always happiness, at least peace of mind. So she reached the end of her book and concluded:

> At this point the three ladies stopped talking and suddenly disappeared; I, Christine, remained, somewhat weary from having written so much, but delighted by the fine results of their worthy lessons, which, having been summarized, reviewed and revised by me, seemed better than ever and most useful for the preservation and improvement of virtuous customs intended to increase the honor of ladies, and, indeed, of women in general, now living and to be born, wherever this work may circulate and be seen.[39]

Christine was not mistaken in her ambitions for this book, or for the *The Book of the City of Ladies*. They were among her most popular books and mark a high point in Christine's career. *The Book of the Three Virtues* was published in three editions and continued to be read for more than 125 years after its composition. The manuscripts of *The Book of the City of Ladies* multiplied into the sixteenth century. None of her previous works, with the exception of *Othéa's Letter to Hector* had enjoyed a comparable success. Christine was well aware of her achievement, and she speaks of it in the most autobiographical of her writings, *L'Avision-Christine (Christine's Vision)* to which she now turned her attention.

John the Fearless, Duke of Burgundy

The Duke of Berry

8

The Search for a Patron

hristine's Vision is the most informative and at the same time the most cryptic of her writings. Presenting her ideas once more in an allegorical vision, Christine continues her analysis of the troubles of French society as she did in *The Long Road of Learning*. While focusing primarily on the country's troubles, however, she elaborates the universal history that was an important element in *The Mutation of Fortune*, this time giving Dame Fortune's role to another allegorical lady, Dame Opinion. To these familiar themes she adds an autobiographical section (Part III) in which she discusses her childhood, her marriage, the problems resulting from her widowhood, and, finally, the consolation she has derived from her now fully launched career as a writer.

These seemingly diffuse elements can best be understood in the light of the situation faced by the country and also by Christine as an individual in the fall of 1405. In August and September there had been a confrontation, a struggle for power, between the duke of Orleans and the queen on one hand and the duke of Burgundy, John the Fearless, on the other. Christine made her contribution to the resolution of the crisis by the letter she wrote to Queen Isabeau on October 5 begging her to be a peacemaker between the two dukes. [1] In the course of the quarrel, the duke of Burgundy had proposed a program of much needed social reforms that Christine appears to have favored at least tacitly.

Christine had already lost her hope that she would receive any particular help from Louis of Orleans when he had been unwilling to give her son a place in his household, and she had lost the best patronage she had enjoyed to date with the death of Philip the Bold. [2] It was therefore to his son and successor John the Fearless that she directed *Christine's Vision*. Although there is no formal dedication to the duke, one of the original copies was presented to him and has figured regularly in the inventories of the Burgundian library ever since. Only two other copies are known to exist, and there is no evidence that either ever belonged to the queen, the duke of Orleans, or the duke of Berry.[3] The work can best be understood as an appeal by Christine to the new duke of Burgundy on behalf of France and of herself.

According to her own testimony, *Christine's Vision* was finished before the end of 1405 or, according to the modern calendar, before Easter 1406. The date suggests that she was once more making common cause with Jean Gerson, her collaborator in the Rose debate. On November 7, 1405, Gerson had preached a sermon at the royal court entitled *"Vivat Rex,"* in which he expressed the official views of the University of Paris with regard to the crisis that had recently taken place through the ambitions of the rival dukes. The university had supported the duke of Burgundy's position and continued to support it even after the crisis had passed and all the royal princes had returned to pursuing their own selfish ambitions.

The chronicler Jean Juvenal des Ursins has left an account of this sermon:

> In that season, a notable doctor of theology named Master Jean Gerson, Chancellor of Notre-Dame de Paris and Curate of St.-Jean-en-Grève, made a noteworthy proposition and took as his theme: *"Vivat rex, vivat rex,* long live the king," which proposition is common enough and written in several places. If they had wished to pay attention to the contents of this in a good policy and government for the kingdom, affairs would have gone well. But it was useless to preach, for the lords and those who surrounded them paid no attention and thought only of their particular interests.[4]

In spite of its lack of success in changing events, however, the sermon is worthy of note as an indication of what intelligent Parisians were thinking about the problems of the day.

Gerson spoke with particular concern for the situation of the dauphin Louis, who was almost completely neglected by his mother and who needed to be trained ("indoctrinated" was the word he used) for his present and future duties. He added that if princes were sometimes called to reign while still young, their very innocence might be an advantage for the realm. Turning to the political situation, Gerson repeated in essence the duke of Burgundy's demands for reform set forth in August, and he reserved for the duke of Orleans a particularly sharp rebuke for his ill-considered and ill-mannered rejection of the university's efforts to mediate in his quarrel with the duke of Burgundy.

As the royal princes could not completely ignore the remonstrances of such an important public figure, a program aimed at a reform of public justice was subsequently devised and debated in Parliament, although without any demonstrable results. Gerson also pressed for a clearer autonomy for the university, which was showing signs of being corrupted by various pressure groups.

The *"Vivat Rex"* provides important background for several of Christine's subsequent works, and most especially for her vision of the state of France at the end of 1405. Undoubtedly, it encouraged her to speak out about the corruption that was evident on every hand.

Christine's Vision differed from earlier allegorical interpretations of the times, *The Long Road of Learning* and *The Mutation of Fortune.* Written entirely in prose, a form chosen, possibly, because it was preferred in Burgundian circles, it is also the last of her long allegorical works; henceforth she addressed herself to the problems of the times more directly. Like so many other medieval treatises, it is divided into three parts in which she engages in dialogues with three supernatural creatures on three different problems.

As she started to write, Christine clearly recalls the opening verses of *The Divine Comedy.* She speaks of finding herself in the middle of life's journey, her pilgrimage, as she calls it. In 1405 she would have been forty years old. Feeling tired, she seeks repose, and her spirit immediately takes leave of her body, transported by the force of various winds to a shadowy distant country. This spiritual journey is also reminiscent of the opening lines of Gerson's *Vision* written in the course of the debate concerning *The Romance of the Rose.*[5]

Having witnessed Nature's process for creating human beings out of Chaos, Christine gives an allegorical account of her own birth in another land and her youthful journey to France, where she met the Crowned Lady who turns out to be the personification of her adopted country. It had been this supernatural creature's duty to oversee the growth of a sprig from the Golden Bough brought from Troy to be replanted in a new garden. Having thus given France the same Trojan origin that had figured in the biography of Charles V, she proceeds to set forth the Crowned Lady's allegorical, and somewhat abbreviated, version of French history. Individual episodes are sometimes obscure, but there is no difficulty in identifying the reign of Charles V, when France prospered, and the subsequent misfortunes marking the reign of his son, who is portrayed as a butterfly turned into a noble bird of prey. At this point, the Crowned Lady interrupts her discourse to speculate on what might have happened if this noble bird had not been struck down by "the turning of Fortune's wheel," a reference to the king's insanity. Then she devotes herself to deploring the power struggle that has resulted from this national misfortune. Many of the ills to which the lady alludes in veiled terms echo those spoken of in greater detail by John the Fearless and Jean Gerson, although there is no mention here of an actual program of governmental reform. There is, nevertheless, a discreet reference to the coming of a strong man who would be able to free the nation from its enemies and restore it to its "rightful heirs." Was this Christine's manner of expressing her support for the duke of Burgundy's program of reforms? It seems quite possible.

In describing the moral decline of France at the time, Christine, speaking through the Crowned Lady, presents the case of the Virtues, Truth, Justice, and Chivalry, all of whom lie in a prison cell while Voluptuousness, Fraud, and Avarice have usurped their places at court. Predictions about disasters that must result from such a state of affairs are buttressed with examples of comparable situations in both sacred and profane history. Ambition, above all, will inevitably spell ruin for the country. In expressing her fears for France, the Crowned Lady compares herself to Cassandra, who was not heeded when she tried to warn the Trojans of impending disaster. She begs Chistine not to give up working on her behalf, however inadequately she may be rewarded for her efforts.

In the second part of *Christine's Vision,* the scene shifts to the halls of the University of Paris, the "second Athens" as Christine calls it. There her attention is caught by a shadowy feminine form hovering over the students and giving off lesser shadows in varied forms and colors. These, in turn, hover about the students who are engaged in discussions and debates, whispering into their ears as they talk. Eventually, a voice from the great shade calls out to Christine: "Bookish daughter, what are you doing here?" It is the voice of Dame Opinion, daughter of Ignorance, creator of the thirst for the knowledge of good and evil. She describes at length her role in human affairs from the Garden of Eden onward. After having caused Adam's downfall, it was she who taught the condemned pair how to survive outside the walls of the Earthly Paradise.

Dame Opinion confesses to Christine that she is not immortal but will disappear when the material world crumbles away, for when eternal truths have been revealed to mankind, she will have no further reason to exist. In the meantime, her service to each individual begins with the awakening of the intellect and diminishes in the measure that natural endowments develop. All mortals, even the greatest and wisest, are subject to her suggestions. It is her mission to inspire people to seek truth but not to achieve it, for she and her cohort do not coexist with Truth. Because of her power over mankind, however, she has been involved in all religious movements, and even after the triumph of Christianity has sown the discord that brought about various heresies.

Dame Opinion's influence on philosophers has been equally potent, as she demonstrates by reviewing the history of philosophical speculation from the early Greeks to Aristotle. It is a question, of course, of natural philosophy, which in Christine's day meant scientific speculation about the nature of the physical world. Much of what Christine has to say here is inspired by Aristotle's *Metaphysics,* which presents an interesting problem because no French translation of the text existed at the time, although it was known in Latin, at least in part, from the twelfth century onward. By her own admission, Christine did not know Greek, and her knowledge of Latin is subject to conjecture, but in *Christine's Vision* she presents the first known French commentary on the Book I of Aristotle's *Metaphysics.*[6] Could she have had in her possession some of her father's notes from the University of Bologna? Or had he even written some sort of commentary on Aristotle's text? A good deal of scientific speculation in the later Middle Ages took the form of commentaries on Aristotle's writings that either disputed or extended his ideas. It is noteworthy that Christine places each of the early Greek philosophers she mentions in his proper setting, noting significant biographical details and particularly important ideas. Such information as this could have come from a text such as Guillaume de Tignonville's *Les Ditz des Philosophes (The Sayings of the Philosophers),* with which she was undoubtedly familiar, but its presence in her text is unusual.

Christine gives considerable attention to Pythagoras and the Neo-Platonic emphasis on experimentation and on mathematics as the basis for an understanding of cosmology. She also was particularly attracted to the Pythagorean theory of numbers, very possibly a reflection of her father's mathematical education. It is interesting, and also significant, that Christine gives evidence of being thoroughly aware of the sort of scientific discussion that was a hallmark of intellectual life in the fourteenth century. Here one catches a glimpse of the intellectual ferment that was an impressive aspect of Charles V's Paris, which Christine recalls from time to time with great regret.[7]

In *Christine's Vision,* however, Dame Opinion is obliged to admit that she cannot discuss all the philosophers because she must speak of her importance in other fields of human endeavor. She wants especially to reproach Christine for underestimating her role in *The Mutation of Fortune.* She points out that human beings owe the outcome of events more to their own power than to the machinations of Dame Fortune, demonstrating this by various cases drawn from ancient history. Dame Fortune is Opinion's servant and therefore subject to her authority; it is Opinion who initiates all strife, dissension, and struggle for power. Christine is referring here to the political quarrels dividing the French court, but Dame Opinion does not fail to remind her that it was she who stirred up the debate over *The Romance of the Rose*.

This criticism of *The Mutation of Fortune* inspires Christine to ask whether she has been similarly led astray in other works, to which question Dame Opinion replies:

> Dear friend, be at peace, for I tell you that even if I blame you for having given the place of honor to Fortune, forgetting that I am the principal one, even if I lead some others to argue, for some say that clerks or priests have written your works for you for they could not come from feminine intelligence. But those who say such things are ignorant, for they are not aware of the writings of other women wiser than you, even prophets who have been mentioned in past times, and as nature is no less powerful now the same thing can still be possible. Others say that your style is obscure and that it is not possible to understand it, so it is not pleasing, and so variously some praise and others withhold their praise. But as it is impossible for anything to be pleasing to everyone, I say to you that truth based on experience is not subject to blame which diminishes true praise, so I urge you to continue your work, which is valid, and not to be afraid of me.[8]

She adds that Christine is unfortunate in the time in which she is living because knowledge is not respected and is, so to speak, out of style, but that in the future she will be read and better understood:

> After your death will come the prince full of valor and wisdom who, because of your books, will wish that he had belonged to your time and would wish to have known you.[9]

The basis of Christine's concern for her own immortality as a writer was, of course, the concept of her importance as an individual. If, in her biography of Charles V, she had shown herself influenced by the new humanistic attitude toward the significance of certain historical figures, in Part III of *Christine's Vision* she showed an equally humanistic concern for autobiography in the desire, quite unusual for her day, to present a portrait of herself in the act of overcoming the problems that had directed the course of her life. In doing this, she not only revealed her remarkable stamina in dealing with both Opinion and Fortune, but also she became the first woman to leave such an autobiography as a record of her evolution both as a writer and as a person.

In Part III she is guided in her quest by Dame Philosophy, inspired primarily, no doubt, by her admiration for Boethius's *The Consolation of Philosophy,* for the lady is quite evidently the same as the one who appeared to offer Boethius comfort in his prison. The dialogue in which Christine engages with her, however, gives the impression that she was also influenced by Petrarch, and through him by St. Augustine's *Confessions.* This last part of *Christine's Vision* is best known to modern readers for the information it furnishes about Christine's life, for her philosophy of life, which is also revealed, and for the path of her progress, under pressure of necessity, from a retiring, timid young woman to the independent woman who was not afraid to become the defender of her sex and, ultimately, of her adopted country.

The dialogue takes place in a brilliantly illuminated study hall of a convent among *"les estudes de Paris,"* which is to say, near the University of Paris. Dame Philosophy is the superior of this hypothetical convent. At the beginning, Christine is admiring the frescoes on the walls of the room, much as she is portrayed in the Munich manuscript of *The Mutation of Fortune.*[10] Her interview with Dame Opinion has depressed her, and in passing through the halls of the convent, she pauses to refresh herself at the Fountain of Knowledge. But she hurries on to the Great Hall in order to quench her fundamental thirst at the Fountain of Wisdom, which she knew she would find sending up its waters there. As the great door opens to admit her, she sees a light so brilliant that she is momentarily blinded. As she falls on her knees, the voice of Dame Philosophy speaks reassuringly to her. The two have met before through Christine's reading of Boethius, and in the hope of finding consolation for her own trials, Christine decides to tell her story to this lady.

Christine reiterates her belief that Dame Fortune has been hostile to her, despite Dame Philosophy's reproof that this has not been the case. She persists in the idea that it was Fortune who had sent Death to summon the benevolent king who had been her family's benefactor, then to her father, then to her husband after only a short period of happy marriage. Next Fortune made use of the services of Fraud and Avarice to reduce Christine's resources to the bare necessities of life. She speaks with feeling of the men who denied her the money owed her husband and the merchants who defrauded her of the money set aside for her children. She recalls plaintively her efforts to keep up appearances so that others would not be aware of her difficulties, adding that she had often shivered under her well-preserved fur-trimmed cloak and passed many sleepless nights in her fine bed. Finally, only one resource was left to her, her writing. But she needed to find a patron, and patrons willing to interest themselves in women were rare indeed. Then Death had again interfered to remove the most promising of her patrons, the duke of Milan and the duke of Burgundy, before they had been able to give her any real assistance.

She is only human in resenting the loss both of wealth and the promise of wealthy protectors and also in failing to grasp the moral value of her trials, but Dame Philosophy immediately points out to her that actually her sorrows have been blessings in disguise. What is more important, she reminds Christine, that no person has the right to question God's will in human affairs.

Having weighed Dame Philosophy's arguments, Christine is persuaded to seek the sort of happiness recommended by Boethius, a complete detachment from worldly desires. This leads to an interesting revelation of Christine's interior life as she struggles to understand the divine plan for her. Dame Philosophy plays the role of Christine's conscience, ultimately leading her to acknowledge that her sufferings have been a mark of God's concern for her and have resulted in a better understanding of herself. This dialogue is above all an encomium of the virtue of Patience.

Dame Philosophy points out to Christine that her numerous sorrows have been counterbalanced by advantages that might be considered unusually great benefits: noble parents, a sound body, and children who are a credit to her. She further reminds Christine of her father's accomplishments and her mother's exemplary virtue. She speaks of her daughter in the royal Abbey of Poissy, where she lives in the company of daughters from France's most noble families, and of her son's sojourn in England and the fact that he is a source of great pride to her. She does not rebuke Christine for her complaints, yet undertakes to make her see that they are largely ill justified. Furthermore, she explains that having survived her tribulations, Christine has come out of them a morally stronger woman and better equipped intellectually than she would have been otherwise; therefore, reverses of Fortune are necessary to prepare the soul for enduring happiness.

Finally, like a physician who has brought a patient safely through a crisis, Dame Philosophy ends by demonstrating to Christine that the path to happiness lies in the endurance of all ills without complaint and the disdain of worldly joys. In doing this, she draws heavily on Boethius, naturally, but also on the Church Fathers. Thus, Christine comes again to the point of view expressed at the end of *The Mutation of Fortune*, basically a Stoic resignation. It was here that the "long road of learning" has brought her. *Christine's Vision* reflects Christine's reading and also her assimilation of what she has read. All this she applies to her observation of the world that surrounds her.[11]

This third part of the book has special significance as an early example of feminine autobiography, just as it must be regarded as a manifestation of Christine's humanist tendencies. The Italian humanists considered the uniqueness of one's feelings, opinions, and experiences worth expressing. It has also been pointed out that this aspiration for individualism corresponds to the development of portrait painting at the same period.[12] It is thus possible to draw an interesting parallel between this autobiographical section of *Christine's Vision* and the portraits of Christine working in her little study that enhance so many of the early manuscripts of her works.

The problem of providing herself with a patron still remains, however, as Christine observes to Dame Philosophy with more than a touch of bitterness:

> I tell you that in spite of the supplications and petitions I have made frequently to the French princes who are still living . . . not soliciting them because of my own merits but because of the love my father formerly enjoyed as their servant, and because of his good deeds, hoping that they might be willing to rescue his little household, now left in my care, but I do not lie . . . when I say that any help was given me reluctantly and not very generously, and even when given, the delayed payment and the need to pursue their treasurers to receive it, has diminished the value of the gesture.[13]

One gathers that she was voicing her disillusionment with both the duke of Orleans, who had disappointed her hopes for her son, and the duke of Berry, who was notorious for not paying his debts. There remained the duke of Burgundy, whose father had made promises, still unfulfilled when he died, and his son John the Fearless, to whom Christine was now addressing her plea.

Christine has all too often been accused of excessive self-interest in her dedications of works to princes and her flattering references to them. It has even been suggested that she transferred her allegiance from the duke of Orleans to the duke of Burgundy because the latter offered her a higher price for her services.[14] In view of the practices of both princes and poets at the beginning of the fifteenth century, such an accusation is thoroughly unjust. Both her father and her husband had been in positions to profit from royal patronage, which ceased with their deaths. As a widow Christine found herself without adequate income and had no choice but to follow the customs of the day. Even such a successful writer as Chaucer was not able to live from his writings and was obliged to devote some of his energies to being a courtier; the highly successful Machaut enjoyed the favors of a succession of patrons; and Eustache Deschamps was first a messenger in the royal service and then, for many years, attached to the household of the duke of Orleans. Most artists, therefore, were dependent on the generosity of patrons. Christine's particular problem was to find a prince who would be willing to protect a woman writer, a novelty to say the least. Moreover, by the time she had begun her career in earnest, Charles VI was no longer capable of continuing his father's role as patron of the arts. Also, none of Charles V's brothers were able to patronize the arts on a scale comparable to his, although each tried to imitate the late king within the limits of his financial resources. The result was that during the years between the French victory at Brétigny and the defeat at Agincourt an interested patronage permitted the arts to continue to flourish in spite of the king's insanity and political rivalries among the princes. Thus the most significant cultural unit was the court of individual princes, modeled ultimately after Charles V's court in Paris. [15]

It is scarcely surprising that Christine should have courted the patronage of the queen by presenting several of her works to her. In return, especially between 1402 and 1405, she received gifts, but these seem to have been limited to silver goblets and tankards. The first of these may have followed the presentation of the collection of letters based on the debate over *The Romance of the Rose,* a time when Christine most definitely sought the queen's support. It is not known how the queen rewarded her for giving the magnificent manuscript of her collected works, now one of the treasures of the British National Library (Ms. Harley 4431), although few things have contributed more favorably to the queen's memory than the dedicatory miniature showing Christine presenting the volume to her as she sits surrounded by her ladies. However, Isabeau is not remembered for her generosity to anyone, not even to her unfortunate husband or her ill-fated children. [16]

Christine's earliest patrons, or potential patrons, seem to have lived in other countries. She herself mentions first Sir John Montague, the earl of Salisbury, a personal friend of Richard II who was sent to Paris during the fall of 1398 to discourage a possible marriage between the duke of Derby (the future Henry IV) and the duke of Berry's daughter Marie, recently widowed because her husband, the count of Eu, had died while a prisoner of Bayazid in Turkey, after the Battle of Nicopolis in 1396. Christine explains that he had heard of her poetry, and it is true that he was a patron of literature and had himself written poetry in French, which unfortunately has all been lost.[17] Touched by the plight of this unusual widow, he offered to take her son Jean into his household as a companion to his own son, the future military genius of Henry V's armies. As a result, Jean spent three years in England, and his mother's works enjoyed an early reputation at the English court. The arrangement ended in misfortune when Salisbury was killed in January 1400 while supporting Richard II's right to the throne. Henry IV immediately took Jean under his protection and tried to attract Christine to his court, but she was profoundly disturbed by events in England and was not tempted to cast in her lot with a monarch she considered a traitor. Through the use of guile, she managed to get her son back to France, a process she described with the rueful comment that it had cost her several of her works.[18] It is not certain which of her works she was referring to, but the translation of the *Cupid's Letter* was made by Thomas Hoccleve shortly after 1400 and the early popularity of *Othéa's Letter to Hector* in England, where it was translated three times in the course of the fifteenth century, point to these two works in any case.[19]

In 1387, the marriage of Louis of Orleans to Valentina Visconti, daughter of the duke of Milan, encouraged new contacts between France and Italy. Again, it is uncertain what brought Christine's poetry to this duke's attention, although a link with Christine's family through her two brothers might have been established by the uprising in Bologna in 1401 when the overthrow of Giovanni Bentivolgio put the city into Visconti hands. It is also possible that an embassy including Marshal Boucicaut and the provost of Paris Guillaume de Tignonville introduced Christine's poetry to the court of Milan. At the end of the summer of 1401, these men were sent to discuss the possibility of a marriage between the duke's oldest son and a daughter of Charles VI. Whatever the reason, Christine received a tempting invitation from the duke to take up residence at his court, and she might have done so had it not been for Giangaleazzo Visconti's unexpected death in September 1402. While blaming Fortune for having betrayed her once more, Christine nevertheless understandably felt some hesitation at abandoning her home in France.[20] The interesting point about these two episodes is that they give evidence of the spread of Christine's reputation as a poet even before she had begun to produce her major works.

Jean's return from England presented Christine with a new problem. As the boy was now about sixteen, she needed to find a situation in life for him. To be sure, although there had been a tendency since the reign of John II for appointments to the royal chancellery to be passed from generation to generation within the same families, the assent of the king was necessary for such an appointment. It may thus have been partially with her son's interests in mind that she made a great effort to gain the patronage of the duke of Orleans. It was at this time that she addressed the ballade to the duke offering him her own services as well as her son's.[21] The earl of Salisbury's interest in the young man may not have helped his cause, inasmuch as the duke of Orleans had favored a marriage that Salisbury had come to France to discourage. But by 1402, Orleans was the sworn enemy of Henry IV, whose rise to power had been Salisbury's undoing. In that year, Orleans also went so far as to challenge the English usurper, as he was called, to a single combat, an encounter that never took place.[22]

In addition, Christine had a number of contacts with the duke's entourage that must have seemed promising. Perhaps the most important of these was Gilles Malet, who was now in charge of Duchess Valentina's household as well as the royal library. Guillaume de Tignonville had been the duke's chamberlain before being appointed provost of Paris in 1401. Jean de Montaigu, the king's counselor and the grand master of his household, was a person to whom Christine owed a debt of gratitude, having already benefited from his benevolence.[23] Jean de Garencières, a poet with whom she enjoyed friendly relations, was the duke's *maître d'hôtel* before becoming bailiff of the town of Senlis and, in 1404, treasurer of France.[24]

Among the courtiers to whom Christine dedicated poems were Charles d'Albret, marshal of France and royal counselor, who was Louis of Orleans's cousin and one of his intimate friends, and Jacques de Bourbon, count of Marche and the duke's ally in several campaigns against Henry IV. With so many friends at the Orleans court, Christine might understandably have held high hopes of attracting the duke's support.

Making a direct approach to the duke himself, Christine dedicated to him several of her early works, beginning with *Othéa's Letter to Hector.* Soon afterward she addressed to him *The Debate of Two Lovers,* asking him for his judgment of the question they were debating. A series of three ballades written in the course of 1402 refer to the duke's interests, celebrating a tournament between seven knights of his household and seven English knights that took place on May 19 near Bordeaux. The contest was supervised in person by the duke and his knights were victorious, although there is no record of any significant issues having been settled.[25]

It is difficult to determine just what Christine's relationship with the Orleans court really was, just as in the appeal she made on her son's behalf it is impossible to know how much of her praise is genuine and how much merely conforms to the conventions required when addressing a prince:

> This is my only son, who in his youth
> Would like to find a way to use his time,
> And serve as best he could, in truth,
> According to the ways you might assign.
> For this I beg, prince, so valiant and fine.
> If it please you to take him in your hand,
> I make a gift of him, yours to command;
> Make of him what you will, and do believe
> He would heartily serve at your demand,
> If, noble duke, you would my son receive.

And she concludes with this *envoi:*

> Excellent prince, by all prized and acclaimed,
> For asking this boon may I not be blamed
> Nor forgotten, for by your gracious leave
> My service I offer you to be claimed
> If, noble duke, you would my son receive.

There is no evidence that the duke paid any attention to Christine's plea. In any case, Jean de Castel eventually entered the Burgundian household under the patronage of Duke John the Fearless.[26]

Before Christine had lost hope of the duke's patronage, however, she dedicated to him *Le Dit de la Rose (The Tale of the Rose),* dated February 14, 1402.[27] The setting of the poem is a gathering at one of the duke's Parisian residences, a social occasion that was sufficiently familiar to Christine to permit her to describe it with considerable charm. The guests were entirely aristocratic, which suggests the possibility that Christine was enlisting their support for her position in the debate with her less-than-noble opponents about the merits of Jean de Meun's poem.

The Tale of the Rose opens with a salutation to princely lovers, knightly nobles, all lovers in general, and also to ladies of good repute, young women who are beloved, as well as all other honorable women. There follows the description of the supper that is supposed to have taken place in the latter part of January 1402. At the end of the evening, the guests are dazzled by the appearance of a beautiful woman who proclaims herself "Lady and Goddess of Loyalty." Singing a new motet so harmoniously that it is as though one were in paradise, her attendants distribute bouquets of roses to the guests, whereupon the goddess, speaking in a series of ballades, explains that the God of Love has charged her to bring a message to the assembly. She is to offer support to his true servants against their enemies, presumably the admirers of Jean de Meun. Therefore, each guest, on accepting one of the roses, is required to vow loyalty to the opposite sex, a promise that is by no means to be taken lightly. The guests, without exception, take the vow and Loyalty promises to report the good news to the God of Love. After she has vanished, her companions remain to entertain the company with their sweet singing and to heap more roses on them.

At the end of the festivities and in a happy frame of mind, Christine retires to the room assigned to her. She explains that the room is "as white as the snow that lies on the branch" because of her special friendship for Diana the moon goddess, whose favorite color is white. Diana was, of course, the goddess of Chastity, a quality that, according to medieval lore, made women equal with men in intellectual powers.[28]

As soon as Christine falls asleep, she has a vision, as might be expected under the circumstances. Loyalty stands before her once more, this time to report that the God of Love is much disturbed by the evil ways into which men have fallen. Even noblemen indulge in certain vices because they lack courage. After a review of the qualities traditionally associated with *courtoisie* (good breeding), Loyalty deplores the state into which Honor has fallen, condemning especially the practice of vilifying women, although the habit of speaking ill of men is also to be deplored. The Order of the Rose has been founded, Loyalty explains, to correct these bad habits, and Christine is expected to make this fact known wherever potential supporters for the cause are to be found. The goddess then disappears, leaving on Christine's pillow the charter of the Order, written in blue letters on golden parchment. On one side of the folio is a portrait of the God of Love, his feet resting on a leopard, and on the other side the goddess of Loyalty herself is portrayed. Because of this vision, Christine takes it as her duty immediately to proclaim the Order of the Rose, enlisting the support of true lovers everywhere on their special day, the Feast of St. Valentine.

Whether the Order of the Rose actually existed is a question that has been debated on various occasions, but there is no real evidence that it was more than a creation of Christine's imagination.[29] Such chivalric orders were popular, and all princes and important noblemen wanted to found one with an identifying emblem. The duke of Orleans had founded the Order of the Porcupine, but Christine's Order of the Rose is more reminiscent of the Marshal Boucicaut's Order of the Green Shield with the White Lady, devoted to the protection of women. That, too, may have been only the expression of an ideal.[30] In any case, Christine had invented a charming fiction to engage the attention of an aristocratic audience while calling attention to her efforts to protect women against denigration. The Order of the Rose was undoubtedly intended to remind her readers of the discrepancy between the ideal and the actuality where women were concerned.

The most curious, and possibly most significant, fact about the poem was that when Christine revised her original collection of poetry after 1402, she dropped *The Tale of the Rose*. Was it because the duke of Orleans did nothing either for her or her son, or did she decide, in view of subsequent events, that he was not a worthy sponsor for such an order? The former explanation is suggested by her account in *Christine's Vision* of her son's return from England. Here she says:

> I sought for him a great and powerful master who by his grace might be pleased to retain him, but as the abilities of the young child were not very noticeable in the throng of important people at that court, he remained in my charge without my drawing any profit from his services. And so Fortune disappointed me in one of my good friends and in one of my hopes.[31]

Her disappointment in the duke of Orleans is perhaps even more clearly reflected in a comment about the vagaries of patronage in *The Book of the Three Virtues*. Here she speaks of a certain court where a person reputed to be wise was invited on various occasions, apparently pleasing the lord with her poetry and wisdom and providing for him several services worthy of remuneration. At the same time, the court was frequented by a buffoon who made the company laugh at his worthless and foolish jokes. In the end the fool was far more generously rewarded than the poet.[32] Louis of Orleans is known to have received popular entertainers at his court, and the poet Eustache Deschamps has left a vivid picture of him carousing in the midst of his courtiers on at least one occasion.[33] On the whole, the duke of Orleans illustrates well Christine's observations about noblemen with double standards. There is certainly no record of generosity on her behalf and it is unlikely that she dedicated any further works to him after 1404.

In fact, in 1403, she had already expressed her admiration for the court of Philip the Bold, duke of Burgundy, who had, according to her own words, "come to have affection for me through his acquaintance with my books and volumes." She was thus inspired to write a ballade about the Court of Burgundy with a refrain based on the old proverb *"Selon Seigneur Voit on Maignée Duite"* ("A Household Can Be Judged by Its Master"):

> It is good to see how a court may shine
> With folk so noble in bearing and deed.
> So fair, so gentle, it's a joy sublime
> To see it, for it has not any need
> Of haughty pride, so it is great indeed.
> And in arms there's no better in any year
> On any field to be seen, far or near.
> And if all are full ready to hold the line
> It but shows once more by example clear
> Just like the lord, so are his courtiers fine.[34]

At the end of this same year, Christine offered to the duke the first copy of *The Mutation of Fortune.* A few weeks later, he commissioned her to write the biography of Charles V, which he did not live to see finished. Not only did she speak of his loss in *Christine's Vision,* but also she had immediately given expression to her regrets in another ballade, in which she called on the king, the duke of Berry and the other dukes, the queen and other members of the court, and, finally, all of France to join her in weeping because of their common loss.[35] This exhortation was not all rhetoric. The duke of Burgundy's death had upset the delicate balance of power in Paris and set in motion the deadly rivalry between his son John the Fearless and his nephew Louis of Orleans.

Christine's personal fortunes, however, seem to have been improved by her presentation of *Christine's Vision* to John the Fearless, for he was willing to pay his father's debt to her and even showed an interest in making further use of her talents. The Burgundian accounts record a payment of 100 écus, a considerable sum, to Christine de Pizan on February 20, 1406,

in compensation for two books which she presented to my lord, one of which was commissioned by my late lord the duke of Burgundy, my lord's father, may God forgive him, shortly before he died, and my lord has received it in his stead. The other my lord wished to have, which books and others of her letters and poems are pleasing to my lord; and also for compassionate reasons and as a gift to be used for the dowry of a poor niece of hers whose marriage she has just arranged.[36]

The first volume mentioned is quite obviously the biography of Charles V, but which is the second? *The Book of the Three Virtues,* dedicated to the duke's daughter, Marguerite of Guyenne, or *Christine's Vision?* Both were written in the months preceding the gift. And which letters and poems were especially pleasing to John the Fearless?

Without any indication of the works that were being rewarded, other gifts are noted on November 17, 1407; June 17, 1408; and December 3, 1412. The duke's interest also encouraged the patronage of other members of his family: his brother Anthony, duke of Brabant, made payments to Christine in 1407 and 1408, and his younger brother, Philip of Nevers, rewarded her as well. She was to deplore the deaths of both brothers at Agincourt in her *Epistre de la Prison de Vie Humaine (Letter concerning the Prison of Human Life).* Although no record of specific gifts has been preserved, Christine speaks of the kindness of their sister Marguerite, countess of Hainaut, in *The Book of the City of Ladies.*[37] One must conclude that Christine's attachments to the Burgundian court were multiple and that she found there an appreciative audience, in particular for her didactic works. Her writings formed an important section in the Burgundian library; seven volumes were recorded in the inventory made in 1420, shortly after the death of John the Fearless, and others were added later.[38]

On the other hand, Burgundian tastes had their part in the change of direction to be observed in Christine's writings from 1405 onward. Burgundian interests were inclined toward history, education of the young, and political reform. If the taste for history originally had focused the attention of this very literate family on Christine, the other two concerns would be reflected in her writings for the next several years. One inevitably regrets, however, that the relative security she must have felt at finding her works appreciated discouraged further revelations of her personal life and problems. Her autobiographical writings ceased until the very last years of her life. One must learn what one can about the next stage of her career from the ideas she expressed in a series of prose works that comment on the deteriorating situation in France with which she, like all loyal French subjects, had to contend.

Christine Instructs Her Son

The Dauphin Listens to His Teacher

9

The Education of the Dauphin

Traditionally, accounts of life during the Middle Ages have focused attention on large events, and private concerns such as family life and the education of children have been largely overlooked, even in the case of children who might eventually influence national destiny. The matrimonial policy of the House of Burgundy is well known, but less has been written about its concern for its children's education. The dukes of Burgundy shared with Christine an interest in this matter. The Burgundian inventories record numerous books bought for instruction, from the "two pairs of Hours of Our Lady with illustrations" bought by Philip the Bold for his grandchildren, Philip and Marguerite, in 1403, to the translation of Xenophon prepared for the instruction of Charles the Bold.[1] It was, of course, John the Fearless who responded to Christine's concern for establishing her son and provided the necessary dowry for the niece whose marriage she had arranged. Even before concerning herself with the education of this same duke's daughter, Christine had written two texts for the education of her son. These are *Les Enseignemens Moraux (Moral Teachings)* and *Les Proverbes Moraux (Moral Proverbs)*. She had also provided an introduction to the study of classical mythology in *Othéa's Letter to Hector* written when her son Jean, like Hector, was about fourteen years old. This text was copied and read at the Court of Burgundy throughout the fifteenth century.

Like the early Italian humanists, Christine was concerning herself with the *moral* education of the young. In her son's case, she knew it was the only real treasure she could give him. She began her *Moral Teachings* with the explanation:

> Son, I have here no great treasure
> To make you rich, but a measure

> Of good advice which you may need;
> I give it hoping you'll take heed. . . .
>
> Study carefully to inquire
> How best you may Prudence acquire.
>
> Mother she is of every virtue,
> Who Fortune's treasons can undo.[2]

Although these quatrains are addressed first of all to her son, Christine eventually shows her concern for the various undertakings of other young men, be they rulers, soldiers, churchmen, or merchants. She admonishes them all to be kind and generous:

> Great Pity have for all the poor
> Whom you find starving at your door;
>
> Help you can give them don't deny—
> Remember someday you must die.

But in addition to striving to follow virtuous ways, one should also cultivate his mind:

> Willingly read fine books of tales
> Whenever you can, for it never fails
>
> That examples such books comprise
> Can help you to become more wise.

The *Moral Proverbs* are obviously patterned after the *Distics of Cato,* a popular school text, yet Christine's two little books were popular, too, the proverbs being published by Caxton in an English translation.[3] Christine had a sufficiently good understanding of children to know that verse helps the youthful memory to retain useful precepts. Indeed, a number of her pedagogical ideas seem to have been in advance of her times.

In the program of education she proposes for a young princess in the first part of *The Book of the Three Virtues,* Christine suggests that the governess should tell the child stories to engage her attention and then make use of them to teach her the behavior that is expected of her. She should also play games with the little girl and sometimes give her small, attractive trinkets to win her confidence and affection, so that she can correct her when the need arises without bringing about rebellion.[4] Although Christine had obviously had considerable experience from the upbringing of her own children, it is extraordinary to find her advocating these methods just at the time they were being incorporated into the first humanistic educational programs in Italy. *The Book of the Three Virtues* is contemporary with both Giovanni Dominici's *La Regola del Governo di Cura Familiare (Rule for the Government of Family Care)* and the influential treatise by Petrus Paulus Vergerius entitled *De ingenuis moribus,* written for the Carrera family of Padua. Christine was ten years older than the early humanist educator Guarino da Verona, and she wrote *The Book of the Three Virtues* ten years before Francesco Barbaro's *De Re Uxoria (On Wifely Duties).* [5] One must suspect that Christine's advanced educational ideas were a part of her Italian heritage. Although she was not sufficiently well educated to advocate a program of classical reading as advanced as those developed by the Italian humanists, she nevertheless insisted on the importance of a moral education for civic responsibility based on the lessons of history, mythology, and the example of famous people. Obviously, Christine was familiar with some of Boccaccio's works, but Venice may have been the common bond she shared with the early educators. As early as the fourteenth century, Venetians were concerned with providing a good education for their children, although all too little is known of just what this involved. Venice may also have provided a bond between Christine and John the Fearless, who had spent the winter of 1397 there on his way home from his Turkish captivity. [6] He was met in Venice by Dino Rapondi, the Italian merchant and banker whose skill and far-reaching commercial relations had been instrumental in bringing about his release. Rapondi's continuing role in the ducal family was so important that he was eventually buried with its members in the Charterhouse of Champmol, near Dijon. It is not too surprising that Christine's Italian educational ideas should have found favor with Duke John.

After the book for the duke's daughter, Christine's interest turned— or perhaps was directed—toward the education of his son-in-law Louis of Guyenne, the dauphin. The formation of the "perfect prince" was another favorite concern of humanist writers, who stressed the importance of moral values and civic duty based on a study of the Latin classics. There was no doubt that the dauphin had need of guidance and that Christine's interest in his future was shared by many others, notably Nicolas Clamanges, Jean de Montreuil, and Jean Gerson. All were in sympathetic agreement with the young prince's tutor Jean d'Arsonval, who was already trying to provide a proper education for him. Although their efforts were influenced by the new ideas from Italy, they also followed a great body of medieval literature from Saint Augustine's *City of God* to certain works translated at Charles V's command, such as John of Salisbury's *Polycraticus* and Egidio Colonna's *The Regiment of Princes*.[7]

Unfortunately, the young prince was not equal to their efforts. Born in Paris on January 22, 1396, four years after the onset of his father's insanity, Louis was his parents' third son and eighth child and became heir to the throne in 1401 after the death of his two brothers. Although he lived longer than these brothers, he died while still young, in December 1415, after having been the nominal head of the French government for several turbulent years. He made his first appearance on the political scene in 1403 at the age of seven when he was betrothed to Marguerite of Nevers. Two years later, in August 1405, his mother and uncle, Louis of Orleans, tried to kidnap him in order to keep him out of the clutches of John the Fearless, starting an altercation that brought about the first actual show of arms between the rival dukes.[8] From that time onward, Louis was the object of constant maneuvers by ambitious courtiers hoping to control the government through him, for even at his tender age he was expected to be his father's official representative during his "absences," as the king's spells of mental derangement were called. Thus the boy was inevitably surrounded by a perpetually shifting group of courtiers whose influence varied as greatly as their political ambitions. Those who were interested in prescribing an education for him were also hoping to influence him by turning him into an enlightened ruler of the sort his grandfather, Charles V, had been.

Louis of Guyenne is best known to posterity through the unflattering portrait given by Shakespeare in *Henry V*.[9] In reality, he probably had both the abilities and shortcomings observable in other members of his family. His mother and his uncle, Louis of Orleans, were both known for their excessive love of pleasure, as had been his father during his youth. His passion for collecting art objects reflected the interest of his great-uncles the dukes of Anjou, Berry, and Burgundy. Even in a short lifetime Louis was able to amass a remarkable collection of gold and silver ornaments and show an interest in collecting illuminated manuscripts worthy of his grandfather.[10] The royal library included at least twelve volumes that were gifts to him, handsome manuscripts the duke of Berry lost no time in claiming after Louis' death. He also showed signs of becoming a patron of artists. Records mention a certain Haincelin of Hagenau as a favorite and there is also reference to a payment made to Christine for a book he received from her between 1408 and 1410.[11]

Christine's first mention of the young dauphin is in a prayer that forms a passage in her *"Oryson Notre Dame"* ("Prayer for Our Lady"), probably written around 1403, where she asks a blessing for his future responsibilities:

> Peace, a good life and a good end
> To my lord, the young dauphin, pray send,
> With wisdom to rule in good fame
> Over the people whose love extends
> To him loyally, and so to such ends
> Like his father, long may he reign.[12]

It is possible to see in these verses the ideal that Christine was to develop at considerable length in *Le Livre du Corps de Policie (The Book of the Body Politic)*. This book is probably the one for which his payment is recorded. It was finished some time before the assassination of the duke of Orleans on November 23, 1407, for there is a reference to him as living and concerning himself with the education of his children.[13]

Once more following the pattern of dividing the work into three parts, Christine devotes the first to the education of princes, the second to knights and noblemen, and the third to the rest of the social order in which she includes scholars at the University of Paris, merchants, artisans, and laborers.

The idea of the human body as an analogy for the organization of society, the basic concept of the work, is not original with Christine. It had been used by Egidio Colonna, who cited as his source a supposed letter written by Plutarch to the emperor Trajan. It had been repeated by Philippe de Mézières in *The Dream of the Old Pilgrim*, written for the instruction of Charles VI in his youth. Indeed, in his version it is Dame Prudence's attendant Droiture (Rectitude), no doubt the inspiration for Christine's Virtue of the same name, who recounts the story of King Nebuchadnezzar's statue to illustrate the parallel between the structure of society and the human body.[14] Nor was it the first time Christine had made use of the comparison herself. In *The Long Road of Learning* she had written:

> Plutarch said, and leaves the record
> Telling us that civil concord
> Is like a body vivified,
> And as God's gift is sanctified,
> But governed is by Temperance
> From Reason in good ordinance,

> Of which body is the prince the head,
> By which all members will be led,
> For as the head is over all,
> The members must await his call
> Which governs all the rest at will
> Giving commands which then fulfill
> The senses which control the rest.[15]

More recently, the comparison had been used by Gerson in his sermon *"Vivat Rex,"* delivered in November 1405, and it seems probable that Christine was immediately inspired by Gerson, for there are other similarities between his sermon and the first part of *The Book of the Body Politic:* the representation of a king as the good shepherd of his flock, reference to the need to pay French armies so that they do not plunder the population they are supposed to protect, and, especially, a concern for the lot of poor peasants. As in Gerson's sermon, *The Body Politic* contains numerous illustrative examples drawn from the pages of Valerius Maximus.[16]

A new translation of the Roman history of Valerius Maximus, *Facta et Dicta Memorabilia (Memorable Deeds and Sayings),* with a commentary, had been undertaken by Simon de Hesdin at the command of Charles V but had been left unfinished after the king's death. It was finally finished, on the duke of Berry's suggestion, by Nicholas de Gonesse toward the end of 1401. A copy of the entire text was presented to the duke as a New Year's Day gift at the beginning of 1402. The translation apparently was an immediate success, and a number of copies were soon made of it, two of which were illustrated by the Cité des Dames Master around 1405.[17] Christine quotes both the text and the commentary without always discriminating between them.

In common with other treatises on the education of princes, Christine insists on virtue as the only proper basis for ruling a country. She outlines the qualities he must cultivate in order to prepare for his future responsibilities, but she insists somewhat more than others on his early instruction, saying that it is essential to provide the child with a tutor of excellent character who is capable of instructing him with kindness as well as firmness, teaching him above all to recognize the difference between good and evil, and, if he shows any aptitude, opening for him "the way of philosophy" by introducing him to the pleasure that can come from learning.[18]

At the same time, the young prince should be exposed to more than theory, and as soon as he is capable of understanding what is going on he should be present at meetings of the royal council to hear discussions of the affairs of state. He should also be given the opportunity to learn about other countries and their customs, especially about their governments, and from his contacts with the royal counselors he should learn about the needs of various groups among his subjects. He should learn to appreciate the merits of various social classes, since the welfare of the whole body politic is essential to the well-being of the state. Throughout these instructions reminiscences of Charles V are mingled with examples drawn from Valerius Maximus selected to demonstrate that merit is more important in society than nobility of birth.

After devotion to God and a concern for his subjects untainted by personal interest, the good prince should love justice. In ruling he should be assisted by advisers of high moral character as well as of observable competence. Cicero is quoted to call attention to the fact that such men as these would be inclined to defend the rights of all subjects. Christine also recommends Cicero's advice that young men be excluded from the high councils in favor of more seasoned and experienced counselors.

In her insistence that justice apply to everyone, Christine takes up the cause of the poor and the humble, pointing out with noteworthy courage that it is a disgrace that they should be burdened with heavy taxes from which the rich and powerful are too often exempt. She also speaks out against dishonest tax collectors who feather their own nests at the expense of the poor, citing the superiority of Rome over France in methods of managing such problems. [19]

Of particular interest is the importance accorded to eloquence and oratorical skill in a future ruler, essential for convincing his subjects to do his will. Here Christine cites the talents of Charles V, adding that both Louis of Orleans and Philip of Burgundy had developed oratorical skill to good purpose. This quality was also highly regarded by humanists.

Christine's concept of the perfect prince varies only in detail from the long series of treatises on the subject beginning with Xenophon's *Cyropedia,* written in the fourth century B.C. for the education of Cyrus, the king of Persia. In common with most other writers on the subject, she asserts that the personal moral virtues of the prince affect the prosperity of the land and that Christian goodness can be a cure for human woes.

At the beginning of her book, Christine speaks of the nobles and knights as the arms and hands of the body politic. Turning to these in part two, she bases their value on six principles that she illustrates liberally with examples of Roman leaders drawn from Valerius Maximus and occasionally from Livy. In the first place, knights should love the profession of arms and be willing to devote themselves wholeheartedly to perfecting their skill. In the second place, they should be brave and of such constant courage that they would neither flee from battle nor sacrifice their country to save their own blood. The third condition is that they be prepared to encourage each other and urge their companions on to do their best; the fourth is that they be truthful and faithful to their given word; the fifth that they cherish honor above all worldly things; and the sixth that they be wise and wary not only where the enemy is concerned but in all other military undertakings as well. The ideal that Christine holds out to the knights is not too far removed from the one that would be set forth by Baldassare Castiglione for his courtiers slightly more than a century later. His courtier, too, was to be first of all a good military man.[20]

The second part of *The Book of the Body Politic* would also provide the basis for *Le Livre des Fais d'Armes et de Chevalerie (Feats of Arms and of Chivalry)*, which Christine wrote two or three years later, and one may well ask what inspired her to write as she did in 1406. Around the same time, Jean de Montreuil wrote the first version of a treatise entitled *A Toute la Chevalerie (To All Knighthood)*. He presented a version in Latin to Louis of Guyenne in 1408 and offered an extended French version several years later.[21] Some of his admonitions are similar to Christine's. In addition to a limited number of references to Roman military prowess, he retells at length glorious episodes from French history, some of which Christine had also recounted in *The Deeds and Good Customs of the Wise King Charles V.* Clearly a need was felt by both writers to rally the morale of the French armies, which were about midpoint between the defeat of Nicopolis and the disaster that awaited them at Agincourt. It is a fact that few revisions or improvements were made in the French military establishment between the reigns of Charles V and Charles VII.

In many respects, the third part of the treatise is the most interesting of all dealing as it does with the common people, about whom so little history has been recorded. They are called the stomach, the legs, and the feet of the body politic, and Christine makes a great point of their importance to the general welfare, dwelling on the necessity of all parts of the body to function harmoniously together. She therefore insists that it is important for all subjects to remain loyal to their rulers and especially to avoid revolting against them. Clearly, the possibility of a civil war is present in her thinking.

Turning to the University of Paris, Christine shifts her attention to the intellectual life of the city, one of its most exhilarating aspects. These chapters underscore once more Christine's genuine devotion to learning and to those who give their lives to the pursuit of knowledge. On the rewards of such a life she comments: "There is nothing more perfect than to know the truth and the explanation of all things, which is the purpose of knowledge."[22]

Returning then to a subject that had already concerned her in *Christine's Vision,* she speaks of the contributions of early philosophers to human knowledge, adding the curious detail that among the books known to have been collected by Plato was the poetry of Sappho, whom she considered to be one of her principal models as a poet.[23] (It is not known how she gleaned this information.) Above all, Christine insists that the possession of knowledge has little merit in itself if one makes no effort to make it available to others; for learned men who keep their knowledge to themselves, or use it for evil ends, are more blameworthy than the ignorant.

Focusing her attention next on the merchants, Christine insists on the distinction between wealthy merchants, those who were considered nobles in certain Italian cities, and small businessmen. Her description of the first category quite obviously refers to the Italian merchants and bankers who had established themselves in Paris and with whose life she was familiar, (she had described their wives in *The Book of the Three Virtues).*[24] Here, as elsewhere, she makes it clear that she considers these prosperous merchants a particularly stable and useful element in society because they are unable to underwrite the projects of the nobility and even the royalty (they were well known as moneylenders), and at the same time they exercise a calming influence on the volatile nature of artisans and workers. Thus, their cooperation is particularly important to the health of the body politic, and their presence should be welcome, a situation that was not invariably appreciated by the Parisians.[25]

Finally, Christine turns her attention to artisans and agricultural workers. She expresses great respect for the latter, although her sympathy for them is less obvious than for their female counterparts. She honors the dignity of their work, recalling that the common ancestors of all members of society were farmers and shepherds. As for artisans, she praises the quality of their work but expresses considerable reservation about their morals, in particular, their fondness for frequenting taverns. She had already admonished their wives in *The Book of the Three Virtues* against encouraging them in this bad habit. It would appear that bohemian life was already in full flower in Paris at least a generation before François Villon arrived on the scene to immortalize it in his poetry.

In contrast to her disapproval of this undisciplined sort of existence, Christine sees a possibility for contentment in the lives of the poor, perhaps an echo of Boccaccio's *Fates of Illustrious Men*. She points out that they have no reason to fear treason, poison, or robbery.

She ends the book, rather surprisingly, by quoting Ptolemy's *Almagest* to the effect that the happy man is the one who does not care in whose hands the world finds itself, no doubt a consoling thought for anyone living in Paris during the troubled years of 1406 and 1407.[26] More important than prescribing an education that will turn a self-indulged youth into a philosopher-king, Christine is speaking in *The Book of the Body Politic* of the necessity of a society to confront its problems as a unified body, a lesson her contemporaries unfortunately did not heed.

One may well ask what sort of political attitude Christine is expressing here. She appears to fear a civil war and to be in favor of stability at any cost, a point of view with a very practical justification during the period when she was writing. At the same time, one is led to the conclusion that however advanced Christine's educational ideas may have been, in politics she was consistently conservative.[27] It is true that her father, her husband, and eventually her son held official positions in the royal government, but it seems probable that she would have been opposed to violent social changes under any other circumstances as well. Events were soon to show that she had every reason to expect the worst. Throughout the spring and summer of 1407, the rift between the rival dukes widened. Almost everywhere, they worked at cross purposes. Finally, on November 23 the showdown occurred. Late that evening the duke of Orleans was murdered in a Parisian street as he was returning from a visit to the queen in her residence at the Porte Barbette. Although the murderer was soon identified as the Norman knight, Raoul d'Anquentonville, it eventually became known that he had been hired by the duke of Burgundy. After confessing the crime, the duke fled headlong from Paris to his territories in the north, leaving others to deal with the chaos he left behind him.[28]

Once rid of his enemy, John the Fearless embarked on a distinctly bizarre course of publicity to justify his crime sufficiently to gain the pardon of the king. At the royal court, a certain Master Jean Petit of the University of Paris delivered an oration lasting several hours, copies of which were later circulated throughout Europe. The text, "Covetousness Is the Root of All Evil," was the point of departure for demonstrating that Louis of Orleans was a tyrant and that it is permissible, even meritorious, to kill a tyrant.[29] Along with serious arguments borrowed from the Italian legist John of Legnano, the oration contained innuendo based on gossip accusing Louis of dabbling in black magic as well as behaving dishonorably in dealing with England. The suggestion that he had used taxes raised for the war with England for his own purposes was probably somewhat nearer the truth. Jean Petit's efforts were successful: On the day following his speech, John the Fearless was granted a formal pardon by the king.

Later the same year, the duke's prestige in Paris was increased by his victory over the rebellious citizens of Liège at the Battle of Othée. Indeed, this victory enhanced his name throughout Europe. He had shown considerable talent for military organization and tactics and had effectively dealt with the turbulent elements in cities, those who made people like Christine so uneasy. Although his position in France had been uncertain since the murder of his rival, it was now so well repaired that by the end of 1409 he was able to gain personal ascendancy over the queen and the royal council, and on December 28 he was appointed the official governor of the dauphin, an accomplishment that marked his triumph over all political rivals.[30]

The duke of Burgundy lost no time in surrounding the prince with courtiers in whose loyalty he could have confidence. Among his major concerns was the military education of the young man, who had little taste for arms. In 1410 the dauphin was made captain of the royal Château of Creil to give him experience in command and also to encourage him to engage in physical exercise, for which he also had no great liking. In the meantime, the duke of Burgundy's enemies were arming to attack Paris in the hope of restoring their influence there, making obvious the dauphin's need for immediate training.

By 1412 Louis of Guyenne had indeed developed enough signs of leadership to accompany his father-in-law on two expeditions, and Christine's *Feats of Arms and of Chivalry* may have been a factor in this accomplishment. In any case, the duke of Burgundy's plan for the dauphin's military education was certainly the inspiration for this manual on warfare. Understandably, Christine felt somewhat uneasy embarking on a subject in which she was so little qualified, so she made an appeal to Minerva, whose prowess she had already noted in the *The Book of the City of Ladies*:

O Minerva, goddess of arms and of chivalry, which by virtue of your understanding beyond all other women, you founded and instituted among other noble arts and sciences because you initiated the habit of forging arms and harnesses of iron and steel. . . . Lady and high goddess, may it not displease you that I, a simple woman in no way comparable to your greatness in reputed knowledge, should dare to speak of such an institution as that of arms, which you first established in Greece. May it rather please you to be favorable to me because I am somewhat connected with the nation into which you were born, which was then called Greater Greece but is now Apulia and Calabria in Italy, for I am like you, an Italian woman.[31]

Christine tried to make clear from the start that she was not addressing her treatise on warfare to learned men, but rather to practitioners, who could not be expected to know the classics on the subject such as the writings of Vegetius and Frontinus. Considering this objective, it does not seem reasonable to dismiss the *Feats of Arms and of Chivalry* as a mere compilation of material drawn from other sources, as has sometimes been suggested. Her most important source was a translation of Vegetius's *De Re Militari (On Military Affairs)*, which has been characterized as the most influential military treatise in the western world from Roman times to the nineteenth century.[32] It was translated several times in the course of the Middle Ages. She also made extensive use of Honoré Bouvet's *L'Arbre des Batailles (The Tree of Battles)*, a manual on the legal aspects of warfare written toward the end of the fourteenth century and dedicated to Charles VI. These she supplemented by examples drawn from the *Strategemata (Strategems)* of the Roman writer Frontinus and by others from Valerius Maximus. The most original passages of the book, however, are based on conversations concerning military matters with certain contemporaries whom, regrettably, she does not name. One recalls from her earlier writings, however, the names of the seneschal of Hainaut and of Jean Chateaumorand, Marshal Boucicaut's lieutenant in Constantinople. As a whole, the book should be considered as a work of popularization, and it was sufficiently valuable to have been read well into the sixteenth century. It was printed in French by Antoine Vérard, and in English by Caxton, who translated it at the request of the English king Henry VII.[33]

The first two books of Christine's treatise are inspired principally by Vegetius and the other by Bouvet. The opening chapters of Book I, however, are devoted to a discussion of the "just war," reflecting not only concerns of Bouvet, but also of the Italian legist John of Legnano, who had held a chair of civil law at the University of Bologna around the same time that Christine's father was lecturing there. She could have known his treatise *De Bello (On Warfare)* either directly or through Bouvet, who makes extensive use of it. The treatise had also served as one of Jean Petit's sources for his defense of Duke John the Fearless only a short time before. It is particularly noteworthy that Christine cites as an example of a just war Charles V's abrogation of the Treaty of Brétigny in 1369. As in the biography of Charles V, she gives an account that is not entirely free from bias.[34]

In subsequent chapters, she draws a portrait of the ideal commander. He need not be a king or prince, as she wrote in a chapter from *The Deeds and Good Customs of the Wise King Charles V.*[35] It is not always expedient for the king to take part personally in a battle, and he might be better represented by the constable, for whom she also outlined the qualities desirable. She turns then to a discussion of the proper upbringing for young boys, who should be trained to austerity and sobriety, rather than, like Roman youths, indulged by easy living. This remark was clearly intended as a polite, discreet reproach to the upbringing of the lazy and overindulged Louis of Guyenne.

In this discussion, Christine is not merely pilfering Vegetius. She was selecting material to support certain observations she wanted to make about her contemporaries. To make certain that her purpose is understood, she calls attention to important differences between the Roman army and the practices of her day, ignoring, for instance, what Vegetius had to say about the Roman legions in Book II of his treatise. Her interests are practical more than merely historical.

Book II of her own treatise was inspired in large measure by the *Strategems* of Frontinus, which she used to provide examples of exemplary conduct. To these examples, she adds accounts of both the fortification of a castle and plans for besieging such a stronghold. The details of her descriptions throw interesting light on military equipment and techniques typical of the early years of the fifteenth century.

The third and fourth books of the *Feats of Arms and of Chivalry* are devoted to legal questions concerning relationships between military leaders and their men and also between countries at war. The problems examined are typical of those that were constantly debated by diplomatic representatives trying to formulate treaties between France and England and, more frequently, commercial treaties between England and Flanders, where the threat of raiding and piracy in the English Channel to the important wool trade required frequent arbitration.

In these last two sections Christine made extensive use of Honoré Bouvet's *The Tree of Battles,* a source she quite openly admitted, although without mentioning the name of the author. She did, however, describe the appearance of a wise old man who said to her:

> I have come to help you with the present book . . . upon which you are working so hard with great diligence and good will, and to give comfort to your desire to provide material for knights and noblemen who may hear it and make use of it and distinguish themselves all the more in the deeds

which nobility requires. So it is a good thing for you to gather from the Tree of Battles, which is in my garden, some of its fruits and make use of them. I will assist you to complete it as master and you will be my disciple.[36]

There follows a long dialogue between master and disciple, in the style Christine had devised in *The Book of the City of Ladies.* Christine was perhaps clever in judging that this conversation would offer a good way to present rather dry legal material to men of action who, in some cases, were barely literate. The questions discussed ranged from who should pay the soldiers under various circumstances, stressing the importance of paying them in order to prevent them from devastating the territories they traversed, to the rights of noncombatants. In Book IV, the discussions center around safe-conducts, treaties, letters of marque (legalized reprisals), and judicial combats (to which Christine was firmly opposed). The final chapters are devoted to the question of who should be allowed to adopt coats of arms: Christine was of the opinion that only a limited group should be entitled to them.

It is everywhere evident that the essential purpose of the book was to encourage discipline within the army and loyalty to a leader as opposed to the pursuit of the individualistic objectives by knights-errant, who were all too often primarily interested in their own renown, and by common soldiers whose principal concern was acquiring booty. If the ideal upheld by both Christine and Bouvet has been criticized as far removed from the harsh reality of the day, it does provide evidence of a desire to reform chivalric conventions that were no longer useful to society. Both books were immediately popular, an indication that their ideas found favor with many knights, and it was in fact during the course of the fifteenth century that national armies evolved out of the various orders of knighthood. These books are less an indication of the decline of chivalry than of its potential for adapting itself to changing circumstances.

A curious fate awaited Christine's treatise, however. Although there still exists a group of manuscripts naming Christine, there are other copies where no author is mentioned, where the invocation to Minerva at the beginning has been suppressed, and where even masculine pronouns replace the feminine forms in the original text. The scene at the beginning of Book III, where Honoré Bouvet appears to Christine in a dream, offering her any fruit she might find useful from *The Tree of Battles,* is also suppressed, and in the second version Bouvet and Christine are replaced by *L'Aucteur* and *Le Disciple.*[37]

Although Caxton's imprint belongs to the first group, the early

French edition, first printed by Vérard in 1488, reproduces the second text. In general, the first group includes the earlier manuscripts, many of them associated with the Court of Burgundy with which Caxton had close associations. Most manuscripts of the second group appear to have been copied after Christine's death and circulated in Paris, where Vérard had his contacts, as did Philip LeNoir who published the text in 1527. Even so, both printers knew of Christine and printed editions of *The Book of the Three Virtues* with her name on the title page. It can only be concluded that the anonymous version reflects the disbelief that a woman could have written such a text.

By the time Christine had finished her treatise, the situation in France had deteriorated further. The duke of Burgundy's power was now opposed by the young duke of Orleans and his brothers, and especially by his father-in-law, Bernard VII, count of Armagnac, who gave his name to the alliance. The elderly dukes of Bourbon and Berry lent their support to the party, but little more. John the Fearless, for his part, made a strenuous effort to detach the allegiance of the duke of Berry. To further his own ends he busily organized a campaign of propaganda.

It is in this context that Christine's letter to the duke of Berry, dated August 25, 1410, must be read. This was *La Lamentacion sur les Maux de la France (Lamentation on the Troubles of France).*[38] As it develops ideas already familiar from *The Book of the Body Politic,* it is not certain whether it was entirely spontaneous on her part or whether she had been enlisted in the duke of Burgundy's propaganda program. In this public letter, she addresses all French princes and appeals to other sectors of French society as well. Expressing once more her fear of civil war, she accuses the French princes of behaving more like the country's enemies than its sons, for though it is their duty to defend the crown, they now oppose each other, threatening war. She sees even worse to come: famine, plundering troops in the countryside, dissension in the cities, and far worse than any of that, the threat of an English attempt to take advantage of the country's disunity. Christine, like Cassandra, shows herself able to see France's future with remarkable clarity. Above all, she appeals to the women who risk losing their husbands, fathers, and sons; then she speaks once more to the queen, inquiring if she is asleep since she shows so little concern for her children's heritage. In her distress she cries out:

Ah, France, France, formerly glorious realm! Alas! what more can I say? Bitter tears stream unceasingly from my eyes onto the paper so that no dry spot is left where I can continue writing this most distressing complaint.[39]

Then, recalling the noble example of Saint Louis, she begs the duke of Berry to act as peacemaker to save the country, a role that would assuredly bring him great honor and esteem. Unfortunately for France, John of Berry, then as always, lacked the qualities of a hero.

It was not until the summer of 1411 that the opposition had made sufficient headway to undertake military action. In July the armies were drawn up with exchanges of challenges and manifestos in a new war of propaganda, in which the duke of Burgundy still enjoyed considerably more success than the Armagnacs. In June the duke of Burgundy's ambassadors achieved the prolongation of an important commercial treaty between England and Flanders, and negotiations were continuing with a view to arranging a marriage between the Prince of Wales, the future Henry V, and one of the duke's daughters. These meetings served as a pretext for the arrival in France of English troops under the command of the Earl of Arundel. There is no evidence, Armagnac propaganda to the contrary, that Burgundy had asked for their help, nor is there proof of any sort of military treaty at this time.[40] Nevertheless, John the Fearless was not above taking the English forces with him as he rode into Paris, evading the Armagnac army, which was trying to guard the approaches to the city. Once in Paris, he was able to make the king declare the dukes of Orleans and Bourbon outlaws, and all royal subjects were called upon to take up arms against them. The following month, they were defeated at St.-Cloud. Burgundian propaganda had been as effective as its military strength.

By this time, there was a growing desire in Paris for peace, and public-spirited citizens looked to the dauphin for leadership. His efforts, seconded by those of the count of Savoy and the duke of Anjou, succeeded in bringing about the Treaty of Auxerre on August 22, 1412. In speaking of this treaty, the chronicler Jean Juvenal des Ursins added the wry comment that it was probably less a manifestation of God's will than the exhaustion of financial sources on both sides.[41] During the general euphoria following this event, Christine took up her pen to write *Le Livre de la Paix (The Book of Peace),* which she dedicated to Louis of Guyenne in recognition of his role in the reestablishment of peace.[42]

John the Fearless remained in control of Paris, but he now had to take into account the ambitions of the dauphin who on January 20, 1413, reached the age of eighteen. He had already prevailed on his father to encourage the moderation that had helped to bring about the Treaty of Auxerre. Now he became more and more the focus of the Parisians who favored peace at almost any price—the message that is evident in the first pages of *The Book of Peace*.

In spite of the fact that John the Fearless still appeared to be in command of the situation during the early months of 1413, at the end of April a popular rebellion suddenly broke out and brought about his downfall. One might almost say that events conspired against him. On April 28, the so-called Cabochian Revolt began. Named for one of its leaders, Simon Caboche, the head of the powerful guild of butchers, it was the sort of popular uprising that Christine had warned against, and her references to it in Book III of *The Book of Peace* provide considerable insight into the terror it evoked among the Parisians. Although the revolt was occasioned by an understandable desire for governmental reform, it became so violent that it essentially defeated its own purpose. Even John the Fearless was unable to control the mob, and its leaders were his protégés, originally encouraged by him for his own ends.[43]

The first uprising was marked by the presentation of a detailed program for reforms that were certainly not without merit. But the second outburst on May 22 led to the arrest by the mob of the queen's brother, Louis of Bavaria, along with several other members of her household. The mob then forced its way into the dauphin's apartments and seized some of his intimates. This episode was followed on the twenty-sixth and twenty-seventh of May by the promulgation of the Cabochian Ordinance, a program of reforms aimed at making the government less extravagant and more efficient. Unfortunately, it was a program that was never put into effect.

The dauphin's reaction to the violence that had reached his own door was to appeal to the Armagnacs for help. In early August Louis welcomed back to Paris the Armagnac princes, a move supported by those moderate Parisians whose views are represented in Christine's book. By the end of the month, it was the turn of the Burgundians and the Cabochians to flee from Paris.

The events of this turbulent spring and summer are recorded by Christine in *The Book of Peace*, along with an appeal to Louis of Guyenne to take seriously his responsibilities. According to her own statement, this was not her only appeal to the dauphin. She refers to an *"Advision du Coq,"* obviously the French cock that was already a recognized symbol, a work which she had presented to him earlier that year during Lent. Although no other trace of this work remains, it would appear that she had called his attention to examples of divine punishment visited on realms that were not able to control their greed and self-seeking passions.[44]

Following her usual practice, she divided *The Book of Peace* work into three parts, the first of which was started at the beginning of September 1412 and the second a year later, after the return of the Armagnacs to power. She had finished it by the end of the year. On New Year's Day 1414, she presented a copy to the duke of Berry.

Exhorting the dauphin to strive to maintain the peace, she expresses the view that cruelty was the cause of wars and that justice would go far in preventing them. She insists further that a just prince should strive to see that the wicked are punished, the innocent protected, evil prevented, and, finally, that good subjects are rewarded according to their merits. As she had done in *The Book of the Body Politic*, she recalls the admirable Roman system of rewarding civic virtue.

Speaking of the Cardinal Virtue of Fortitude, she insists on the moral rather than the physical qualities implied, recalling once more the military successes of Charles V, achieved with the help of Bertrand DuGuesclin on land and Jean de Vienne at sea, even though he had not personally led his armies in battle. It is evident that she is aware of the prince's continuing distaste for military prowess. At the end of the second part, she repeats the names of some of the knights who had served the former king so that their deeds would not be forgotten.

In the long and diffuse third part, consisting of forty-eight chapters, the most interesting pages reflect Christine's own reactions to the events she has so recently witnessed. More than ever she is obsessed by the dangers of popular rule. In spite of her humanitarian concern for the common people, she insists that they should be held firmly in check to prevent them from terrorizing a city, as they had done recently in Paris. At the same time, she warns the prince against the intrigues of wicked men in power. If this is a veiled reference to the duke of Burgundy's part in preparing the way for the uprising, it must have been a bitter pill for Christine to swallow since he had been her benefactor, but she never hesitated to take a stand for principles she considered important.

To underscore her point, she introduces into the text of her treatise a letter to the common people, warning them once more against rising up against their rulers. She also expresses strong opposition to their holding office or being allowed to bear arms. The recent events had merely confirmed her in her misgivings about popular government. She even permits herself to satirize the ineptitude of those who have found themselves in power:

What mischance had instructed an artisan, who all his life had done only his work . . . and had certainly never frequented legists or lawyers to learn about law and justice, nor had ever experienced honor or known what is good sense, or learned to speak logically with good and evident proof, nor learned any of the things needed to carry on government. And such a fool as this, who can scarcely say his Pater Noster, and knows how to behave himself only in a tavern, now wants to govern others. Heavens! What government! For such as he commonly have little sense, and naturally fools have pride, however limited they may be, so nothing is more harmful than their government. What else could one expect of a buffoon who suddenly becomes a master? . . . But to see them at their councils and assemblies! It would make one laugh if it weren't so dangerous, hearing them explain their points, where the most foolish speaks first, still wearing his apron. It seems more a play performed in jest, for these fellows model their speeches on farces, imagining that one should speak in such a manner, one foot forward and the other behind, hands held at the sides. One has never seen the like.[45]

In another series of chapters, Christine discusses opposing virtues and vices, and from these she moves to the concluding chapters aimed at the prince's known shortcomings. She recommends to him skill in public speaking, deplores unbridled anger (the prince's violent temper has been recorded by the chroniclers), and praises the virtues of marriage at a time when Louis had all but abandoned Duchess Marguerite in favor of a mistress chosen from among his mother's ladies-in-waiting. Recalling the obligations of noblemen to serve their people, she deplores sloth and recommends communication between a ruler and his subjects (Louis was criticized for preferring the society of a few intimate friends). Once more, she stresses the dangers of the ever-present flatterers who surround princes. After a few final words on the necessity of leading a regular life, a virtue she had recommended earlier in *The Book of the Body Politic,* and some remarks about the merits of charity and friendship in a ruler, she concludes her treatise by reaffiming her goodwill toward the prince as well as desires for his success. It is a testimony to Christine's courage and independence of spirit that she dared to take to task this short-tempered and pleasure-loving prince. Apparently, the hopes she held for his future role were more important to her than the danger of his incurring displeasure.

By the fall of 1413, as she was finishing her book, it was the turn of the Armagnacs to avenge themselves after the Burgundians had been forced to flee from Paris. On October 3, the Cabochian Ordinance was revoked soon after the duke of Burgundy had been officially banished. A campaign of propaganda by the Armagnacs was then directed against him, accompanied by the systematic replacement of people in the government who were sympathetic to his cause. By the end of the year, his influence had been almost completely eradicated.

The following April, the Armagnacs were ready for military action against the Burgundians, heading north toward Arras with the mad Charles VI in their company as evidence of the legitimacy of their cause. This time the dauphin appears to have been full of enthusiasm for the expedition, riding forth with his banner adorned with a swan and the enigmatic initials *K* and *L,* marking his infatuation for the young woman named La Cassinelle. Although the siege that was laid before Arras was not a military success, it gave Louis an opportunity to play a major role in the new Treaty of Arras, which was eventually negotiated.[46]

Before this treaty could be put into effect, a new, more serious menace presented itself. In England the ailing Henry IV had been succeeded by the young and ambitious Henry V. Taking advantage of the disarray in France, he seized the opportunity to invade the country, no doubt hoping to find an ally in John the Fearless. The duke, however, did nothing to help the English, perhaps because he had sworn at Auxerre that he would not do so. (Whatever the prince's shortcomings, he was in the habit of honoring oaths.) He was not present at the Battle of Agincourt, either, although both his brothers lost their lives on that battlefield: The futility of traditional chivalric practices, a lesson of the French defeat at Nicopolis so many years before may not have been lost on him at least. Few French princes had a tactical sense as good as his, and he may have foreseen the disaster at Agincourt. In any event, the French defeat there sealed the fate of most of the Armagnac leaders.

Louis of Guyenne was not at Agincourt, though he was the official commander of the French armies. As recommended by *The Feats of Arms and of Chivalry,* he was represented by the constable, Charles d'Albret, who was among the day's victims. Shortly after landing at Harfleur, Henry V had sent a challenge to the dauphin, inviting him to single combat for the future control of France. Henry must have known that it would hardly be an equal contest. Of course such a solution would have been in keeping with chivalric tradition, but it probably would not have greatly changed France's ultimate fate, except that the lives of many Frenchmen might have been spared.

Although Louis was saved from the humiliation of personal defeat and survived Agincourt, he died in Paris at the end of December.[47] Remarkably little regret was expressed at his passing, and history has not dealt kindly with his memory. But in spite of his numerous shortcomings, had he lived he might at least have attenuated some of the disasters of the next few years. He had been trained for kingship and had even begun to show some qualities of leadership, including a desire for moderation. At least there was never any question of his legitimacy, the problem that was the undoing of his younger brother Charles at the terrible Treaty of Troyes in May 1420. It would take the miracle of Joan of Arc to rescue Charles from his dilemma.

The efforts expended on providing a humanistic education for Louis of Guyenne may have seemed in vain, but *The Book of the Body Politic* and *The Feats of Arms and of Chivalry* were translated, printed, and read in both France and England during the next century. If *The Book of Peace* was less well known, it was copied and read at the Court of Burgundy, where its influence can be detected in *Le Livre d'Instruction d'un Jeune Prince (A Book of Instruction for a Young Prince)*, written around the middle of the fifteenth century by the distinguished Burgundian diplomat Guillebert de Lannoy, who had known Christine in his youth, when he was the squire of her friend, the seneschal of Hainaut. The young prince he was addressing was the future Burgundian duke, Charles the Bold. One copy of Christine's book appears to have been prepared for another dauphin named Louis, who would reign as Louis XI.[48] He would be Charles the Bold's bitter enemy, bringing about the downfall of the Burgundian realm, but he would also be called "France's first modern king."

Inside the Courtyard of the Abbey of Poissy Today

Joan of Arc at Orleans

10

The Retreat to Poissy

At the beginning of 1416 Christine, now more than fifty years old, again found herself the victim of Fortune's instability, but this time she was not alone in her misfortune. All of France was in a state of disarray. The defeat at Agincourt and the death of Louis of Guyenne were serious blows, and they were followed by other deaths and often trials. The young duke of Tourraine, who succeeded his brother Louis, lived only until April 5, 1417. Too young and inexperienced to do more than serve as a figure-head, he was soon followed to the grave by Louis of Anjou, king of Sicily, the last of Charles V's brothers. The duke of Berry had already breathed his last on April 15, 1416, leaving his heirs to dispose of his treasures as well as his monumental debts. Much of this duty fell on his daughter Marie, the duchess of Bourbon, whose life was already burdened by responsibility for her husband's territories in central France. (The duke was one of the captives of Agincourt who would never know freedom again.)

In addition to the loss of these royal princes, France lost most of the Armagnac leaders who had controlled the government since the summer of 1413. The only important survivor was Count Bernard VII of Armagnac, the duke of Orleans' father-in-law. He was now named constable of France, Charles d'Albret having died at Agincourt. The appointment of this brutal nobleman to public office not only hardened differences between the Armagnac and Burgundian factions, but also brought about another reign of terror in Paris. Although the duke of Burgundy was more definitively exiled from the capital than ever, the very repressiveness of the government there gave him the excuse he wanted for intervention.

In October 1416, John the Fearless entered into negotiations with Henry V at Calais, but no agreement was actually reached or treaty signed.[1] Then, during the summer of 1417, he organized an all-out military offensive that, though a failure, prevented the Armagnacs from leaving Paris to counter the initial stages of the English conquest of

Normandy. His next move followed the naming of the new dauphin, the future Charles VII, as lieutenant governor of France in his father's name, thereby making him the nominal chief of the Armagnac government in Paris. John the Fearless countered by persuading the queen to spend the winter in Chartres and Troyes, where the two of them set up a rival government. By spring a considerable part of France had recognized this new government. A net was being drawn ever more surely around Paris until, on the night of May 28, 1419, the city gates near St.-Germain-des Prés were secretly opened and Burgundian troops stormed the city at last, spreading violence and terror. Parisians suspected of Armagnac sympathies were murdered in the streets and in their beds. Christine had enjoyed the patronage of two dukes of Burgundy, but her son was now one of the dauphin's secretaries: Her family was fortunate to escape from Paris with their lives. The dauphin, too, made a dramatic flight from the royal palace to the protecting walls of the Bastille and eventually reached safety outside the city, while the count of Armagnac was one of the victims of the massacre. In July the duke of Burgundy, with Isabeau of Bavaria in his company, returned to Paris in triumph.

Already at the beginning of 1418, Christine wrote of the "great worries and failing courage" that had been her lot because of many difficulties which confronted her.[2] It is understandable that neither she nor any other Parisian could have lived very comfortably or securely during those turbulent times. Yet in some ways her personal situation must have been less precarious than it had been in earlier years. Her son Jean was now established as a secretary in the royal chancellery.[3] His signature appears on royal documents from 1409 onward, so he had finally been given the opportunity to follow in his father's footsteps, the normal course in notorial families as long as the royal favor required for an appointment could be obtained. It also seems likely that Christine was living with him. A document recording a suit made against Christine and her son by Jehanne de Sens, the widow of a former counselor of Parliament, involves a house they were renting from her.[4] Her son had already married, or would soon have as his wife a young woman named Jehanette Cotton, the daughter of another royal secretary, and by 1418 the couple's three children had probably been born. As nothing is known to have come from Christine's pen between 1413 and 1418, some of her preoccupation with living in this difficult period may have been tempered by the pleasures of being a grandmother.

It was on a far from happy note, however, that on January 20, 1418, Christine started writing *Letter concerning the Prison of Human Life,* which she dedicated to Marie de Berry, the duchess of Bourbon.[5] She spoke, rather, of having to "restrain the flow of her tears" in order to console the multitude of French women mourning the loss of their husbands, fathers, and sons on the battlefield at Agincourt, and those whose men were prisoners of war in England, some of them never to return to France. Fortunately, two sons of Marie de Berry's third marriage were too young to bear arms, yet she was certainly one who had great losses to mourn, for not only had her husband been captured—and in spite of repeated offers to pay the ransom demanded by his captors, would die in England in 1413—but also the son of her second marriage, Philip of Artois, count of Eu, was also among the captives and did not regain his freedom until 1438. In addition, her daughter Bonne of Artois had been left a widow by the death in battle of her husband Philip of Nevers, the duke of Burgundy's younger brother. Several cousins had also died at Agincourt (among them the French constable, Charles d'Albret). All of these losses were followed by the death of her father in 1416. There could have been few women in France more greatly in need of consolation than she.

On the other hand, it must be said that the Duchess Marie was a woman of unusual intelligence and resourcefulness. Although she was badly treated by the English in the matter of her husband's ransom, she managed his territories with success until her son succeeded to the title. She was also noted for her patronage of writers. Christine expressed gratitude to her for kindnesses that had helped her through the early days of her own widowhood.[6]

It was for her particular benefit, in any event, that Christine developed a theme she had already mentioned in her letter to the duke of Berry in 1410, which is to say that French women were condemned to suffer immeasurably from events beyond their control.[7] The idea of writing this letter had apparently been suggested to Christine by someone other than the duchess whose identity is not known. The true inspiration for Christine's letter, however, was the humanistic tradition of writing letters to give advice to princes, princesses, and other leaders of society. Christine had been attracted to this sort of public letter writing from the time of her involvement in the debate over *The Romance of the Rose;* and ever since writing *The Long Road of Learning,* she had felt called upon to offer advice on various matters to the French princes. In this case, she combined these two interests to produce a letter on one of the most compelling themes of literature, the search for consolation in the face of sudden death and the loss of loved ones.

As was her custom, she developed her literary allusions on a basis of personal experience. The lonely widow of nearly thirty years earlier was now prepared to offer consolation to the bereft women of France in the name of the duchess of Bourbon. In order to do this, she turned to Boethius, in whose book she herself had found solace so many years before. She takes the tone that Dame Philosophy used in her admonitions to Boethius in his prison cell, but the idea of life as a prison was Christine's own addition. Christine attributes her inspiration for the idea to Saint Bernard, although her manner of developing it has distinctly Platonic overtones that would have seemed more usual in the sixteenth century than at the beginning of the fifteenth:

> For, says Saint Bernard, this mortal life can be figured for each one as a prison, for just as the enclosure of the prison detains the prisoner so closely that he cannot follow his own wishes nor carry out his desires, and usually quite the contrary, just so the reasonable soul, man's noblest part, without which the body is no more than dust and ashes, is held imprisoned and bound in the body as long as it is alive, where it is so constrained by the weight and the crudity of the container that it has no more than a slight possibility of following its own wishes and inclinations, but is usually obliged to obey the opposite. However, as the wise Albert (the Great) says so well, when a man dies the soul is released from its prison.[8]

Elsewhere in the letter she names Plato and quotes from his *Phaedo* concerning his belief in the immortality of the soul after death. Death is the common lot of all human beings and those who sacrifice their lives in battle die in a state of grace and, it can be assumed, in the majority of cases go directly to paradise. For others, prayers and memorial masses are more helpful than tears.

On the whole, Christine's consolation may seem rather austere to the modern mind, yet, her ideas have a certain validity for the warriors of any era whose lives risk sacrifice on the battlefield. She insisted, in this instance, that those who had died could not be accused of cruelty, a particularly interesting point in view of Henry V's decision at Agincourt to have the poor and badly wounded slaughtered on the battlefield because they offered little prospect for a large ransom, an act that violated all accepted rules of chivalrous warfare. The essential innocence of these warriors led Christine to a discussion of Fortune's victims and also of tyrants who in the end had paid for their crimes. In this latter group, there might seem to be more than a slight echo of the sufferings of Paris at the hands of the count of Armagnac and his followers, although the examples Christine cites are taken from ancient history and from the

Scriptures. Among the victims of Fortune, she names in particular Alexander the Great, Julius Caesar, Pompey, and Scipio; her tyrants include Cain, Absalom, and Saul from the Bible and such legendary or historical figures as Titus Andronicus, Athalie, Brunehaut, Nero, Julian the Apostate, and Denis the Tyrant, several of whom she had cited on various other occasions in her writings. All these secular figures, as well as others she mentions, are to be found in Boccaccio's *Fates of Illustrious Men,* which was already sufficiently popular in France to have been translated twice. And as a number of the manuscripts of these translations were illustrated by the same artists who worked on Christine's own works, there is every reason to suppose that she knew the text, as she knew *Concerning Famous Women* before she started to write *The Book of the City of Ladies.*

Her second reason for taking comfort in the face of the overwhelming loss of French knights is that they had now escaped from life's prison and were protected against further misfortune and fear of death. As for those whom they left behind them, Christine points out that the Creator has bestowed on mortals three forms of help: Grace; natural qualities, which are internal; and Fortune, which is external. The gift of Grace is human understanding, whereas nature includes such qualities as physical strength, health, beauty, an attractive bearing and behavior. The gift of Fortune included the benefits of a worldly situation such as a successful marriage, good family connections, children. It might be argued that these qualities had been of little benefit to the victims of Agincourt, although it was true that those with the most favorable worldly position were the ones saved for ransom and were at least reasonably well treated in England. It was probably Christine's primary intention to point out to Marie de Berry that she was particularly well endowed with these gifts, which should make it possible for her to go on living in the face of adversity.

Developing further the idea of Grace as understanding, Christine explains that it is ideally accompanied by three virtues: Retention, which, in effect, remembers; Memory, which records what is retained, and Reason, which is the source of prudence or discretion, the quality that prevents virtues from turning into vices. She had already given detailed attention to the problems of virtues and their corresponding vices in an early work entitled *Le Livre de la Prod'hommie de l'Homme (Book of Human Integrity),* which was large inspired by the pseudo-Seneca's (in reality Martin of Braga's) *Formula Honestae Vitae (Formula for an Honest Life),* and she had repeated some of his material in a revised form in *The Book of Peace.*[9] As was her custom, she made reference to her own earlier writings, citing once more, for instance, examples based on the life of Charles V.

These cross-references should not be dismissed as mere repetition, for it is through such passages that one becomes aware of Christine's habit of reexamining and developing certain ideas that she considered especially important. In this case, they lead her to the conclusion that Duchess Marie should not spend her time mourning her losses and instead occupy herself with good works in memory of those she has lost. She had already pointed out in *The Book of the Three Virtues* that in bereavement sorrow must be allowed to express itself for a time, and then one should then get on with the demands of everyday life. This is, in essence, the advice she offers to Duchess Marie.

In addition to her own writings and the work of Boethius, Christine draws material from the pseudo-Seneca's *De Remediis Fortuitorum (On Remedies against Fortune)*, which had been translated for Charles V's library by Jacques Bauchaut. She modifies this text slightly to suit her purposes, as was so often her custom. She also cites the Scriptures and the Doctors of the Church, notably Saint Augustine (both his *Confessions* and his *City of God*), Saint Gregory, Saint Bernard, Saint Isidore of Seville, and Saint Anselm. Among her secular sources, in addition to Boccaccio, are Aristotle, the mythological pastoral poem the *Ecloga Thoeduli,* which had been translated into French by Jean Le Fèvre in the fourteenth century, and, surprisingly, a passage on the immortality of the soul from Xenophon's life of Cyrus, the *Cyropedia.* [10] This history had been all but forgotten during the Middle Ages and would not be translated into either Latin or French until later in the fifteenth century, yet Christine could have known it by way of Cicero, who included this particular passage in his *De Senectute (On Old Age),* translated into French in 1405 by Laurent de Premierfait, the translator of Boccaccio. [11]

However, the most interesting example of Christine's ability to synthesize and develop her sources comes at the end of the treatise. It is there that she describes very movingly the joys of paradise that await the dead who die in grace, not only the victims of Agincourt but also those who mourn and remember them. One is again conscious here of Christine's indebtedness to Dante as well as to Saint Augustine as she describes the ranks of angels, the arrival of the souls of the elect who make their way from star to star until they arrive at final union with God. Ultimately, they will experience an overwhelming vision of the Trinity with a joy unknown to earthly creatures.

They will see with their eyes the imperial throne and glorious majesty, surrounded by cherubim and seraphim giving voice to marvelous melody and continually praising God, setting into motion the fair order in which the glorious creatures are seated in ranks, each according to his merit, all content and fulfilled without seeking, wishing, nor desiring more, living forever in all joy in that Holy Celestial Court, of which Saint Augustine said so well: O! glorious things of thee are spoken, blessed City of God. [12]

In addition to the texts of Saint Augustine and Dante, Christine's words reflect a familiarity with the illustrations of the Celestial Court in early fifteenth-century manuscripts, miniatures in certain copies of the *City of God,* and also in *Books of Hours* or *The Golden Legend.* Some of these had come from the hands of the same artists who illustrated her own manuscripts. For the medieval mind, even at the dawn of the modern era, the glories of Paradise were quite as real as the pains of Hell. [13]

The *Letter concerning the Prison of Human Life* was finished and dated January 20, 1418, with an apology that it had not reached the duchess sooner. But, as Christine explains, "several great trials and troubles of courage" had prevented her from writing and her mind had been for some time "so hindered by sad imaginings and thoughts." There is no clue as to whether these troubles were personal or caused by the difficulties of living in Paris under the Armagnac regime.

The work is preserved in a single manuscript, possibly one prepared by Christine herself, for it has corrections that appear to be in her own hand. There is no way of knowing if it ever actually reached Marie of Berry, but this is not particularly significant in the case of a humanistic letter that is more an essay than a personal missive.

Christine's work inevitably invites comparison with Alain Chartier's *Le Livre de Quatre Dames (Book of Four Ladies),* which sets forth the dilemmas of four ladies whose lovers have met with misfortunes at Agincourt: The first was killed, the second captured; the third lost without a trace, and the fourth was a coward who fled from the battlefield. Although the sorrows of these ladies are genuine cases that were many times repeated in actuality, Chartier's poem lacks the tone of sorrow experienced and overcome that is Christine's. Chartier's *Quadrilogue Invectif (Four-Part Invective)* also dwells on the losses at Agincourt. [14] But neither this nor his *Book of Four Ladies,* in spite of their considerable literary reputation, has the emotional tension or the genuine expression of sympathy for the bereaved characterizing Christine's letter. Years of living with her own sorrow had taught compassion and, in the end, the true meaning of patience.

The political situation in Paris at the beginning of 1418 was far from reassuring. As winter turned into spring and the Burgundian net around Paris tightened, the Parisians must have had some awareness of what was going on and have been bracing themselves for an inevitable crisis. Their troubles were compounded by an unusual snowfall at Easter, followed by an inevitable scarcity of food because supplies could not be brought into the city. The Bourgeois of Paris, writing in his *Journal*, gives some idea of the troubles which beset the city:

> So Paris was falsely governed, and those who did govern hated those who were not of their band so much that they threatened to gather up their opponents in all the streets of Paris and kill them without mercy, and they would drown the women. They had seized linen from the merchants without paying for it, claiming that it was to make tents and pavillions for the king, but it was for sacks to drown those women. And moreover, they insisted that before the Burgundians should come to Paris, or peace should be made with them, they would sell Paris to the King of England.[15]

When the Burgundians finally bought their way into Paris late in May and the dauphin had the good fortune to escape from the city to set up a provisional government in Bourges, many of his subjects were less fortunate.[16] If they were known to be supporters of the Armagnacs and were caught in the city, they were murdered without mercy. All official appointments of the former regime were revoked and the places filled by Burgundian sympathizers. Royal officers such as Christine's son Jean de Castel had no choice but to follow the dauphin into exile if they could. Jean was able to continue his career in the entourage of the dauphin, where confidence in his ability was demonstrated by his appointment as an ambassador to the Court of Castille in 1422, a time when both French governments were eager to cultivate allies in Spain.[17] He is also known to have taken part in the literary dispute stirred up around 1424 by Alain Chartier's *Belle Dame sans Merci (Fair Lady without Mercy)*, whose heroine gives the impression of having been influenced by Christine de Pizan's warnings against the dangers of so-called courtly love in *The Book of the Three Virtues* and *One Hundred Ballades of a Lover and His Lady*.

Unfortunately, this is the last to be heard of Jean de Castel. Like his father, he died young, probably in 1425 at the age of forty-two, leaving behind him the widow and three small children who had followed him into exile. These scant facts are known because of his widow's efforts to rejoin her own family in Paris, an undertaking that did not succeed until 1431 when permission for her return was finally granted by the government of Henry VI.[18]

Little is known of Christine's life during these difficult years, but it is thought that she joined her daughter in the Abbey of Poissy. This assumption not only seems logical, but is also substantiated by a note in the margin of a manuscript in England, written by one of Sir John Fastolf's secretaries, stating that during the English occupation of Paris Christine, was living at Poissy. [19] Both Fastolf and his secretary, William of Worcester, were among the Duke of Bedford's troops, which were occupying Paris at the time. Fastolf admired Christine and was the owner of one of the English translations of *Othéa's Letter to Hector*. If Christine was indeed with her daughter, it must have softened the sorrow of her exile, and it also suggests that she could not have been entirely out of the duke of Burgundy's favor, for Poissy lay in the territory he controlled. He is known to have dined at the abbey with his cousin the princess Marie of France, who was one of the nuns there, during the period of his own exile from Paris. Later, the town was occupied by the English, so Christine would not have been completely removed from contact with political events. [20] Neverthe- less, contact with her son at the court of the exiled dauphin would inevitably have been difficult and news of his death, when it reached her, would have been a new and deeper cause for anguish. The plight of her daughter-in-law and grandchildren could not have failed to remind her of her own early misfortunes.

Very possibly it was Jean de Castel's death that inspired her to write *Les Heures de Contemplation sur la Passion de Notre Seigneur (Hours of Contem- plation on Our Lord's Passion).* [21] It has been suggested that Christine was responding to a national misfortune such as the Treaty of Troyes in 1420, yet her touching evocation of Christ's mother standing at the foot of the cross would seem to reflect a personal tragedy rather than a political event. [22] This entirely religious work would also befit a life behind convent walls: It is a translation of the Passion put into the form of a Book of Hours intended to inspire themes for meditation. It is interesting to compare Christine's compassion for the sufferings of all women here with her highly personal suffering and spirit of rebellion against her fate im- mediately after the death of her husband so many years before. Dame Philosophy had indeed left her mark on Christine. She commends herself to all ladies, and generally to all of the female sex who can profit from her words, expressing to her desire to give comfort as best she can for the misery from the endless tribulations that have been plaguing the kingdom of France and have resulted in the death of friends, exile, expulsions, as well as other sorts of hardships and perils. [23] She herself seeks the consolation of the Scriptures to guide her in the further cultivation of patience. No other remedy remains; she no longer refers to the whims of Fortune.

The single manuscript that preserves this text does not offer any further clues to its history. It is to be found in a collection of religious and philosophical works, with a section devoted to Burgundian history, signed by a-Robert LeJeune, the son of a merchant from Chalons, also in Burgundian territory, and dated 1504. It seems therefore quite far removed from the original that Christine composed in her convent cell, but once more it points to the probability that the Burgundians did not consider Christine a public enemy.

Happily, Christine's career as a writer was to end on a more positive note. Her last poem was inspired by an event that seemed to her no less than miraculous, the appearance of a woman military leader who was able to raise the seemingly hopeless siege of the city of Orleans and triumphantly lead the dauphin to be crowned king of France according to established tradition in the Cathedral of Rheims. In July 1429, soon after these stirring events had taken place, she began to write *Le Ditié de Jeanne d'Arc* (*The Tale of Joan of Arc*), the first poem to celebrate the Maid of Orleans and the only one written during Joan's lifetime.[24]

On the last day of July, when Christine completed and dated her poem, the French had just taken Château-Thierry after the overwhelming victory at Orleans, and the coronation of the dauphin as Charles VII had been accomplished. The new king was expected to reenter Paris at any moment and thereby end the English occupation and the long years of civil war.

Having begun the poem with a reference to her eleven years in the abbey cloister, Christine speaks of Joan's progress from Vaucouleurs to Chinon, her reception there by the dauphin, and the other events leading up to his triumphal entry into a number of towns on the route to Paris. The poem vibrates with the excitement generated by these stirring days. As is the case with the *Hours of Contemplation of Our Lord's Passion,* no copy of the poem remains that seems directly connected with Christine. The best one is to be found in a collection containing other documents relating to Joan of Arc and bears the signature of a Nicolas de Pleissy who, in July 1430, was appointed an official of the city of Sens.[25] The compilation appears to date from 1428, so it is possible that Christine's poem was added soon after it was written, making this one the earliest copy in existence. A fragment is also preserved in Grenoble as part of a collection of documents prepared for the future Louis IX in 1456.[26] Matthieu Thomassin, who was charged with making the collection, noted that he thought both Joan of Arc and Christine had brought honor to their sex, saying:

Of all the signs of love sent by God to this Realm, there has been none so great nor so marvelous as that Maid. And because of this, great chronicles have been written about her, and among others by a notable woman named Christine, who has written several books in French (I have often seen her in Paris) who has made of the coming of the aforesaid Maid and of her deeds a treatise of which I will put here only the part having to do with the Maid. . . . And I have wished to put here the treatise of the aforesaid Christine rather than the others in order always to honor the feminine sex by means of which all Christendom has had so much good, by the Virgin Mary, the reparation and restoration of all mankind, and by the aforesaid maid Joan, the reparation and restoration of the Kingdom of France, which was entirely laid low and in danger of being lost if she had not come. . . .[27]

It is probable that the poem had its greatest success in the official circles surrounding the new king, where Christine undoubtedly continued to be remembered and honored even after the death of her son Jean.

Although the poem cannot be considered one of Christine's masterpieces, in a certain sense it does serve to crown her literary career, and it is valuable as an historical document. Christine's main idea is to rejoice at God's grace in having brought back the sun and spring into her own life after the desolate years of her exile while at the same time miraculously restoring France's fortunes and providing the country with its rightful king. She responds to this miracle on three levels: As a devout Christian she expresses her thanks to God for Joan's mission; as a Frenchwoman she rejoices in the victory over the English invader, which she hopes will end both foreign occupation and civil war and lay the foundations for a lasting peace; and, finally, as a woman she sees her defense of all women as vindicated and rewarded by Joan's triumphs.

In the course of the poem, she returns to a number of familiar themes, but one change in her outlook is striking. It is now Providence that guides human destiny rather than a capricious Dame Fortune. It is Providence that has ordained Joan's role. Beyond the restoration of peace in France this will surely lead to new crusades to conquer the Holy Land. Thus she revives Philippe de Mézière's (and also Henry V's) dream of a final effort to vanquish the enemies of Christianity.

She compares Joan with a series of Old Testament heroines, including such as Esther, Judith, and Deborah, who were chosen by God to carry out the designs of Providence, yet she does not neglect to mention that her coming had been foretold by Merlin, Bede, and the Tiburtine Sibyl whose prophecy of Christ's coming had inspired the final chapter and illustration in *Othéa's Letter to Hector.*

In her exaltation as a patriotic Frenchwoman, Christine sees the vindication of her long series of writings devoted to the welfare of France, dating from her ballades on the combat of seven Frenchmen against seven Englishmen commemorating an event of the year 1402. Although she had shown her opposition to the Lancastrian regime on various occasions, she had always expressed her greater concern for the cause of international peace, from *The Long Road of Learning* in 1403 to *The Book of Peace,* finished ten years later.

The defense of women, too, had been especially close to Christine's heart, and Joan's unbelievable achievements were the culminating joy inspired by the change in French fortunes. Here was the incontrovertible proof that she had been correct in her assumption about feminine potentialities and the evidence that what had been possible in the past, as demonstrated in *The Book of the City of Ladies,* could also be accomplished in the present. Joan of Arc was a modern Amazon capable of performing wonders:

> What honor this for womankind,
> Well-loved of God, it would appear,
> When that sad crowd to loss resigned
> Fled from the kingdom in great fear
> Now by a woman rescued here
> (Which 5,000 men could not do)
> Who made the traitors disappear.
> One could scarcely believe it true.[28]

From her retreat in the country she could not resist reproving the Parisians for their fickleness in changing alliances so readily. They were apparently reluctant to receive their deliverer:

> O Paris, city ill-advised,
> Foolish people undone by fear,
> Would you now rather be despised
> Than your own royal prince revere?
> In truth, you so perverse appear
> You'll be destroyed, aren't you aware?
> Unless with contrite hearts sincere
> Mercy you beg. If not, beware.[29]

She ends by expressing her hopes that in the end the king will overcome the doubts of his people:

> I pray to God he will prevail,
> To make your courage so increase
> That this cruel storm no more assail
> And this long war at last will cease
> So you may live your lives in peace.
> Your loyalty to your rightful lord,
> May it never more know surcease,
> So a good lord he may be to you.[30]

Then having dated the poem, Christine laid down her pen forever, insofar as is known. She was now approaching sixty-five, a venerable age for a person of her day, and she had survived many years of hardship and tribulation. One cannot avoid hoping that she did not survive long enough to learn of the capture of her heroine before the walls of Compiègne in May 1430, or of her trial and execution in Rouen the following May. Both Joan's defeat and knowing that the trial was undoubtedly devised to discredit by association Charles VII would have caused her profound sorrow and disillusionment. Charles did not reenter Paris until 1437.

Before that time, Christine had unquestionably breathed her last, for the Burgundian courtier Guillebert de Mets, recording his memories of Paris in 1434, speaks of her in the past tense.[31] It is also possible that the permission granted by Henry VI's government for her daughter-in-law to return to Paris at the end of 1431 was related to the fact that her voice was no longer able to speak out in behalf of the French king or against the English usurpers in the French capital.

In addition to her writings, Christine left behind her three grandchildren. Through a curious medieval habit, the two grandsons seem both to have been named Jean for their father, at least so they are known to posterity. One was a notary, a public official and eventually, like his father and grandfather before him, a royal secretary. He apparently died sometime before the beginning of 1474. The other Jean became a Benedictine monk in 1439. It is recorded that in 1459 he was rewarded by the king for presenting him with a "role of parchment containing several poems written by him in praise of Our Lady." With the advent of Louis XI in 1461, he was appointed a royal historian, the king having taken a dislike to the official chronicle written at the Abbey of St.-Denis. Some idea of his ambitious nature can be gleaned from two poems that he addressed to Charles de Gaucourt, one of the new king's counselors, expresssing the hope that Gaucourt would intercede on his behalf in obtaining further favors from the king. He also exchanged ballades with the Burgundian poet and chronicler Georges Chastellain, and in 1468 he dedicated to the bishop of Poitiers Jean de Bellay a long moralizing poem entitled *Le Specule des Pêcheurs (The Looking-Glass for Sinners)*.[32] In 1472 Jean's ambitions were rewarded by an appointment as Abbot of St.-Maure-des-Fossés near Paris where he died in 1476. Although his literary career would certainly have been a joy to Christine, his writings show him to have followed her inspiration less than that of François Villon. In any case, Martin LeFranc considered him one of the best poets of his day, and Jean Molinet spoke of him as "a great chronicler of France."

Their sister Jeanne was married to a French knight named Pierre Petit but does not seem to have lived long thereafter, for her husband's second marriage to the widow of a provost of Paris is also recorded.

It was undoubtedly the first Jean whose descendants are still to be found in Paris and have provided Christine with one of her modern biographers.[33] In the end, her years of struggle had not been without substantial rewards, both personal and literary.

Christine Presents a Copy of Her Othéa's Letter to Hector *to
Sir John Fastolf*

Burgundian Ladies Attend the School of the Virtues

11

Renown At Last

In reading the works that Christine left behind her, one is struck repeatedly by her intense desire to be remembered by posterity. This trait links her firmly to the new intellectual era that was spreading north from Italy to France in which the quest for fame was considered one of the legitimate objectives of life as opposed to the otherworldliness of the true Middle Ages. It is not without significance that Christine was born the year Petrarch was engaged in writing the section of *I Trionfi (The Triumphs)* devoted to fame.[1]

Regardless of other troubling concerns, Christine seems to have been confident that her fame would endure. Toward the end of *The Book of the Three Virtues*, she writes, for instance:

> And to this end I thought that I would multiply this work in various copies throughout the world, whatever the cost might be, so that it can be presented in various places to queens, princesses, and noble ladies . . . that through their efforts it may be circulated among other women, which thought and desire I have already put into effect. . . . Thus it will be seen and heard by many valiant ladies and women of authority both at the present time and in times to come. . . .[2]

She concludes *The Book of the Body Politic* in a similar vein, by saying:

> I ask that in recompense [for my work] that those now living and their successors, very noble kings and other French princes, who will recall my name through the memory of my poems in the future when my soul has left my body, that by prayers and devout supplications offered by them or because of them, they may appeal to God for indulgence and remission of my shortcomings in my behalf. And likewise I beg of knights and noble Frenchmen, and all others in general, wherever they may be, when because of reading or hearing read my trifling things they think of me, that they will say in recognition a Pater Noster.[3]

As it turned out, Christine did not greatly underestimate her prospects for the future. Her works continued to be read without interruption for more than a hundred years after her death. Although many manuscripts have undoubtedly been lost, an impressive number are still known, and from time to time an additional one turns up from its hiding place in some private library. Although most of the copies from the presses of early printers are also lost, or probably simply worn out from usage, enough are still to be found in rare-book collections to give some idea of their original appearance and contents. From these remaining manuscripts and incunabula, it is possible to form some idea of Christine's success and enduring reputation.

Judging by this evidence, Christine's writings had four particular periods of popularity. During her lifetime, she was certainly known for her courtly poetry, for her role in the debate over *The Romance of the Rose,* for her long allegorical poems, and, to some extent, for her books about women and her treatises on ideal government addressed to Louis of Guyenne. Many of the early manuscripts containing these works were handsomely copied and illustrated in a manner to make them worthy of taking their places in such princely libraries as those of the dukes of Berry and Burgundy. To this period belong, for instance, the duke of Berry's *Othéa's Letter to Hector* and his *The Book of the City of Ladies,* the duke of Burgundy's copy of *The Mutation of Fortune,* and Queen Isabeau's volumes of Christine's works. Much has been learned in recent years about the production of such manuscripts, notably through the efforts of the late Professor Millard Meiss, whose studies of the workshops where such manuscripts were illustrated have given such interesting results. It was he who, above all, identified the work of the two most important artists of this group, assigning the names the Epître d'Othéa Master and the Cité des Dames Master. Thus it has been possible to follow their work in other manuscripts and also to gain some idea of groups of manuscripts that were produced in Paris at more or less the same period. This has shown better than before what books were available to Christine as she worked and what texts were enjoying a particular popularity.

Through a slightly different sort of evidence, the influence of Christine's advice to young women can be seen reflected around 1425 in the controversy which arose over Alain Chartier's *The Fair Lady without Mercy.* Chartier's heroine who refuses offers of love that certainly would lead to her ultimate unhappiness, is a perfect illustration of Christine's theories about the dangers of so-called courtly love. This debate was, in turn, referred to in two of the discussions recorded in Marguerite of Navarre's

Heptameron. It may even have had an indirect influence on Pantagruel's consultation with Doctor Rondabilis on the subject of marriage in Rabelais's Third Book.[4]

Cupid's Letter, where Christine first raised the issue of the attitude toward women in society, was soon translated into English by the poet Thomas Hoccleve, Chaucer's disciple.[5] He modified the work somewhat for his own purposes, but then the poem and the letters inspired by *The Romance of the Rose* were for the most part forgotten, along with the manuscripts into which they were copied.

Christine's second period of popularity, directly related to the first, was at the Court of Burgundy around the middle of the fifteenth century. All of her works found a place in the library of the first two dukes, Philip the Bold and John the Fearless, but during the great proliferation of manuscripts of many sorts during the lifetime of the third duke, Philip the Good, many of the original manuscripts were copied and put into circulation again, and in a few cases they were even revised to conform to the taste of the day. *Othéa's Letter to Hector,* in particular, was not only copied several times, but also was revised by one of Philip the Good's most prolific copyist-editors, Jean Miélot, and provided with a hundred new illustrations by one of the duke's most popular artists, Loyset Liedet. In explaining the reasons for his revisions, Miélot said in his introduction: "Because often brevity has made the subject matter obscure to the readers and so that the hundred glosses written for the hundred authorities . . . may be equal in length, as are the four lines of text, from each of the authorities a new addition has been made."[6] This addition was primarily made up of quotations from Boccaccio's *On the Genealogy of the Gods,* Virgil's *Aeneid,* and Ovid's *Metamorphoses,* bearing witness to the growing humanistic interests at the Burgundian court. Both *The Book of the City of Ladies* and *The Book of the Three Virtues* were popular, and copies were made for the libraries of such notable bibliophiles among the Burgundian courtiers as the Croys, Louis de Gruythuse of Bruges, and probably for the Créquys. Jean de Créquy's wife Louise de la Tour was one of the earliest women known to have had books of her own.[7] It was also at this period that a copy of *The Book of the Three Virtues* was sent by the duchess of Burgundy, Isabel of Portugal, to her niece, the queen of Portugal, a copy that formed the basis for the Portuguese translation published in 1518. A Flemish translation of *The Book of the City of Ladies* also dates from this time, made at the request of the Baenst family, important officials of Bruges.[8] Perhaps even more significant is a considerable group of paper copies of Christine's principal didactic works, many of them emanating from Lille, which was at the time the administrative center of the Burgundian realm. These manuscripts provide evidence that the works were beginning to attract a wider audience among middle-class public officials and their increasingly literate wives and daughters, an important step in preparing the way for the success of printing.

The third period of Christine's popularity centered in Paris in the second half of the fifteenth century, to judge by copies of her works in the libraries of the Houses of Bourbon, Brittany, and Orleans. Agnes of Bourbon was a younger sister of Philip the Good, and both she and her numerous children spent extended periods at the Burgundian court. She was a book collector in her own right and was undoubtedly responsible for some of the Christine de Pizan manuscripts in the Bourbon library. Her interest was shared by her daughter-in-law Anne de France, who was inspired by *The Book of the Three Virtues* in writing a book of advice for her daughter Suzanne de Bourbon, *Les Enseignements d'Anne de France à sa Fille (Anne de France's Teachings for Her Daughter).*[9] Marie, duchess of Orleans, who was the third wife of the poet Charles of Orleans and mother of King Louis XII, was Philip the Good's niece and had been reared at his court, where her literary tastes had first developed. She had a copy of *Othéa's Letter to Hector* prepared for her personal library in 1475, although she may also have inherited copies of one or two others of Christine's works from her husband's mother, Valentina Visconti.[10]

Most important of all, however, was the interest shown by Anne of Brittany in these works, which were admirably suited to the tastes of the coterie of intelligent women who surrounded her at court. In the manuscripts dedicated to her, she was often shown surrounded by ladies, members of some of France's leading families. Although this is perhaps not the most significant group of Christine's manuscripts, it is important in that it provided the basis for some of the first printed texts, several of which emanated from the entourage of Anne of Brittany.

Nevertheless, it is unexpected to discover that Christine's writings were first printed in England and by William Caxton. Especially noteworthy is his printing of Anthony Woodville's translation of the *Moral Proverbs*. At one time, Woodville was the owner of the handsomely illustrated manuscript prepared for Isabeau of Bavaria, now in the British National Library.[11] During the English occupation of Paris, it was acquired by the duke of Bedford, Henry VI's regent during his minority. This and other manuscripts from the royal library in the Louvre eventually made their way to England, where they came into the possession of the duke's widow Jacquette of Luxembourg, whose signature still appears in several of them. This lady was Anthony Woodville's mother by a second marriage.

After his father and older brother were executed for treason during the reign of Henry VI, Anthony became Lord Rivers. Closely allied with the House of York, he was an intimate of Edward IV and served as the governor of his ill-fated sons, the two princes of the Tower. He was also an early patron of Caxton's, which accounts for the printing of his translation, very possibly intended for the edification of his royal charges, just as the original had been devised for the instruction of Christine's son Jean de Castel. The proverbs were printed in decasyllabic couplets, with a colophon added by Caxton himself:

> Go thou little quire and recommend me
> Unto the good grace of my special lord
> The Earl Rivers, for I have emprinted thee
> At his commandment, following every word
> His copy, as his secretary can record,
> At Westminster of Feverer the xx day
> And of King Edward the xvii year vraye.
> > Emprinted by Caxton
> > In Feverer the cold season.

During the same year that Caxton printed these proverbs, he was primarily involved in printing his edition of *The Canterbury Tales,* but the success of the *Moral Proverbs* was at least sufficiently important for them to be reprinted by Richard Pynson in 1526.[12]

A Norman by birth, Pynson came to London from Rouen between 1486 and 1489. He became the King's Printer in 1508, the year when he used the first Roman type seen in England. Christine's text was one of some 370 volumes he printed before his death in 1530.

Caxton also printed another text of Christine's before the end of his career. This was his own translation of *The Feats of Arms and of Chivalry,* her treatise on the art of warfare and the profession of knighthood, which she wrote in around 1410. Although one of Christine's principal sources, Honoré Bouvet's *Tree of Battles,* was an important and popular text that was read by Frenchmen and Englishmen alike and was printed nine times in forty years and translated into four languages (Anglo-Scots, Castilian, Catalan, and Provençal), it was Christine's treatise that Caxton chose to print in his own version in 1489.[13]

Caxton's text correctly attributes the original text to Christine and is obviously based on one of the manuscripts dating from her lifetime. To judge from some twenty copies still extant, it must have been one of his most successful books, more copies being known of only three others. The translation was undertaken at the request of Henry VII and the circumstances add an interesting note to the project. Caxton, a lifelong Yorkist because of ties and convictions of some forty years' standing, did not take readily to Tudor patronage after Henry VII's victory at Bosworth in 1485. It was not until three years later that he was willing to accept the new king's patronage, possibly through the intercession of Queen Margaret, to whom he had always remained devoted, and the earl of Oxford, who played a major role in the king's request to have Caxton translate Christine's text.

The work "being in French," as Caxton explained in his Prologue, "was delivered to me William Caxton by . . . my natural and sovereign lord King Henry VII in his palace by Westminster on 23 January 1489." The king "desired and willed me to translate this said book . . . and to emprint it to the end that every gentleman born to arms and all manner of men of war, captains, soldiers, vituallers and all others should have knowledge how to behave them in the faytes of war and of battles, and so delivered me the said book then my lord the Earl of Oxford awaiting on his said Grace."[14] Surely Christine's spirit must have rejoiced at this manifestation of the king's tribute to her efforts, in spite of her earlier reservations about English politics.

The purpose of the king's request was more completely revealed as Caxton continued: "For to have the name to be one of the little servants to the highest and most Christian King and prince of the world, whom I beseech Almighty God to preserve, keep and continue in his noble and most redoubted enterprises as well in Brittany, Flanders, and other places that he may have victory, honor, and renown to his perpetual glory. For I have not heard nor read that any prince has subdued his subjects with less hurt et cetera, and also helped his neighbors and friends out of his land."

Caxton's word can be taken to reflect the events of the spring and summer of 1489. In April the king, who had made a treaty of alliance against France with Brittany, Flanders, and Spain, sent an expeditionary force to Brittany, and in June he won a battle in Flanders for the emperor Maximilian. Caxton's propaganda was aimed not only at glorifying the king but also at justifying the unpopular taxation his campaigns required by extolling his military accomplishments. As a reward for his endeavors, he became the printer of the statutes of Henry's first three parliaments, a curious destiny for Christine's treatise written for the education of a French prince in 1410.

Perhaps even more unexpected is the fact that this work continued to arouse the interest of military men. The copy now preserved in the Harvard University Library, a late fifteenth-century copy written on paper, bears the signature of Napoleon Bonaparte's aide-de-camp, Baron Gaspar Gourjoud.[15]

One of Christine's most popular works, *Othéa's Letter to Hector,* was not printed until about ten years after both the French text and the English version of *The Feats of Arms and of Chivalry.* More than forty manuscripts remain from the fifteenth century, but it was not printed until the last year of the century, almost exactly a hundred years after its composition. In the meantime, the first two of three English translations had circulated in England, one dating from the middle of the fifteenth century made by Stephen Scrope, stepson and ward of Sir John Fastolf, who had spent the years of the English occupation in Paris where he would have had ample opportunity to learn of Christine's reputation. A second translation by Anthony Babington was made some years later, and, after the first French publication, there was still a third translation by the printer Robert Wyer, who published this himself around 1540.[16] Few French works of the period aroused sufficient interest to be translated so often in a comparable span of time.

Once printed in France, the text went through five or six editions in the next twenty-five years. The format of Pigouchet's first edition is unusual in that it reproduces one of the earliest manuscripts in which the layout of the page, with the text in the center surrounded by the glose and the allegory, recalls the page of a legal text or a commented literary text such as Diogini da Borgo San Sepulcro's commentary on Valerius Maximus or Benvenuto da Imola's gloses on Dante's *Divine Comedy.* It also reproduces Christine's original dedication to Louis of Orleans, suggesting once more that Christine's original concept of the work was as an interpretation of ancient mythology from a humanistic point of view. But, evidently, this concept was not widely accepted by her contemporaries because a more conventional presentation is to be found in most manuscripts, with the allegory and glose following the text. This is also the case with most of the printed editions. The first imprint, with its illustrations, was reprinted by Philippe LeNoir in 1522. Pigouchet had changed the title to *Les Cent Histoires de Troie (The Hundred Tales of Troy),* relegating Othéa to the subtitle.

Between the editions of Pigouchet and Philippe LeNoir, there had been one, and possibly two, editions printed by Widow Trepperel in 1518 and perhaps 1521. The evidence for two separate editions is that two different colophons are to be found in the surviving copies. The title of the Trepperel editions varies slightly from Pigouchet's. It reads:

> Here follows the letter of Othéa, goddess of Prudence, moralized, in which are contained several good and notable teachings for all persons wishing to follow virtue and flee vice, by Christine de Pisan. . . .

What appears to be the second edition ends with the note: "Newly printed at Paris in the Rue Neufve Nostre Dame, at the sign of the Ecu de France."[17]

There was one more edition printed in Rouen by Raulin Gaultier, undated, but certainly before 1534, the year when this printer ceased activity. An interesting footnote to this edition is that the single known copy is preserved in the Columbiana Library in Seville, Spain, once the property of Fernando Columbus.[18] Less certain are an edition of 1497 mentioned in a note in a Brussels manuscript and a Lyons edition of 1419 of which no definite trace remains. In any case, there is a sufficient evidence to prove the popularity of the work well into the sixteenth century. By any count, *Othéa's Letter to Hector* was the most successful of Christine's works. A close second is *The Book of the Three Virtues,* of which there were three French editions—in 1497, 1503, and 1536—as well as the Portuguese translation printed in 1518 under the patronage of Queen Leonor of Portugal.[19]

The Book of the Body Politic, a translation of *Le Livre du Corps de Policie,* was printed in England by John Skot in 1521, the year that also saw the publication of *The Book of the City of Ladies* by John Pepwell.[20]

The last of Christine's works to be published was a curious prose version of *The Long Road of Learning* made by a Jean Chaperon, of whom nothing else is known. It was published in 1549 by Estienne Grolleau who, like Widow Trepperel, had a printing press on the Rue Neuve-Notre-Dame, along the western side of the Cathedral. The adapter's preface speaks of the need of making a new version of Christine's original text so that it will be comprehensible to sixteenth-century readers. He says:

> In order to have full intelligence of the present work, entitled the *Chemin de Longue Estude,* kind reader, you must understand the intention of Dame Christine of Pisa, who composed it with a certain emotion in Romance rhythm and dedicated it to the high and powerful king of France, Charles VI, may God forgive him. First you must understand that after the death of her husband, not wishing to remain idle of producing good fruit nor rendering her Muse idle, she was able to use her talents for the praise of kings and the education of the people. She composed the present work of the Long Road of Learning, which signifies the desire she had to occupy herself with sacred and profane letters, in order to profit from both and thus give understanding of them to all sorts of people, principally kings, princes, and knights, of the way to live happily in this world, avoiding misfortune and infamy, in order to arrive successfully at eternal beatitude.[21]

Although this explanation does not entirely obscure Christine's original intentions, it gives some idea of how far her readers had moved away from understanding her thoughts and even her language. By this time, her works had been read for 150 years, and it is apparent that times and tastes were changing.

Up to this point in the middle of the sixteenth century, she was also frequently spoken of by other writers who knew her writings and, in some cases, continued to be influenced by them. She was known, for instance, to the two Marots, father and son; to Jean, no doubt, because of his position as secretary to Anne of Brittany. He praised her great wisdom, and his son Clément spoke of her in a rondeau to Jeanne Gaillarde of Lyon to whom he recommended Christine's "science and doctrine." It is not certain from what they said whether the two poets were acquainted with her poetry or just her didactic works, the ones that had appealed particularly to Anne of Brittany. Jean Marot's verses make it clear that he knew *The Book of the City of Ladies* and was aware of its author's role in defense of women against unfair slander:

> Read of Deborah the wise,
> Read of Thamar the paintress
> Who was art's great mistress
> . . . .
> And Christine's wisdom prize.[22]

Jean Molinet, on the other hand, in composing an epitaph for Isabelle of Castille, honoring the ceremony performed at the Burgundian court after her death in 1504, compared the Spanish queen to the "prudent Othéa." It was also Othéa who was mentioned in an anonymous English poem, "The Assembly of Gods," written in the second half of the fifteenth century.[23]

Some years later, in 1538, Jean Bouchet of Poitiers, composing a *Tabernacle des Illustres Dames (Tabernacle of Illustrious Ladies)*, which formed one section of a longer work called *Le Temple de Bonne Renommee (The Temple of Good Renown)*, gave Christine a place immediately after famous Roman women, praising not only her skill as a rhetorician, but also calling attention to the fact that she was the mother of Jean de Castel, whose talents he held in equally high esteem.

It is somewhat unexpected to find Christine remembered as a rhetorician, although a certain number of observations on rhetoric are to be found in her writings. She had inherited a healthy respect for this art from her father, whose education at the University of Bologna presumably included an exposure to it.

Bouchet was even more extravagant in his praise of Christine in his *Jugement Poétique de l'Honneur Fémenin (Poetic Judgment of Feminine Honor),* also published in 1538, two years after the third edition of *The Book of the Three Virtues,* where he said: "I could not forget the epistles, rondeaux, and ballades in the French language by Christine, who knew Greek and Latin, and was the mother of Castel, a man of perfect eloquence."[24] There is no reason to believe that Christine knew Greek, yet this is not the only reference to her knowledge of Latin, and she may well have known it. In any case, it is interesting to observe how her memory had taken on the qualities considered suitable for a writer of the Renaissance.

By this time, there was a new generation of intelligent and capable women who were making their mark in Europe. Isabelle of Castille had been dead for some years, but in 1531 Marguerite of Navarre, Francis I's sister, had published *Le Miroir de l'Ame Pêcheresse (The Mirror of the Sinful Soul)* and in 1533 Catherine de Medicis, the future regent of France, arrived in France to marry Henry II. In the North, Margaret of Austria had served as regent for her nephew Emporer Charles V, as his sister Mary of Hungary was called on to do after their aunt's death at the end of 1529. Louise of Savoy was the French regent during the minority of her son Francis I. Margaret of Austria, Mary of Hungary, and Louise of Savoy all had Christine's books in their libraries and may well have been influenced by her writings, for they were all exemplars of some of her ideas.

The Book of the City of Ladies continued to be read as part of the vogue for the lives of illustrious men and women inspired by the translations of Boccaccio. Evidence of this is to be found in Symphorien Champier's *Nef des Dames (Ship of Ladies)* printed in Lyons in 1503 and Pierre de Lesnauderie's *Louenge de Mariage (Praise of Marriage),* first printed in Caen in 1523, in which he recommends *The Book of the City of Ladies* "which is good for women to see and read, being that it was composed by a woman."

By the middle of the sixteenth century, however, literary tastes had changed and medieval literature in general was forgotten in the enthusiasm for new forms and new ideas to express a new era. Admiration for the Greek and Latin classics and the desire to imitate them lasted for the next two centuries.

In view of the general disdain for the works of an earlier day, it is interesting to discover that Gabriel Naudé, an official of the royal library in Paris during the seventeenth century, was aware of the existence of some of Christine's manuscripts and expressed a wish to publish *The Book of the Three Virtues* and *The Book of Peace,* although nothing came of his project.[25] In general, however, such interest as there was in Christine centered around her biography of Charles V, which Denys Godefroy in 1653 felt should be better known and of which the Abbot Choisy quoted several passages in *L'Histoire de Charles Cinquième (History of Charles V)* (1689).[26]

During the eighteenth century, the interest was slightly greater. The eighteenth-century Italian scholar Ludovico Antonio Muratori spoke of the intention to publish her biography of Charles V, of which the Abbot Lebeuf did in fact include extracts in his *Dissertation sur l'Histoire Ecclésiastique et Civile de Paris (Dissertation on the Ecclesiastical and Civil History of Paris)*. Jean Boivin de Villeneuve and the Abbot Sallier both wrote short biographical notices of Christine; Prosper Marchand included an article on her in his historical dictionary, published in La Haye (1758–59); and Baron Holbach cited her biography of Charles V once more.[27] Obviously, it was Christine the historian who was remembered during this long period, but at least she was not forgotten altogether, even if Voltaire knew her so little that he spoke of her as "Catherine, daughter of that astrologer of Pisa, who wrote in French."[28]

Toward the end of the eighteenth century appeared the first of a long series of feminist histories. In 1787 Madmoiselle de Kéralio published extracts from Christine's writings in a *Collection des Meilleures Ouvrages Composé par des Femmes (Collection of the Best Works Composed by Women)*. Christine had become merely one of a considerable company of women writers. Around the same time, Horace Walpole discovered Christine, mentioning her on several occasions in his letters and praising one of his correspondents, Miss Hannah More, by telling her that she was worthy of dwelling in the City of Ladies. Walpole was probably also responsible for circulating the legend about a love affair between Christine and the earl of Salisbury, in whose household Jean de Castel had lived in England. Clearly, the Romantic period was at hand.[29]

With the rediscovery of the Middle Ages in the early years of the nineteenth century came a new period of interest in Christine and her writings, of which the first evidence was the curious invention of a woman poet called Clothilde de Surville, who never existed, although her poetry was printed in several volumes in Paris, and who was sponsored by no less an important literary figure than Charles Nodier. This woman was a sort of combination of Christine and the women poets of the early years of the nineteenth century, and so very much to the taste of her day. Henry Wadsworth Longfellow praised her poetry enthusiastically in his literary lectures in Boston.[30]

The true rediscovery of Christine's writings, however, began in 1838 with the publication of Raimond Thomassy's *Essai sur les Ecrits Politiques de Christine de Pizan* (*Essay on the Political Writings of Christine de Pizan*), in which he spoke of her in the highest terms and made a good deal of her friendship and long association with Jean Gerson. Around the same date, a manuscript of *The Tale of Joan of Arc* was discovered in Bern. These events started off a series of new editions of Christine's works, notably *The Long Road of Learning,* published by Robert Püschell in Berlin and Paris in 1881, and three volumes of her poetry published by Maurice Roy for the Société des Anciens Textes Français in Paris between 1886 and 1896. On the basis of such efforts as these, Christine's writings began to be known and discussed once more. However, opinion about their merit was divided. In contrast to Thomassy's unbridled enthusiasm came Gustave Lanson's wry comment in the first edition of his history of French literature, published in 1894, that Christine was "the first in that line of insufferable bluestockings, whose indefatigable facility was equaled only by her universal mediocrity."[31] The reply to this ill-tempered observation was, not surprisingly, a spate of feminist theses across Europe pointing out Christine's value as a woman writer. Studies such as Mathilde Kasteburg's *Die Stellung der Frau in den Dichtungen der Christine de Pisan* presented at Heidelberg in 1909, Rose Rigaud's thesis for the University of Neufchâtel in 1911 on *Les Idées Féministes de Christine de Pisan,* Mathilde Laigle's study of *Le Livre des Trois Vertus* published in Paris in 1912, and Lula M. Richardson's *The Forerunners of Feminism in French Literature of the Renaissance. Part I, From Christine de Pisa to Marie de Gournay,* a dissertation for John Hopkins University, published in 1929. The most important of these studies, however, was the biography prepared by Marie-Josèphe Pinet as a thesis at Lyons in 1927, the most complete study of Christine and her writings to date, and one which has never been entirely superseded.

The principal problem that remained for the restoration of Christine to her proper place in literature was the publication of all her works so that it would be possible for all those interested to read them. In the past fifty years, gradual progress has been made toward this objective, so that now only two or three of the important works are not available except in manuscript. With the use of these editions and of a growing number of individual studies, the time is finally arriving when it is possible to view Christine's life and works as a whole and to form a valid opinion of their merit.

There still remains the problem of judging her as a woman as well as a writer. As has already been observed, opinion has swung from admiration that she could have accomplished what she did at all to disdain for the fact that she did not do what she never intended. This controversy continues in almost the same terms as at the time of the Quarrel of the Rose. It should scarcely be necessary to point out that Christine was by no means a feminist in the modern sense of the term, but neither was she the prude that she has been accused of being by certain modern critics. One must hope that the time has finally arrived when it is possible to view her as an individual of tremendous goodwill—toward women, toward France, and toward humanity in general—and as a writer whose complexity is endlessly revealed by a careful reading of all that she wrote. She herself knew that she was not fortunate to have written at the time when she did. She spoke of this in her *Vision,* putting the words into the mouth of Dame Opinion:

> In the times to come, more will be said of you than during your lifetime, for . . . you have lived in a bad time, when sciences are not held in great esteem . . . but after your death there will come a prince full of valor and wisdom who, through knowing your volumes, will wish that you had lived during his lifetime and would have liked to know you. . . .[32]

There is no doubt that, on the whole, it has been possible to arrive at a more just view of her merits in the twentieth century. Perhaps nobody has done this more tellingly than the modern critic, Daniel Poirion, who has said of her in recent years:

> For the first time in France, the study of a literary production cannot be separated from the study of the writer. Here, in the true sense of the word, is our first *author,* and that author is a woman. And because she is a woman, she avoids many faults, from those which Pascal denounced in the professional writer in contrast with human qualities, and even the feminine pedantry which irritated Lanson, for he was too affected by pedagogical misogyny. . . . In her poetry as well as in her philosophical works, she made a cause of the feminine condition, and her personal experience became a system and a style.[33]

Christine de Pizan had reason to speak with confidence of her literary immortality, and one must join Martin le Franc in the judgment of her he expressed in 1442, only a few years after her death: "Though death may draw the curtain around her body, her name shall still endure."[34]

❧

Notes

I   A Child of Two Worlds

1. *Le Livre de la Mutacion de Fortune*, ed. S. Solente (Paris, 1959–1966). Vol. 2, p. 19 (vv. 4753–4826).
2. For Venice at this period, see especially P. Braunstein and R. Delort, *Venice, Portrait Historique d'une Cité* (Paris, 1971); F.C. Lane, *Venice, a Maritime Republic* (Baltimore, 1973); *La Civiltà Veneziana del Trecento,* Fondazione Giorgio Cini (Florence, 1955); *Venezia e Bisanzio,* catalogue of an exhibition held in the Palazzo Ducale, June–September 1974 (Venice, 1974).
3. P. Ziegler, *The Black Death* (London, 1970), pp. 37–45.
4. J. Seznec, *The Survival of the Pagan Gods,* trans. B. F. Sessions (New York, 1961), pp. 37–63.
5. L. Bertolotti, *I Comuni della Provincia di Bologna nella Storia e nell'arte* (Bologna, 1964), p. 341.
6. P. O. Kristeller, "Learned Women of Early Modern Italy: Humanists and University Scholars," in *Beyond Their Sex; Learned Women of the European Past,* ed. P. H. Labalme (New York-London, 1980), pp. 101–102.
7. E. H. Wilkins, *Life of Petrarch* (Chicago, 1963), p. 193.
8. N. Jorga, *Philippe de Mézières, 1326–1405, et la Croisade au XIVe Siècle* (Paris, 1896). Early in her widowhood Philippe de Mézières bought from Christine property she had inherited from her father near Melun. See *Le Livre des Fais et Bonnes Meurs du Sage Roy Charles V,* ed. S. Solente (Paris, 1936). Vol. 1, p. xviii.
9. E. H. Wilkins, pp. 123–124.
10. M. Bishop, *Petrarch and His World* (Bloomington, 1963), pp. 349–351.
11. *L'Avision-Christine,* ed. M. L. Towner (Washington, D. C., 1932), p. 150.
12. *L'Avision,* p. 150.
13. Notably, Philippe de Mézières and Nicole Oresme were critical. See G. W. Coopland, *Nicole Oresme and the Astrologers* (Cambridge, Mass., 1952), pp. 6–16.
14. *L'Avision,* p. 153; *Le Livre des Fais et Bonnes Meurs* . . . , Vol. 1, p. 41.
15. A. C. Crombie, *Augustine to Galileo* (Cambridge, Mass., 1961). Vol. 1, pp. 89–112; Vol. 2, pp. 80–86.
16. This manuscript is now No. 164 of St. John's College, Oxford. See the catalogues of the exhibitions *La Librairie de Charles V* (Bibliothèque Nationale, Paris, 1968), No. 199 and Planche 5, and *Les Fastes du Gothique, le siècle de Charles V* (Paris, Grand Palais, October 1981–February 1982), No. 289, pp. 335–336. For Pélerin de Prusse, see R. Delachenal, *Historie de Charles V* (Paris, 1900–1931). Vol. 2, pp. 278–279; 367–368, and L. Thorndike, *A History of Magic and Experimental Science* (New York, 1934). Vol. 3, pp. 586–587.

17. This idea is strongly suggested by *Le Songe du Verger*. Charles V's copy is now London, British Library Ms. Royal 19 C IV. See *La Librairie de Charles V*, No. 187 and *Les Fastes du Gothique*, No. 282, pp. 327–328; also M. Lièvre, "Notes sur le manuscrit originel du *Songe du Verger*," *Romania* 77 (1956), pp. 352–360.

18. M. Bloch, *Les Rois Thaumaturges, Étude sur le Caractère Surnaturel Attribué à la Puissance Royale Particulièrement en France et en Angleterre* (Paris, 1961), p. 232, and C. R. Sherman, *The Portraits of Charles V of France, 1338–1380* (New York, 1969), p. 14n.

19. *Fais et Bonnes Meurs*, Vol. 2, p. 193; *L'Avision*, p. 151.

20. The details of Charles V's Paris are based on Christine's information in *Fais et Bonnes Meurs* and *Le Livre de la Paix*, ed. C. C. Willard (The Hague, 1958), and also on J. Th. de Castelnau, *Le Paris de Charles V, 1364–1380* (Paris, 1930) and the exhibition catalogue of *Les Fastes du Gothique*, pp. 49–53.

21. *Fais et Bonnes Meurs*, Vol. 2, pp. 84–85; *Le Livre de la Paix*, p. 139.

22. *Fais et Bonnes Meurs*, Vol. 1, pp. 50–51; *Le Livre de la Paix*, p. 72.

23. Guillebert de Mets, "Description de la Ville de Paris" in Le Roux de Lincy and L. M. Tisserand, *Paris et ses Historiens aux XIVe et XVe Siècles* (Paris, 1867), p. 159. Charles V's copy of Jean Golein's translation of Durand's treatise is now Paris, B. N. Ms. fr. 437. See *La Librairie de Charles V*, No. 176.

24. *Fais et Bonnes Meurs*, Vol. 1, p. 46. For details of these collections, see Paris, B. N. Ms. fr. 2705, "Inventaire général des joyaux de Charles V," published by J. Labarte (unpublished documents, Paris, 1897); *La Librairie de Charles V*, pp. 33–42, and especially, *Les Fastes du Gothique*. Also, Delachenal, Vol. 1, pp. 63ff.

25. For the artists employed by Charles V, see *Les Fastes du Gothique*, especially pp. 429–435 and C. R. Sherman, *The Portraits of Charles V*, pp. 57–63.

26. *Fais et Bonnes Meurs*, Vol. 2, pp. 42–46.

27. C. R. Sherman, pp. 17–32 and F. Avril, *L'Enluminure du XIVe Siècle à la Cour de France* (Paris, 1978). The king's copy of the *Nine Judges of Astronomy* is now Brussels, Bibl. Royale, Ms. 10319.

28. Brussels, Bibl. Royale Ms. 9505, fol. 1. See *La Librairie de Charles V*, No. 202 and C. R. Sherman, "Some Visual Definitions in the Illustrations of Aristotle's Nicomachean *Ethics* and *Politics* in the French translation of Nicole Oresme," *The Art Bulletin*, 69 (1977), 320–330.

29. In *La Librairie de Charles V*, p. 91, there is mention of these manuscripts of Bolognese origin in the library.

30. J. Destrez, *La "Pecia" dans les Manuscrits Universitaires du XIIIe et du XIVe siècle* (Paris, 1958); L. Febvre et H.-J. Martin, *L'Apparition du Livre* (Paris, 1958). Introduction, pp. 1–24.

2   The Wheel of Fortune Turns

1. I. Origo, *The Merchant of Prato, Francesco di Marco Datini* (New York–London, 1957).

2. *L'Avision*, pp. 161–162; *La Mutacion de Fortune*, Vol. 1, p. 21 (vv. 413–430).

3. *Le Livre de la Cité des Dames*, Brussels, Bibl. Roy. Ms. 9393, fol. 54; *The Book of the City of Ladies*, trans. E. J. Richards (New York, 1982), pp. 154–155.

4. *L'Avision*, pp. 151–152; A. Thomas, "Documents sur la Vie de Jean Castel," *Romania* 21 (1892), 274.

5. B. Prost, *Inventaires Mobiliers et Extraits des Comptes des Ducs de Bourgogne* (Paris, 1902). Vol. 1, no. 1595 and p. 297n; *Fais et Bonnes Meurs*, Vol. 1, p. 14n.

6. L. Delisle, *Recherches sur la Librairie de Charles V* (Paris, 1907). Vol. 1, pp. 10–30; *Fais et Bonnes Meurs*, Vol. 1, pp. lxxvi–lxxvii.

7. *La Mutacion de Fortune,* Vol. 1, pp. 43–44 (vv. 982–1024).

8. *L'Avision,* p. 152.

9. R. Delachenal, Vol. 5, pp. 422–423.

10. M. Nordberg, *Les Ducs et la royauté* (Uppsala, 1964), especially pp. 61–75; R. Vaughan, *Philip the Bold* (London, 1962), pp. 39–58.

11. M. Meiss, *French Painting in the Time of Jean de Berry. The Late XIV Century and the Patronage of the Duke* (London, 1967); A. De Champaux and R. Gauchery, *Les Travaux d'Art Executés pour Jean de France, Duc de Berry, avec une Étude Biographique sur les Artistes Employés par ce Prince* (Paris, 1894).

12. A. C. Crombie, *Science in the Middle Ages* (Cambridge, Mass., 1979), p. 231; Paris, B. N. Ms. lat. 11201, fol. 1–13 *(Traité sur la Pierre Philosophale);* L. Thorndike, *A History of Magic and Experimental Science* (New York, 1923–1958). Vol. 3, ch. 36. For Christine's comments on alchemists, see, for instance, *L'Avision,* pp. 137–140.

13. *L'Avision,* p. 153.

14. *L'Avision,* pp. 153–154.

15. G. Fantuzzi, *Notizie degli Scrittori Bolognesi* (Bologna, 1789). Vol. 7, pp. 54–59; *L'Avision,* p. 169.

16. For an account of the organization and operation of the royal chancellery at this period, see O. Morel, *La Grande Chancellerie Royale et l'Expédition des Lettres Royaux de L'Avènement de Philippe de Valois à la Fin du XIVe Siècle* (Paris, 1900), especially ch. II, "Les Secrétaires et les Notaires du Roi," pp. 53–100.

17. *L'Avision,* pp. 154–155.

18. *Le Livre du Corps de Policie,* ed. R. H. Lucas (Geneva, 1967), pp. 13–14; *Le Livre des Trois Vertus,* Boston Public Library Ms. 1528, fol. 81v°–84.

19. *L'Avision,* p. 174. It has been pointed out recently that the first, great epidemic of the Black Death was followed by subsequent epidemics, lasting throughout the fifteenth century. See R. S. Gottfried, *The Black Death, Natural and Human Disaster in Medieval Europe* (New York–London, 1983), especially pp. 129–160.

20. *Fais et Bonnes Meurs,* Vol. 1, p. 179.

21. The date of Salisbury's sojourn in Paris has been established by J. C. Laidlaw, "Christine de Pizan, the Earl of Salisbury and Henry IV," *French Studies,* 36 (1982), 129–43.

22. *Oeuvres Complètes de Froissart,* ed. Kervyn de Lettenhove (Brussels, 1896). Vol. 15, pp. 88–89; S. Moreay-Render, *Le Prieuré Royal de Poissy* (Colmar, 1968).

23. M. Roy, *Oeuvres Poétiques de Christine de Pisan,* Vol. 2, (Paris, 1891), pp. xv–xvii; 159–222.

24. *L'Avision,* p. 163.

25. E. Deschamps, *Oeuvres,* ed. Queux de Saint-Hilaire and G. Raynaud (Paris, 1873–1903). Vol. 7, pp. 216ff.

26. *L'Avision,* p. 157. For a discussion of this first "edition," see F. Lecoy, "Notes sur Quelques Ballades de Christine de Pisan" in *Mélanges . . . Robert Guiette* (Anvers, 1961), pp. 107–114. M. Meiss, *French Painting in the Time of Jean de Berry: The Limbourgs and Their Contemporaries* (New York, 1974), pp. 7–14.

27. Brussels Bibl. Royale Ms. 9393, fol. 29v°; *The Book of the City of Ladies,* p. 85.

28. *Le Livre du Corps de Policie,* p. 197.

29. *Fais et Bonnes Meurs,* Vol. 1, pp. 7–8.

30. C. C. Willard, "An Autograph Manuscript of Christine de Pisan?", *Studi Francesi,* 37 (1065), 452–457. There is also the testimony of Guillebert de Mets in his "Description de Paris en 1407" ('Leroux de Lancy et L. M. Tisserand, *Paris et ses Historiens aux XIVe et XVe Siécles* (Paris, 1868), p. 234, who speaks of Christine "Qui dictoit toutes sortes de choses en français et en latin," which could be taken to mean either that she composed poetry in both French and Latin, or that she dictated to

scribes texts in both languages. As far as is known, Christine's own poetry was written entirely in French, but at the beginning of the fifteenth century, copies of manuscripts were still produced by dictating to several scribes at one time. In an illustration of *L'Epître d'Othéa* (B. N. Ms. fr. 606, fol. 15), Io is to be seen dictating to her disciples, a scene that could have had more than a purely aesthetic significance here. For the practice of dictating under these circumstancs, see C. Bühler, *The Fifteenth Century Book* (Philadelphia, 1960), pp. 15–39.

31. Roy, Vol. 2, pp. 1–27; S. Solente, "Un Traité Inédit de Christine de Pisan, l'Epistre de la Prison de Vie Humaine," *Bibl. de l'Ecole des Chartes*, 85 (1924), 263–301.

32. M.-J. Pinet, *Christine de Pisan, 1364–1430*, pp. 449–450.

33. J. de Montreuil, *Opera*, I: Epistolario, ed. E. Ornato (Turin, 1963), esp. p. lxxiv, and F. Simone, *Miscellanea di Studi e Recerche sul Quattrocento Francese*, (Turin, 1967), Introduction, p. xi.

3   The Beginnings of a New Life

1. *L'Avision*, pp. 164–165.

2. D. Poirion, *Le Poète et le Prince, l'Évolution du Lyrisme Courtois de Guillaume de Machaut à Charles d'Orléans* (Paris, 1965), pp. 19–37.

3. P. Champion, *La Librairie de Charles d'Orléans* (Paris, 1910), pp. viii–ix.

4. A. Piaget, "La Cour Amoureuse, Dite de Charles VI," *Romania* 20 (1891), 416–454; C. Bozzolo and H. Loyau, *La Cour Amoureuse Dite de Charles VI: Etude et Edition Critique des Sources Manuscrites* (Paris, 1981).

5. C. C. Willard, "Lovers' Dialogues in Christine de Pizan's Poetry from the *Cent Ballades* to the *Cent Ballades d'Amant et de Dame*," *Fifteenth Century Studies*, 4 (1981), 167–180; for Muriel Kittel's translation, see *An Anthology of Medieval Lyrics*, ed. A. Flores (New York, 1962), p. 165.

6. N. Wilkins, *One Hundred Ballades, Rondeaux and Virelais* (Cambridge, U. K., 1969), Introduction; see also his "Structure of Ballades, Rondeaux and Virelais in Froissart and in Christine de Pisan," *French Studies* 23 (1969), 337–348.

7. Eustache Deschamps, *Oeuvres complètes*, Vol. 7, pp. 266–292; R. Dragonetti, "La poésie . . . ceste musique naturelle," *Mélanges . . . Robert Guiette*, pp. 49–64.

8. *Anthology of Medieval Lyrics*, trans. Muriel Kittel, p. 166.

9. Roy, Vol. 2, pp. 295–301; Deschamps *Oeuvres*, VI, p. 251.

10. Christine de Pisan, *Ballades, Rondeaux and Virolais*, edited by K. Varty (Leicester, U. K., 1965), p. xxxi; N. Wilkins in *French Studies* 23, 344–345.

11. Virelai X (Roy, Vol. 1, pp. 111–112).

12. Virelai I (Roy, Vol. 1, pp. 101–102).

13. K. Varty, pp. xxix–xxxi, N. Wilkins in *French Studies* 23, 340–344.

14. Rondeau III (Roy, Vol. 1, pp. 148–149).

15. Rondeau XLIII (Roy, Vol. 1, p. 171).

16. Rondeau LI (Roy, Vol. 1, p. 176).

17. C. C. Willard, "*Les Cent Ballades d'Amant et de Dame*: Criticism of Courtly Love," in *Court and Poet*, ed. G. S. Burgess (Liverpool, 1981), pp. 359–360.

18. *Les Cent Ballades, poème du XIVᵉ siècle composé par Jean le Seneschal, publié par G. Raynaud*, (Paris, 1905).

19. Roy, Vol. 1, p. 86; *Anthology of Medieval Lyrics*, trans. Dwight Durling, pp. 170–171.

20. *Charles d'Orléans, Poésies*, ed. P. Champion, Vol. 1, (Paris, 1966), pp. 108–113; Alain Chartier, *La Belle Dame sans Merci et les Poésies Lyriques* (Lille-Geneva, 1949).

21. F. Lecoy, "Notes sur quelques ballades de Christine de Pisan," pp. 107–114. J. C.

Laidlaw, "Christine de Pizan—An Author's Progress," *The Modern Language Review* 78 (1983), 532–544.

22. E. H. Wilkins, *Life of Petrarch*, especially pp. 243–249.

23. Roy, Vol. 2, pp. 1–27.

24. Roy, Vol. 2, p. 6, vv. 159–164.

25. Roy, Vol. 1, pp. 220–221; 303–304.

26. Roy, Vol. 2, p. 13, vv. 389–397.

27. Roy, Vol. 2, p. 24. vv. 732–734.

28. Thomas Hoccleve, *Letter of Cupid* in *The Babbatyne Manuscript*, ed. W. Tod Ritchie (Edinburgh-London, 1930). Vol. 4, pp. 49–64; J. Mitchell, *Thomas Hoccleve. A Study in Early Fifteenth Century English Poetic* (Urbana, 1968), pp. 22–23; 77–84.

29. Andreas Capellanus, *The Art of Courtly Love*, trans. with notes and introduction, John Jay Perry (New York, 1941; rpt. 1959).

30. E. Hoepffner, ed., *Oeuvres de Guillaume de Machaut* (Paris, 1908). Vol. 1, "Le Jugement dou Roy de Behaigne," pp. 57–135; "Le Jugement dou Roy de Navarre," pp. 137–291.

31. Roy, vol. 2, pp. 49–157; Roy, vol. 1, pp. 245–46.

32. Kervyn de Lettenhove, ed., *Oeuvres Complètes de Froissart*, Vol. 23 (table des noms historiques) (Brussels, 1876), pp. 285–286. There is mention of Werchin's pilgrimage to Compostela, during which he matched arms with both French and Spanish knights, taking place in the late summer and fall 1402.

33. Roy, Vol. 2, pp. 49–109; C. C. Willard, "A Re-Examination of *Le Débat de Deux Amants*," *Les Bonnes Feuilles*, 3 (1974), 73–88.

34. Jean de Werchin's poetry has been studied by A. Piaget in "*Le Songe de la Barge* de Jean de Werchin, Sénéchal de Hainaut (1404)," *Romania* 38 (1909), 7–110 and "Ballades de Guillebert de Lannoy et de Jean de Werchin," *Romania* 39 (1910), 324–368.

35. Roy, Vol. 2, pp. 159–222.

36. Roy, Vol. 2, pp. 223–294; C. C. Willard, "Christine de Pizan's "Dit de la Pastour," in *Mélanges de Langue et Littérature Françaises du Moyen Age et de la Renaissance Offerts à Charles Foulon* (Liège, 1981). Vol. 2, pp. 293–300.

37. The copy of Virgil made for the duke of Berry's treasurer is now Florence, Bibl. Laurenziana, Med. Pol. 69. See G. Ouy, "Le 'Pastorium Carmen,' Poème de Jeunesse de Gerson et la Renaissance de l'Eglogue en France à la Fin du XIVe Siècle," *Romania*, 88 (1967), 175–231; D. Cecchetti, "Un 'Egloga Inedita de Nicolas de Clamanges," in *Miscellanea de Studi e Ricerche sul Quattrocento Francese, a cura di Franco Simone*, (Turin, 1967), pp. 27–57. E. Picard, "Le Château de Germolles et Marguerite de Flandre," *Mémoires de la Société Éduenne* NS 40 (1912), 147–218.

38. P. Lacroix, ed., *Le Bon Berger ou le Vrai Régime et Gouvernement des Bergers et Bergères Composé par le Rustique Jean de Brie* (Paris, 1879); G. Sarton, *Introduction to the History of Science* (Baltimore, 1948). Vol. 3, pp. 1631–1632; R. Grand and R. Delatouche, *L'Agriculture au Moyen Age de la Fin de l'Empire Roman au XVIe Siècle* (Paris, 1950), pp. 494–501.

39. Roy, Vol. 2, p. 293, vv. 2260–2262.

4   The Quarrel of the Rose

1. D. W. Robertson, Jr., *A Preface to Chaucer in Medieval Perspectives* (Princeton, 1962), pp. 361–62; J. V. Fleming, "Hoccleve's 'Letter to Cupid' and the 'Quarrel' over the *Roman de la Rose*," *Medium Aevum*, 40 (1971), 21–40.

2. G. Ouy, "Paris, l'un des Principaux Foyers de l'Humanisme en Europe au Début du XVe Siécle," *Bulletin de la Société d'Histoire de Paris et de l'Ile de France*, (1967–1968) 71–98; M. Meiss, *French Painting . . . The Limbourgs*, pp. 19–23; L. Mirot, *Etudes Lucquoises* (Nogent-le-Routrou, 1930).

3. E. H. Wilkins, *Petrarch*, pp. 214–215; F. Simone, *Il Rinascimento Francese, Studi e Ricerche* (Turin, 1961), pp. 47–48; J. Huizinga, *The Waning of the Middle Ages* (New York, 1956), p. 325; J. Monfrin, "La Connaissance de l'Antiquité et le Problème de l'Humanisme en Langue Vulgaire dans la France du XVe Siècle," in *The Late Middle Ages and the Dawn of Humanism Outside Italy* (Louvain–The Hague, 1972), pp. 130–143.

4. On the popularity of humanistic debates, see P. O. Kristeller, *Renaissance Thought II* (New York, 1965), pp. 27–28; 54–56.

5. *The Romance of the Rose*, trans. H. W. Robbins (New York, 1962), pp. 3–4.

6. Recent studies of *The Romance of the Rose* and its importance include A. M. Gunn, *The Mirror of Love; A Reinterpretation of the Romance of the Rose* (Lubbock, Texas, 1952); J. V. Fleming, *The Roman de la Rose; A Study in Allegory and Iconography* (Princeton, 1967); D. Poirion, *Le Roman de la Rose* (Paris, 1973); C. Dahlberg, "Love and the *Roman de la Rose*," *Speculum* 44 (1969), 568–584; L. Friedman, "Jean de Meun's Antifeminism and Bourgeois Realism," *Modern Philology* 57 (1950), 13–23; J. V. Fleming, "The Moral Reputation of the *Roman de la Rose* before 1400," *Romance Philology* 8, (1964–1965), 430–435; Y. Badel, *Le Roman de la Rose au XIVe Siècle; Étude de la Réception de l'oeuvre*, (Geneva, 1980).

7. E. Hicks, ed., *Le Débat sur le Roman de la Rose* (Paris, 1977), p. 6.

8. R. Eder, "Tignonvillana Inédita," *Romanische Forschungen* 33 (1915), 815–1022.

9. Roy, Vol. 2, pp. 49ff.

10. J. de Montreuil, *Opera* vol. I: *Epistolario*, ed. E. Ornato. (Turin, 1963); E. Hicks and E. Ornato, "Jean de Montreuil et le Débat sur le *Roman de la Rose*," *Romania*, 98 (1977), 34–36; 186–219.

11. E. Hicks, *Le Débat sur le Roman de la Rose*, p. xlviii. Further references to the documents of the debate will be to this edition, which supercedes all others. See also M. Liberman, "Chronologie Gersonienne," *Romania* 83 (1962), 7–73.

12. E. Hicks, *Débat*, pp. 9–11.

13. E. Hicks, *Débat*, pp. 11–22.

14. E. Hicks, "The 'Querelle de la Rose' in the *Roman de la Rose*," *Les Bonnes Feuilles*, 3 (1974), 152–163.

15. *The Romance of the Rose*, p. 319.

16. E. Hicks, *Débat*, p. 20.

17. M. Laigle, *Le Livre des Trois Vertus et son milieu historique et littéraire* (Paris, 1912), p. 24; *Le Religieux de Saint-Denis*, Vol. III, pp. 268ff.

18. J. Huizinga, *The Waning of the Middle Ages* (New York, 1956), p. 109.

19. E. Hicks, *Débat*, p. 23.

20. E. Hicks, *Débat*, p. 25.

21. For the history of this "first edition," see F. Lecoy, *Mélanges . . . Robert Guiette*, pp. 107–114.

22. E. Hicks, *Débat*, pp. 59ff; E. Langlois, "Le Traité de Gerson contre *Le Roman de la Rose*," *Romania* 45 (1918), 23–48.

23. E. Hicks, *Débat*, p. 71.

24. E. Hicks, *Débat*, pp. 68 and 73 and the illustrations from the University of Valencia Ms. 387 reproduced in J. Fleming, *The Roman de la Rose*, figs. 26, 41 and 42. If, as F. Avril points out in "La Peinture Français au Temps de Jean de Berry," *Revue de l'Art*, 38 (1975), 50, the artist who illustrated this manuscript is the same who

illustrated the copies of Christine's *Le Livre de Chemin de Long Estude* (1503), Christine's remarks take on particular significance. The *Rose* illustrations would have offended her.

25. E. Hicks, *Débat*, pp. 89–112.

26. E. Hicks, *Débat*, p. 97.

27. E. Hicks, *Débat*, p. 100.

28. E. Hicks, *Débat*, pp. 109–110.

29. E. Hicks, *Débat*, p. 149.

30. E. Hicks, *Débat*, pp. 173–175.

31. E. Hicks, *Débat*, pp. 180–181; L. Mourin, *Jean Gerson, Prédicateur Français* (Bruges, 1952), pp. 138–148.

32. E. Hicks, *Débat*, p. 43; J. de Montreuil, *Opera*, Vol. 1, p. 220.

33. E. Hicks, *Débat*, p. 54.

34. Roy, Vol. 3, pp. 168–169; the letter as a whole, pp. 162–171.

35. Poirion, *Le Poète et le Prince*, pp. 174 and 268; A. Piaget, "Alain Chartier, Chanoine de Notre-Dame de Paris," *Romania* 32 (1904), 393.

36. T. F. Crane, *Italian Social Customs of the Sixteenth Century*, (New Haven, 1920), pp. 118–19. This point of view is not strictly in agreement with that of E. Telle in *L'Oeuvre de Marguerite d'Angoulème, Reine de Navarre, et la Querelle des Femmes* (Toulouse, 1937), although R. Marichal in his edition of *La Coche* has demonstrated that she imitated there Christine's *Le Livre du Dit de Poissy* and *Le Débat de Deux Amants* (Geneva–Paris, 1971), 3–21.

5   The Long Road of Learning

1. The catalogue of the exhibition *Boccace en France* organized by the Bibliothèque Nationale (Paris 1975) calls attention to the early diffusion of this work in France, as demonstrated by B. N. Ms. lat. 8956, which was copied in Paris toward the end of the fourteenth century (No. 85, p. 47).

2. *L'Avision*, p. 164.

3. There is no modern edition of the original French text, but for one of three early English translations, see C. F. Bühler, ed., *Sir Stephen Scrope, The Epistle of Othéa* (London, 1970).

4. P. O. Kristeller, *Renaissance Thought, II*, pp. 8–9; G. Kohl and R. G. Witt, eds., *The Earthly Republic* (Manchester, 1978), p. 5.

5. For her use of the *Histoire Ancienne jusqu' à César*, see P.-G.-C. Campbell, *L'Epître d'Othéa; Étude sur les Sources de Christine de Pisan* (Paris, 1924), pp. 80–109; S. Solente, *La Mutacion de Fortune*, Vol. 1, Introduction, pp. lxiii–xcii.

6. P. Meyer, "Les Premières Compilations Françaises d'Histoire Ancienne," *Romania* 14 (1885) p. 36ff; B. Woledge, *Bibliographie des Romans et Nouvelles en Prose Française Antérieurs à 1500* (Geneva-Lille, 1954), pp. 55–58, nos. 77–79). At the beginning of the fifteenth century, a handsomely illustrated copy of this text was prepared for the duke of Berry's library (now B. N. Ms. fr. 301). This was a new version of an earlier Italian manuscript already in his library (now British Library Royal Ms. 20 D I). See F. Avril, "Trois Manuscrits Napolitains des Collections de Charles V et de Jean de Berry," *Bibliothéque de L'Ecole des Chartes*, 127 (1969), 291–328.

7. Lyons, Bibl. Mun. Ms. 742 (c. 1390) and B. N. Ms. fr. 373 (1400). See M. Meiss, *French Painting . . . The Limbourgs*, pp. 24–33. To be compared with B. N. Ms. fr. 835–836 (Christine's poetry).

8. Ballade III (Roy, Vol. 1, pp. 3–4).

9. B. N. Ms. fr. 606, fol. 28v°.

10. The duke of Berry's copy has been identified as B. N. Ms. fr. 166 (see M. Meiss, *French Painting... The Limbourgs*, pp. 81–101). Christine speaks of this Moralized Bible in *Fais et Bonnes Meurs*, Vol. 2, p. 43, as one of the translations sponsored by Charles V, describing it as "the Bible in three manners, which is to say the Text, then the Text and the Glose together, and then another allegorical interpretation."

11. *L'Avision*, pp. 162–163.

12. *Fais et Bonnes Meurs*, Vol. 2, p. 176.

13. See A. Thomas, "Jacques de Longuyon, trouvère," in the *Histoire de Littérature Française*, T. XXXVI (Paris, 1924), pp. 1–35.

14. For a discussion of Hector in art, see M. R. Scherrer, *The Legends of Troy in Art and Literature* (New York, 1963).

15. B. N. Ms. fr. 606, fol. 2v°. C. C. Willard, "Christine de Pisan's 'Clock of Temperance'," *L'Esprit Créateur* 2 (1963), 149–159.

16. B. N. Ms. fr. 606, fol. 17; M. Meiss, *French Painting... The Limbourgs*, pp. 27–28.

17. P. G. C. Campbell, *Sources*, p. 124.

18. B. N. Ms. fr. 606, fol. 17.

19. M. Meiss, "Atropos-Mors: Observations on a Rare Early Humanist Image," in *Florilegium Historiale: Essays Presented to Wallace K. Ferguson* (Toronto, 1971), pp. 152–159.

20. Narcissus, B. N. Ms. fr. 606, fol. 10; Pygmalion, fol. 12v°; Hero and Leander, fol. 20 and Roy, Vol. 1, p. 4.

21. B. N. Ms. fr. 606, fol. 6.

22. J. Seznec, *The Survival of the Pagan Gods*, trans. B. F. Sessions (New York, 1961), pp. 70–76.

23. B. N. Ms. fr. 606, fol. 1v°.

24. B. N. Ms. fr. 606, fol. 8.

25. This artist is known almost exclusively through his illustrations of Christine's works. See M. Meiss, *French Painting... The Limbourgs*, pp. 40–41.

26. See C. M. Reno, "Feminist Aspects of Christine de Pizan's *Epistre d'Othéa à Hector*," *Studi Francesi* 71 (1980), pp. 271–276.

27. Minerva, B. N. Ms. fr. 606, fol. 8; Ceres, fol. 13v°; Isis, fol. 13v°; Aesculapius, fol. 19v°; Bacchus, fol. 12.

28. B. N. Ms. fr. 606, fol. 15.

29. B. N. Ms. fr. 606, fol. 48. The duke of Berry's two manuscripts are *Les Belles Heures*, now at The Cloisters, New York, and the well-known *Les Très Riches Heures* in the Musée Condé, Chantilly. In the duke's copy of the *Othéa*, the miniature of the sibyl and the emperor is attributed to the artist known as the Edgerton Master, who is thought to have painted the similar miniature in *Les Belles Heures*. (M. Meiss, *French Painting... The Limbourgs*, p. 40.)

30. Rosemund Tuve, *Allegorical Imagery* (Princeton, 1966), pp. 31–34. For the manuscripts and printed versions of the text, see G. Mombello, "Per un'Edizione Critica dell' *Epistre Othéa* di Christine de Pizan," *Studi Francesi* 24 (1964), pp. 1–12.

31. The duke of Berry's copy of *The Long Road of Learning* is now B. N. Ms. fr. 1188, the duke of Orleans' Ms. fr. 1643, and the duke of Burgundy's Brussels, Bibl. Royale, Ms. 10928. The relationship with the Valencia Ms. is discussed by F. Avril in *La Revue de l'Art* 38 (1975), p. 50.

32. *Le Livre du Chemin de Long Estude*, ed. Robert Püschel, (Berlin-Paris, 1881; rpt. Geneva, 1975).

33. R. Püschel, ed., p. 11, vv. 253–259.

34. R. Püschel, ed., p. 21, vv. 492–497.

35. She knew, in any case, Boccaccio's *De claris mulieribus*, a principal source for *The*

Book of the City of Ladies, as well as the *Moralized Ovid,* both of which retell the story of the sibyl Almathea. As for contemporary copies of *The Aeneid* in French translation, in 1403 the duke of Berry's treasurer acquired a manuscript of *The Aeneid* and *The Bucolics* (now Florence, Bibl. Laurenziana, Med. Pol. 69), and Gontier Col's copy of the *Aeneid* is still in existence. Virgil's popularity at the time can be judged from Gerson's *Pastorium carmen,* discussed by G. Ouy, *Romania* 88 (1967), 175–231. See also M. Meiss, *French Painting . . . The Limbourgs,* pp. 55–61. In view of Christine's contacts with others who knew Virgil directly, there is no reason to think that she did not know it.

36. R. Püschel, ed., vv. 1101–1102 (p. 48).
37. R. Püschel, ed., vv. 1128–34 (p. 49).
38. C. C. Willard, "The Duke of Berry's Multiple Copies of the *Fleur des Histoires d'Orient,*" in *From Linguistics to Literature, Romance Studies Offered to Francis M. Rogers* (Amsterdam, 1981), pp. 281–292.
39. See M. Toynbee, "Christine de Pisan and Sire John de Maundeville," *Romania* 21 (1922), pp. 228–239.
40. J. W. Barker, *Manuel II Palaeologus, 1391–1425: A Study in Late Byzantine Statesmanship* (New Brunswick, N. J., 1969), pp. 154–199.
41. R. Püschel, ed., pp. 91–93, vv. 2109–45. See also C. C. Willard, "Christine de Pizan, the Astrologer's Daughter," in *Mélanges à la Mémoire de Franco Simone* (Geneva, 1980). Vol. 1, pp. 95–111.
42. R. Püschel, ed., p. 264, vv. 6253–6259.
43. For a recent discussion of the possibility that Christine might have written the account of Boucicaut's exploits, see J.-L. Picherit, "Christine de Pisan et *Le Livre des Faits du bon messire Jean le Maingre, dit Boucicaut, maréchal de France et Gouverneur de Gennes,*" *Romania* 103 (1982), pp. 300–331.
44. See especially H. R. Patch, *The Goddess Fortuna in Medieval Literature* (Cambridge, Mass., 1927; rpt. New York, 1967) and P. Courcelle, *La Consolation de Philosophie dans la Tradition Littéraire* (Paris, 1967).
45. Roy, Vol. 1, p. 8.
46. Roy, Vol. 1, p. 13.
47. B. N. Ms. fr. 606, fol. 35.
48. The duke of Burgundy's copy is now Brussels, Bibl. Roy. Ms. 9508 and the duke of Berry's The Hague, Kon. Bibl. Ms. 78 d 42. The two other manuscripts prepared at the same time are Chantilly, Musée Condé Ms. 494 and another, formerly in the collection of Pierre Berès, rare book dealer in Paris, which was sold by Sotheby, London, in July 1976. See S. Solente, ed., vol. 1, pp. xcic–cxlii and M. Meiss, *French Painting . . . The Limbourgs,* pp. 291–292. J. C. Laidlaw, "Christine de Pizan—An Author's Progress," pp. 546–548.
49. R. Püschel, ed., p. 47, vv. 1081–1098.
50. S. Solente ed. I, pp. 14–23, vv. 211–468.
51. S. Solente ed., I, pp. 51–53, vv. 1325–1416.
52. H. R. Patch, *The Goddess Fortuna,* pp. 126–46; S. Cigada, "Il Tema Arturiano del Château Tournant: Chaucer e Christine de Pisan," *Studi Medievali* 3d. ser. 2 (1961), 576–606.
53. H. R. Patch, *The Goddess Fortuna,* pp. 42–48.
54. S. Solente, ed., Vol. 1, pp. c–ciii; cx–cxi; cxiv–cxvii; cxix–cxx; cxxiii–cxxix and M. Meiss, *French Painting . . . The Limbourgs,* pp. 126–146.
55. S. Solente, ed., Vol. 2, pp. 133–134, vv. 8065–8068.
56. B. N. Ms. fr. 9–10.
57. S. Solente, ed., vol. 4, pp. 79–80, vv. 23, 569–523, and 636.

6   The Lessons of History

1. *Fais et Bonnes Meurs,* Vol. 1, pp. 6–8.
2. Now Vatican Library, Ms. lat. 4791. See A. Thomas, "Un Manuscrit de Charles V au Vatican. Notice Suivie d'une Étude sur les Traductions de Bernard Gui," *Mélanges d'Archéologie et d'Histoire de l'Ecole Française de Rome* 1 (1881), pp. 259–283.
3. The duke of Burgundy demonstrated in a number of ways that he was a devoted father and grandfather who took seriously Aristotle's admonition, as explained by Oresme in his translation of the *Ethics* and shown by the dedicatory miniature in Charles V's copy (Brussels, Bibl. Roy. Ms. 9509, fol. 2v°). See L. M. J. Delaissé, *Miniatures Médiévales dans la Librairie de Bourgogne au Cabinet des Manuscrits de la Bibliothèque Royale de Bruxelles* (Brussels, 1969), pp. 78–81 and C. R. Sherman, *The Portraits of Charles V of France, 1338–1380* (New York, 1969), pp. 28–30.
4. For a detailed discussion of this issue, see M. Nordberg, *Les Ducs et la Royauté* (Uppsala, 1964), pp. 61–75.
5. S. Solente was of the opinion that Christine knew both the poem and the prose version, but it is that latter that figured in the Burgundian library, in a manuscript contemporary with some of Christine's own works (Bibl. Roy. Ms. 10230). M. Meiss, *French Painting . . . The Limbourgs,* p. 357.
6. An important discussion of humanistic theories of biography is to be found in M. R. Gilmore's essay "The Renaissance Concept of the Lessons of History," in *Humanists and Jurists* (Cambridge, Mass., 1963), pp. 1–37. See also P. O. Kristeller's observation: "There was the model of Plutarch and of other ancient writers, but there obviously was a great contemporary demand for biographies. . . . Like the portrait painting of the time, the biographical literature reflects the so-called individualism of the period, that is, the importance attached to personal experiences, opinions, and achievements, and the eagerness to see them perpetuated in a distinguished work of art or literature," *Renaissance Thought, II,* p. 11.
7. M. R. Gilmore, p. 19.
8. *Fais et Bonnes Meurs,* Vol. 1, p. xxxvi.
9. *Fais et Bonnes Meurs,* Vol. 1, pp. li–lvi. The *Flores Chronicorum* had been used by Raoul de Presles for a description of Paris at the beginning of his translation of St. Augustine's *City of God,* finished around 1371. This antiquarian interest, suggesting that Paris had a distant past worth recalling, reflects Petrarch's enthusiasm for Rome's past. It was in this tradition that Christine repeated the legend of the transmission of studies from Constantinople to Rome and then to Paris, a theme already used by Charles V's envoy to Avignon in 1367 to dissuade the papal court from returning to Rome.
10. *Fais et Bonnes Meurs,* Vol. 1, pp. 12–14.
11. R. Delachenal corrects this error in his article "La date de la naissance de Charles V," *Bibliothèque de l'Ecole des Chartes* 40 (1879), pp. 195–197, and in his *Histoire de Charles V,* Vol. 1, pp. 1 and 11.
12. R. Delachenal, Vol. 1, pp. 186–187.
13. *Fais et Bonnes Meurs,* Vol. 1, p. 34.
14. It is abundantly evident that this was the image the king himself undertook to promote. See C. R. Sherman, "Representation of Charles V . . . as a Wise Ruler," pp. 83–96.
15. *Fais et Bonnes Meurs,* Vol. 1, p. 41.
16. *Fais et Bonnes Meurs,* Vol. 1, pp. lxxxi–lxxxii; R. Delachenal, Vol. 2, p. 368.
17. *Fais et Bonnes Meurs,* Vol. 1, pp. 39–48. R. Delachenal Vol. 3, p. 110 questions whether the king could really have carried out such a schedule on a daily basis.

18. *Fais et Bonnes Meurs,* Vol. 1, pp. 48–49.

19. *Fais et Bonnes Meurs,* Vol. 1, pp. 49–51.

20. *Fais et Bonnes Meurs,* Vol. 1, pp. 53–57; *Le Livre des Trois Vertus,* Book I, chapt. xii; R. Delachenal, Vol. 1, pp. 26 and 45; M. Meiss, *French Painting in the Time of Jean de Berry: The Late XIV Century and the Patronage of the Duke,* pp. 99–107.

21. Roy, Vol. 1, pp. 255–257; *Fais et Bonnes Meurs,* Vol. 1, p. 109.

22. *L'Arbre des Batailles,* ed. E. Nys (Brussels-Leipzig, 1883); *The Tree of Battles of Honoré Bonet. An English Version with Introduction,* ed. G. W. Coopland (Liverpool, 1949); N. A. R. Wright, "The Tree of Battles of Honoré Bouvet and the Laws of War," in *War, Literature and Politics in the Late Middle Ages,* ed. C. T. Allmand (Liverpool, 1976), pp. 12–31.

23. The king's own copy of *Le Songe du Verger* is now London, British Library Ms. Royal 19 C. IV. See *La Librairie de Charles V,* no. 187; *Les Fastes du Gothique,* no. 282; M. Schnerb-Lièvre, "Evrart de Trémaugon et le *Songe du Verger,*" *Romania* 101 (1980), 527–530. For the revision of the Treaty of Brétigny, see R. Delachenal, Vol. 2, p. 248; Vol. 4, pp. 50–51.

24. *Fais et Bonnes Meurs,* Vol. 1, pp. 180–184.

25. *Fais et Bonnes Meurs,* Vol. 1, pp. 184–202.

26. *Fais et Bonnes Meurs,* Vol. 1, p. 191.

27. Charles de la Roncière, *L'Histoire de la Marine Française* (Paris, 1899–1934), II, pp. 1–69; C. F. Richmond, "The War at Sea," in *The Hundred Years War,* ed. K. Fowler (London, 1971), pp. 96–121.

28. *Fais et Bonnes Meurs,* Vol. 1, p. 243.

29. *Fais et Bonnes Meurs,* Vol. 2, pp. 33–34.

30. Nicole Oresme, *Le Livre du Ciel et du Monde,* ed. A. D. Menut and A. J. Denomy, (Madison, Wisc., 1968).

31. *La Librairie de Charles V,* pp. xv–xxi; *Les Fastes du Gothique,* pp. 276–282.

32. M. Meiss, *French Painting . . . XIV,* pp. 99–125.

33. *Fais et Bonnes Meurs,* Vol. 2, pp. 48–49.

34. *Fais et Bonnes Meurs,* Vol. 2, p. 84n; L. de Mas Latrie, ed. *La Prise d'Alexandrie* (Geneva, 1877). See also W. Calin, *A Poet at the Fountain: Essays on the Narrative Verse of Guillaume de Machaut* (Lexington, Ky., 1974), pp. 203–226.

35. Paris, B. N. Ms. fr. 2813. See especially R. Delachenal, Vol. 5, pp. 61–117; M. Thomas, *La Visite de l'Empereur Charles VI en France d'après l'Exemplaire des 'Grandes Chroniques' Exécuté pour Charles V, Congrès International des Bibliophiles* (1969) (Vienna, 1971), pp. 85–89.

36. *Fais et Bonnes Meurs,* Vol. 2, pp. 111–113.

37. *Fais et Bonnes Meurs,* Vol. 2, pp. 126–127.

38. *Fais et Bonnes Meurs,* Vol. 2, pp. 133–36; R. Delachenal, Vol. 5, pp. 120–122.

39. *Fais et Bonnes Meurs,* Vol. 2, pp. 137–138; 139–152; 155–159 and R. Delachenal, Vol. 5, pp. 12–22.

40. R. Delachenal, Vol. 5, pp. 389–401.

41. *Fais et Bonnes Meurs,* Vol. 1, pp. lvi–lx; R. Delachenal, Vol. 5, p. 399; B. Hareau, "Notice sur le n° 8299 des Manuscrits Latins de la Bibliothèque Nationale," *Notices et Extraits* 31, pp. 275–291.

42. *Fais et Bonnes Meurs,* Vol. 2, pp. 186–188. R. Delachenal (vol. 3, p. 92n) saw in the king's words addressed to the crown the inspiration of Valerius Maximus, one of Christine's favorite sources.

43. R. Delachenal, Vol. 5, pp. 422–423.

44. *Fais et Bonnes Meurs,* Vol. 1, pp. lxxxiii–lxxxv; R. Delachenal, Vol. 1, pp. viii–x.

7   A Feminine Utopia

1. The manuscripts of St. Augustine's *Cité de Dieu* are Paris, B. N. Ms. fr. 23–24 and 174; see M. Meiss, *French Painting . . . The Limbourgs*, p. 381. For the two Boccaccio manuscripts, Ms. fr. 12420 (the duke of Burgundy's copy) and 598 (the duke of Berry's copy), see *Boccace en France*, pp. 53–54 and C. Bozzolo, *Manuscrits des Traductions Françaises d'Oeuvres de Boccace*, (Padua, 1973), pp. 23–25; 92–93; 86–98. See also M. Meiss, *French Painting . . . The Limbourgs* pp. 287–290.

2. A. Jeannroy, "Boccace et Christine de Pisan: le 'De Claris Mulieribus' Principale Source du 'Livre de la Cité des Dames'," *Romania* 48 (1922), 92–105.

3. M.-J. Pinet discusses this work in a section devoted to "Les Translations," pp. 363–376 in *Christine de Pisan, 1364–1430*.

4. *Le Songe du Vieil Pèlerin*, ed. G. W. Coopland (Cambridge, U. K., 1969), pp. 536–595; 621–624.

5. B. N. Ms. fr. 606, fol. 4; *The Epistle of Othéa*, ed. C. F. Bühler p. 132; see also C. F. Bühler, "The *Fleurs de Toutes Vertus* and Christine de Pisan's *L'Epître d'Othéa*," *PMLA*, 62 (1947), 32–44.

6. Brussels, Bibl. Roy. ms. 9393, fol. 6; E. J. Richards, trans., *The Book of the City of Ladies*, p. 15.

7. M. Meiss, "The First Fully Illustrated Decameron," in *Essays in the History of Art Presented to Rudolph Wittkower* (London, 1967), pp. 56–61; *French Painting . . . The Limbourgs*, pp. 377–378.

8. *Les Lamentations de Matheolus et le Livre de Léesse, de Jehan Le Fèvre de Ressons (Poèmes Français du XIV* Siècle)* (Paris, 1905).

9. Christine had also discussed the Amazons in *The Mutation de Fortune*. The source for her information was undoubtedly a passage of the *Histoire Ancienne* based ultimately on the *Historiae adversus Paganos* of Orosius. See P. Meyer, "Les Premières Compilations Françaises d'Histoire Ancienne," *Romania* 14 (1885), 36–76.

10. Brussels, Bibl. Roy. Ms. 9393, fol. 24; *The Book of the City of Ladies*, pp. 68–69; Boccaccio, *De claris mulieribus*, ch. 28; Dante, *Inferno* XX, 55ff.

11. Brussels, Bibl. Roy. Ms. 9393, fol. 25; *The Book of the City of Ladies*, pp. 75–76 (Ceres); pp. 69–70 (Circe).

12. Brussels, Bibl. Roy. Ms. 9393, fol. 28; *The Book of the City of Ladies*, p. 78.

13. Brussels, Bibl. Roy. Ms. 9393, fol. 27v°; *The Book of the City of Ladies*, p. 77.

14. C. Bozzolo, "Il *Decameron* come Fonte del *Livre de la Cité des Dames* de Christine de Pisan" in *Miscellanea di Studi e Recerche sul Quattrocento Francese*, pp. 3–24.

15. Brussels, Bibl. Roy. Ms. 9393, fol. 42; *The Book of the City of Ladies*, p. 118. Christine was probably not only reacting against the ideas of Mathéolus, but also against Jean de Meun's comments on marriage in *The Romance of the Rose*, especially in the diatribe of the Jealous Husband (vv. 9097–9360) and the comments of the Friend that grow out of the discussion of the Earthly Paradise (vv. 8455–8744).

16. Brussels, Bibl. Roy. Ms. 9393, fol. 53v°–54; *The Book of the City of Ladies*, pp. 153–155.

17. Brussels, Bibl. Roy. Ms. 9393, fol. 54; *The Book of the City of Ladies*, p. 154.

18. Brussels, Bibl. Roy. Ms. 9393, fol. 54; *The Book of the City of Ladies*, pp. 154–155.

19. Brussels, Bibl. Roy. Ms. 9393, fol. 73; *The Book of the City of Ladies*, pp. 211–212. Christine also speaks of this lady in the *Fais et Bonnes Meurs*, Vol. 2, pp. 69; 88–89.

20. E. McLeod, *The Order of the Rose*, p. 131.

21. Brussels, Bibl. Roy. Ms. 9393, fol. 82; *The Book of the City of Ladies*, p. 240.

22. Brussels, Bibl. Roy. Ms. 9393, fol. 87; *The Book of the City of Ladies*, pp. 256–257.
23. A. de Montaiglon ed., *Le Livre du Chevalier de la Tour Landry pour l'Enseignement de ses Filles* (Paris, 1854); G. E. Brereton and J. M. Ferrier, eds., *Le Menagier de Paris* (Oxford, 1981).
24. Boston Public Library, Ms. 1528, fol. 39v°.
25. Boston Public Library, Ms. 1528, fol. 8.
26. Boston Public Library, Ms. 1528, fol. 92–93.
27. *Les Quinze Joies de Mariage*, ed. J. Crow (Oxford, 1969); see also E. Deschamps, *Miroir de Mariage*. Vol. 8 of *Oeuvres*, which treats a number of similar themes.
28. Boston Public Library, Ms. 1528, fol. 79.
29. Boston Public Library, Ms. 1528, fol. 37v°.
30. Boston Public Library, Ms. 1528, fol. 64v°–65.
31. *Chroniques du Religieux de Saint-Denis*, Vol. 3, pp. 289–291; M. Laigle, *Le Livre des Trois Vertus de Christine de Pisan et Son Milieu Historique et Littéraire* (Paris, 1912), p. 21.
32. Roy, Vol. 3, pp. 59–189; *The Book of the Duke of True Lovers*, trans. A. Kemp-Welch (London, 1908).
33. Roy, Vol. 2, pp. 223–294; C. C. Willard, "Christine de Pizan's 'Dit de la Pastoure,'" in *Mélanges . . . Charles Foulon*. Vol. 2, pp. 293–300.
34. Boston Public Library, Ms. 1528, fol. 50.
35. Boston Public Library, Ms. 1528, fol. 83.
36. Boston Public Library, Ms. 1528, fol. 89v°.
37. Boston Public Library, Ms. 1528, fol. 95.
38. *La Mutacion de Fortune*, Vol. 1, p. 127 (vv. 3480–3490).
39. Boston Public Library, Ms. 1528, fol. 97v°.

8   The Search for a Patron

1. R. Thomassy, *Essai sur les Écrits Politiques de Christine de Pisan, Suivi d'une Notice Littéraire et de Pièces Inédites* (Paris, 1838), pp. 133–140; M. D. Legge, *Anglo-Norman Letters and Petitions from All Souls Ms. 182* (Oxford, 1941), pp. 144–150.
2. *L'Avision*, p. 166.
3. Brussels, Bibl. Roy. Ms. 10309; Paris, B. N. Ms. fr. 1176; ex-Phillips Ms. 128, sold by Sotheby's in 1872 and at the Hôtel Drouot in 1974, and now in a French private collection. This third manuscript will form the basis for a new critical edition edited by Professor Christine Reno of Vassar College. Although there is a note glued to the inside of the binding of the Paris manuscript claiming that it once belonged to the duke of Berry, there is no indication in the records of his library that he owned this copy, according to M. Meiss and S. Off, "The Bookkeeping of Robinet d'Estampes and the Chronology of Jean of Berry's Manuscripts," *Art Bulletin* 53 (1971), 225–235.
4. J. Juvenal des Ursins, *Histoire de Charles VI*, ed. J. A. C. Buchon (Paris, 1875), p. 426; M.-J. Pinet, pp. 129–130; L. Mourin, *Jean Gerson, Prédicateur Français* (Bruges, 1952), pp. 169–175.
5. E. Hicks, *Le Débat de la Rose*, pp. 59ff.
6. *L'Avision*, Introduction, p. 38; *Fais et Bonnes Meurs*, Introduction, p. xxxvi.
7. C. C. Willard, "Christine de Pizan, the Astrologer's Daughter," *Mélanges . . . Franco Simone*, pp. 95–111.
8. *L'Avision*, pp. 143–144.
9. *L'Avision*, p. 145.
10. Bayerische Staatsbibliothek, Ms. gall. 11. fol. 503.

11. Maureen S. Durely, in an article entitled "The Crowned Dame, Dame Opinion and Dame Philosophy: the Female Characteristics of Three Ideals in Christine de Pizan's *L'Avision Christine,*" in *Ideals for Women in the Works of Christine de Pizan,* pp. 29–50 (Michigan Consortium for Medieval and Renaissance Studies, 1981), presents a somewhat different interpretation.

12. P. O. Kristeller, *Renaissance Thought and its Sources* (Columbia University, 1979), p. 30.

13. *L'Avision,* p. 168.

14. R. Vaughan, *Philip the Bold; The Formation of the Burgundian State* (London, 1966), p. 198; D. Poirion, *Le Poète et le Prince,* p. 245.

15. *Le Poète et le Prince,* especially pp. 21–57.

16. M. Thibault, *Isabeau de Bavière, Reine de France, La Jeunesse, 1370–1405* (Paris, 1903); J. Verdon, *Isabeau de Bavière* (Paris, 1981).

17. J. C. Laidlaw, "Christine de Pizan, the Earl of Salisbury and Henry IV," *French Studies* 36 (1982), 129–143; G. Mombello, "J.-M.-L. Coupé et H. Walpole: Gli Amori de Christine de Pizan," *Studi Francesi,* 16 (1972), 5–25.

18. *L'Avision,* pp. 165–166.

19. P. G. C. Campbell, "Christine de Pisan en Angleterre," *Revue de Littérature Comparée,* 5 (1925), 660–670; J. C. Laidlaw, "Christine de Pizan—An Author's Progress," p. 545.

20. *L'Avision,* p. 166.

21. *Autres Ballades* XXII, Roy, Vol. 1, pp. 232–233.

22. M. Nordberg, *Les Ducs et la Royauté,* pp. 115–15; Christine refers to this exchange of letters in the *Fais et Bonnes Meurs,* Vol. 1, p. 171.

23. *Fais et Bonnes Meurs,* Vol. 1, p. 179.

24. Y. A. Neal, *Le Chevalier Poète, Jehan de Garencières, 1375–1450* (Paris, 1953); M. Nordberg, p. 42.

25. *Autres Ballades* XXIX, XXX and XXI; Roy, Vol. 1, pp. 240–244 and 305–306.

26. Roy, Vol. 1, pp. 232–233; *L'Avision,* p. 167.

27. Roy, Vol. 2, pp. 29–48.

28. Christine had already discussed the qualities attributed to Diana in *Othéa's Letter to Hector,* see B. N. Ms. fr. 606, fol. 13 and also V. L. Bullough, "Medical and Scientific Views of Women," in *Marriage in the Middle Ages,* ed. J. Lyerly (Los Angeles, 1973), p. 497, for the association of chastity with women's mental powers.

29. See especially E. McLeod, *The Order of the Rose,* pp. 73–76, and C. C. Willard, "Christine de Pizan and the Order of the Rose," in *Ideals for Women in the Works of Christine de Pizan,* pp. 51–67.

30. The founding of this order is described in *Le Livre des Faits du Bon Messire Jean LeMaingre, dit Boucicaut,* published in *Les Chroniques de Froissart,* ed. J. A. C. Buchon (Paris, 1835), vol. 3, pp. 609–612.

31. *L'Avision,* p. 166.

32. Boston Public Library, Ms. 1528, fol. 34v°.

33. D. Poirion, *Le Poète et le Prince,* p. 158; Y. A. Neal, *Jehan de Garencières,* pp. 67–69.

34. *L'Avision,* p. 167; Roy, Vol. 1, pp. 251–252.

35. Roy, Vol. 1, pp. 257–258.

36. Dijon, Arch. de la Côte d'Or, B1543, fol. 107.

37. G. Doutrepont, *La Littérature Française à la Cour de Bourgogne* (Paris, 1909), especially pp. 274–278; *The Book of the City of Ladies,* trans. E. J. Richards, p. 212. Christine speaks of her as "one woman among others whom you love singularly as much for the goodness of her virtues as for the favors she has extended to you and to whom you are much beholden. . . ."

38. G. Doutrepont, p. 478, points out that she was the writer represented by the most works in the Inventory of the Burgundian library of 1420.

9   The Education of the Dauphin

1. G. Doutrepont, p. 198; D. Gallet-Guerne, *Vasque de Lucène et la Cyropédie à la Cour de Bourgogne* (Geneva, 1974).
2. Roy, Vol. 3, pp. 27–57 includes both *Les Enseignements Moraux* and *Les Proverbes Moraux.*
3. Caxton published in 1478 the translation of the *Moral Proverbs* by Anthony Wydville, Count Rivers; these were reprinted by R. Pynson in 1526 along with Chaucer's works. A facsimile of Caxton's edition was printed in Amsterdam and New York, 1970.
4. *Le Livre des Trois Vertus,* Book I, Chapt. xxiv, Boston Public Library, Ms. 1528, fol. 39–40.
5. W. H. Woodward, *Studies in Education during the Age of the Renaissance, 1400–1600* (Cambridge, U. K., 1906; rpt. Columbia U., 1967), especially pp. 1–47; E. Garin, *L'Education de L'Homme Moderne,* trans. J. Humbert (Paris, 1968).
6. R. Vaughan, *Philip the Bold,* pp. 72–75; B. A. Pocquet du Haut Jussé, "Le Retour de Nicopolis et la Rançon de Jean sans Peur. Compte Inédit de Maître Oudart Douay pour le Duc de Bourgogne," *Annales de Bourgogne* 9 (1937), 296–302.
7. E. K. Born, "The Perfect Prince," *Speculum,* 3 (1928), 470–504; A. Thomas, *Jean de Gerson et l'Éducation des Dauphins de France* (Paris, 1930).
8. L. Mirot, "L'Enlèvement du Dauphin et la Première Prise d'Armes entre Jean sans Peur et le Duc d'Orléans," *Revue des Questions Historiques* 95 (1914), 329–355 and 369–419. M. Nordberg, *Les Ducs et la Royauté,* pp. 185–207.
9. *Henry V,* 2.4, 3.5,7; and 4.3,5. Shakespeare shows the dauphin at Agincourt although he was not actually present at the battle.
10. L. Pannier, "Les Joyaux du Duc de Guyenne, Recherches sur les Goûts Artistiques et la Vie Privée du dauphin Louis, Fils de Charles VI," *Revue Archéologique,* 26 (1873), 158–170; 209–225; 305–320 and 26 (1874), 31–42.
11. B. N. Ms. fr. 32511, fol. 4; *Fais et Bonnes Meurs,* Vol. 1, pp. xxiv–xxv.
12. Roy, Vol. 3, pp. 3–4.
13. R. H. Lucas, ed., *Le Livre du Corps de Policie,* p. 9.
14. *Le Songe du Vieil Pèlerin,* ed. G. W. Coopland, I, (Cambridge, U. K., 1969), pp. 572–574.
15. *Le Chemin de Long Estude,* vv. 5487–5500, pp. 233–34.
16. The *Vivat Rex* is analyzed by L. Mourin, *Jean Gerson, Prédicateur,* pp. 169–87, and M. Nordberg, *Les Ducs et la Royauté,* pp. 207–212.
17. The duke of Berry's copy is now Paris, B. N. Ms. fr. 282. See M. Meiss, *French Painting . . . The Limbourgs,* p. 7.
18. R. H. Lucas, ed., p. 9.
19. R. H. Lucas, ed., pp. 31–41.
20. *The Book of the Courtier,* trans. C. S. Singleton (New York, 1959), p. 32. Count Ludovico da Canossa defines the Courtier in these terms: "I hold that the principal and true profession of the Courtier must be that of arms; which I wish him to exercise with vigor; and let him be known among others as bold, energetic, and faithful to whomever he serves."
21. Jean de Montreuil, *Opera: l'Oeuvre Historique et Polémique,* ed. N. Grévy, E. Ornato, and G. Ouy (Turin, 1975), pp. 91–135.
22. R. H. Lucas ed., p. 177.
23. R. H. Lucas ed., pp. 178–179.
24. *Le Livre des Trois Vertus,* Book III, Chapt. iii, Boston Ms. 1528, fol. 79v°–81v°.
25. R. H. Lucas ed., pp. 183–194.

26. R. H. Lucas ed., p. 203.
27. G. Mombello, "Quelques aspects de la vie politique de Christine de Pizan," in *Culture et Politique en France à l'Epoque de l'Humanisme et de la Renaissance* (Turin, 1974), pp. 43–103; C. Gauvard, "Christine de Pizan, a-t-elle eu une Pensée Politique?" *Revue Historique* 250 (1973), 417–429.
28. Nordberg, pp. 225–37; L. Mirot, "Raoul d'Anquentonville et le Prix de l'Assassinat du duc d'Orléans," *Bibliothéque de l'Ecole des Chartes* 72 (1911), 445–458; R. Vaughan, *John the Fearless* (London, 1966), pp. 44–48.
29. A. Coville, *Jean Petit et la Question du Tyrannicide au Commencement du XVe Siécle* (Paris, 1932); R. Vaughan, pp. 68–79.
30. R. Vaughan, pp. 81–82.
31. Brussels, Bibl. Roy. Ms. 10476, fol. 4.
32. *Military Institutions of the Romans by Flavius Vegetius Renatus*, ed. Brig. Gen. T. R. Phillips (Harrisburg, Pa., 1960), p. 1.
33. *The Book of the Fayttes of Armes and of Chyvalrye translated and printed by William Caxton from the French original by Christine de Pisan*, ed. A. T. P. Byles (London, 1932), p. xxix.
34. *The Tree of Battles*, ed. G. W. Coopland, pp. 25–36; *Fais et Bonnes Meurs*, Vol. 1, pp. 127–128.
35. *Fais et Bonnes Meurs*, Vol. 1, pp. 131–133.
36. A. T. P. Byles, ed., pp. 189–190.
37. A. T. P. Byles, ed., pp. xiv–xvi.
38. *"Lamentacion sur les Maux de la France,"* ed. A. J. Kennedy, in *Mélanges . . . Charles Foulon*, (Rennes, 1980). Vol. 1, pp. 177–185.
39. A. J. Kennedy, ed., pp. 181–182.
40. R. Vaughan, p. 97; *Documents pour Servir à l'histoire des Relations entre l'Angleterre et la Flandre. Le Cotton Ms. Galba B I*, ed. E. Scott and L. Gilliods van Severen (Brussels, 1896), no. 139.
41. *Histoire de Charles VI*, ed. J. A. C. Buchon, p. 473.
42. *The Livré de la Paix of Christine de Pisan, a Critical Edition with Introduction and Notes*, ed. C C. Willard (The Hague, 1958).
43. A. Coville, *Les Cabochiens et l'Ordonnance de 1413* (Paris, 1888).
44. C. C. Willard, ed., p. 152.
45. C. C. Willard, ed., p. 131.
46. R. Vaughan, pp. 197–200.
47. *Journal de Nicolas de Baye, Greffier du Parlement de Paris, 1400–1417*, ed. A. Tuetey (Paris, 1885–1888). Vol. 2, pp. 331–332; *Chronique du Religieux de Saint-Denis*, Vol. 5, p. 587.
48. For Guillebert de Lannoy's treatise, see *Oeuvres de Guillebert de Lannoy, Voyageur, Diplomate et Moraliste*, ed. C. Potvin (Louvain, 1878) and D. M. Bell, *L'Idéal Éthique de la Royauté en France au Moyen Age* (Geneva-Paris, 1962), pp. 140–150; for a later Burgundian copy of *Le Livre de La Paix*, see C. C. Willard, "An Unknown Manuscript of Christine de Pizan's *Livre de la Paix*," *Studi Francesi* 64 (1978), pp. 90–97. M. G. A. Vale, *War and Chivalry* (London, 1981), pp. 14–28.

10   The Retreat to Poissy

1. A useful discussion of the events of this period is provided by R. Vaughan, *John the Fearless*, pp. 209–227.
2. *Epître de la Prison de Vie Humaine*, Paris, B. N. Ms. fr. 24, 786. See also S. Solente,

"Un Traité Inédit de Christine de Pisan, *l'Epistre de la Prison de Vie Humaine*," *Bibliothèque de l'Ecole des Chartes* 85 (1924), 263–301.

3. A. Thomas, *Romania* 21 (1892), 273–274.

4. Paris, B. N. pièces orig. 17, doss. 426, fol. 239.

5. B. N. Ms. 24, 786, fol. 37.

6. S. Solente, "Un Traité Inédit," p. 270.

7. A. J. Kennedy, ed., p. 181.

8. B. N. Ms. fr. 24, 786, fol. 41.

9. Book III of *Le Livre de la Paix* devotes a series of chapters to Clemency, Liberality, and Truth, along with the corresponding vices of Pride, Greed, and Falsehood. In *Le Livre de Prudence*, a revision of the earlier *Livre de la Prod'hommie de l'Homme*, one chapter is entitled, "Cy dit du Mal qui Ensuit des Susdittes Vertus à qui les Pervertie en Vices," B. N. Ms. fr. 605, fol. 19.

10. D. Gallet-Guerne, *Vasque de Lucène, et la Cyropédie à la Cour de Bourgogne*, p. xv.

11. G. Doutrepont, *La Littérature Française à la Cour de Bourgogne*, p. xvi. One copy of Laurent de Premierfait's translation of Cicero is to be found in Milan, Bibl. Trivulziana, Ms. 693, dated c. 1410 by M. Meiss, *French Painting . . . The Limbourgs*, pp. 21; 375.

12. B. N. Ms. fr. 24, 786, fol. 95.

13. For a discussion of the Celestial Court in French manuscript illustration, see E. Panofsky, *Early Netherlandish Painting* (Cambridge, Mass., 1953), pp. 213–217 and A. de Laborde, *Les Manuscrits à Peintures de la Cité de Dieu* (Paris, 1909). Examples associated with Christine's illustrators would be, for instance, Paris, B. N. Ms. 23–24 and 174 (Saint Augustine) and 414 (Voragine's *The Golden Legend*).

14. G. Hirschel, *Le Livre des Quatre Dames von Alain Chartier. Studien zur franz. Minnekasuistik des Mittelalters.* (Diss. Heidelberg, 1929; *Le Quadrilogue Invectif*, ed. E. Droz (Paris, 1923); P. Champion, *Histoire Poètique du Quinzième Siècle* (Paris, 1966). Vol. 1, pp. 11–17; 29–59.

15. *Journal d'un Bourgeois de Paris sous Charles VI et Charles VII.* Preface and notes by André Mary (Paris, 1929), p. 93.

16. M. G. A. Vale, *Charles VII* (Berkeley, 1974), pp. 25–31.

17. A. Thomas, *Romania* 21 (1892), p. 273.

18. A. Thomas, *Romania* 21 (1892), p. 273.

19. British Library, Royal Ms. 18 B XXII; P. G. C. Campbell, "Christine de Pisan en Angleterre," 669; M.-J. Pinet, p. 181n.

20. C. F. Bühler, "Sir John Fastolf's Manuscript of the *Epître d'Othéa* and Stephen Scrope's Translation of this Text," *Scriptorium* 3 (1949), 123–128; S. Moreau-Rendu, *Le Prieuré Royal de Saint-Louis de Poissy* (Colmar, 1968).

21. B. N. nouv. acq. 10059, fol. 114–144.

22. S. Solente, *Bibliothèque de l'Ecole des Chartes* 85, pp. 267–268.

23. B. N. nouv. acq. 10059, fol. 114.

24. Christine de Pisan, *La Ditié de Jeanne d'Arc*, ed. A. J. Kennedy and K. Varty (Oxford, 1977). See also T. Ballet-Lynn, "The Ditié de Jeanne d'Arc: Its Political, Feminist and Aesthetic Significance," *Fifteenth Century Studies* 1 (1978), 149–157; L. Dulac, "Un Écrit Militant de Christine de Pizan: La Ditié de Jeanne d'Arc," *Aspects of Female Existence*. Proc. from the St. Gertrude Symposium "Women in the Middle Ages," Copenhagen, 1978 (Gyldebdal, Denmark, 1980), pp. 115–134; D. Fraioli, "The Literary Image of Joan of Arc: Prior Influences," *Speculum* 56 (1981), pp. 811–830.

25. Bern, Ms. 205; A. J. Kennedy and K. Varty eds., pp. 2–4.

26. Grenoble, Ms. U 909 Rés; A. J. Kennedy and K. Varty eds. pp. 4–6.

27. A. J. Kennedy and K. Varty eds., p. 5.

28. A. J. Kennedy and K. Varty eds., p. 34 (vv. 265–272).

29. A. J. Kennedy and K. Varty eds., pp. 38–39 (vv. 433–440).

30. A. J. Kennedy and K. Varty eds., pp. 39–40 (vv. 473–480).
31. *Description de la Ville de Paris. . . .*, ed. Le Roux de Lancy and Tisserand, p. 234.
32. He also wrote a *Mirouer des dames et damoyselles et de tout Sexe Feminin.* See G. A. Brunelli, "Jean Castel et le 'Mirouer des dames'," *Le Moyen Age* 62 (1956), 93–117; A. Bossuat, "Jean Castel, Chroniqueur de France," *Le Moyen Age* 64 (1958), 285–304; 499–538.
33. Madame E. Du Castel, *Ma Grand-mère Christine de Pizan* (Paris, 1936).

I I   Renown at Last

1. E. H. Wilkins, *The Life of Petrarch* (Chicago, 1963), p. 194.
2. Boston Ms. 1528, fol. 98.
3. Lucas ed., pp. 204–205.
4. *La Belle Dame sans Mercy,* ed. A. Piaget (Lille-Geneva, 1949), Introduction; Marguerite de Navarre, *Nouvelles,* ed. Y. Le Hir (Paris, 1967), pp. 86 and 300; Rabelais, *Le Tiers Livre,* ch. XXXII.
5. J. Mitchell, *Thomas Hoccleve, A Study in Early Fifteenth Century English Poetic,* (Urbana, 1968), pp. 22–23; 77–84.
6. Brussels, Bibl. Roy. Ms. 9392; Christine de Pisan, *L'Epître d'Othéa, Déesse de la Prudence, à Hector, Chef des Troyens, Reproduction des 100 Miniatures du Manuscrit 9392 de Jean Miélot* par J. Van den Gheyn (Brussels, 1913); G. Mombello, *La Tradizione Manoscritta,* pp. 147–153.
7. G. Doutrepont, *La Littérature Française à la Cour de Bourgogne,* p. 39.
8. C. C. Willard, "A Portuguese Translation of Christine de Pisan's *Livre des Trois Vertus,*" *PMLA* 78 (1966), 433–444; for the Flemish translation (British Library Add. Ms. 20698), see S. Solente in *Histoire Littéraire de la France.* Vol. 45, p. 30.
9. *Les Enseignements d'Anne de France à sa Fille Suzanne de Bourbon.* Original text published by A.-M. Chazaud (Moulins, 1878); H. De Chabannes et I. de Linarès, *Anne de Beaujeu* (Paris, 1955), pp. 139–153.
10. G. Mombello, *La Tradizione Manoscritta dell'Epistre Othea di Christine de Pizan,* pp. 334–35.
11. Harley Ms. 4431.
12. G. D. Painter, *William Caxton, A Quincentenary Biography of England's First Printer* (London, 1976), pp. 90–91.
13. See Byles edition of the *Book of Fayttes of Armes and of Chyvalrye* and J. C. Coopland edition of *The Tree of Battles; William Caxton, an Exhibition to Commemorate the Quincentenary of the Introduction of Printing into England,* The British Library, 24 September 1976–31 January 1977 (London, 1976), No. 84, p. 82.
14. G. D. Painter, pp. 160–170.
15. C. C. Willard, "Christine de Pisan's Treatise on the Art of Medieval Warfare," *Essays in Honor of Louis Francis Solano,* eds. R. T. Cormier and U. T. Holmes (Chapel Hill, 1970), pp. 179–191.
16 See C. F. Bühler's edition of *The Epistle of Othea,* pp. ix–xiii; also Anthony Babington's translation, *The Epistle of Othea to Hector,* ed. J. D. Gordon (Philadelphia, 1942).
17. G. Mombello, *La Tradizione Manoscritta,* pp. 361–362.
18. J. Babelon, *La Bibliothèque Française de Fernand Colombe* (Paris, 1913), pp. 28–29.
19. C. C. Willard, "A Portuguese Translation," 433–444.
20. *The Middle English Translation of Christine de Pisan's Livre du corps de policie,* ed. D. Bornstein (Heidelberg, 1977); M. C. Curnow, "*The Boke of the Cyte of Ladyes,*" an English Translation of Christine de Pisan's *Le Livre de la Cité des Dames,*" *Les Bonnes Feuilles,* 116–137.

21. Paris, B. N. Rés. Y². 2020. *Le Chemin de Long Estude de Dame Christine de Pise, Où Est Décrit le Débat Esmeu au Parlement de Raison, pour l'Élection du Prince Digne de Gouverner le Monde.* Traduit de langue romanne en prose françoyse, par Jean Chaperon, dit Lassé de Repos (Paris; Estienne Groulleau, 1549), Aux Lecteurs.

22. Jean Marot speaks of her in his *Doctrinal des Princesses et Nobles Dames.* See M. Laigle, *Le Livre des Trois Vertus de Christine de Pisan et Son Milieu Historique et Littéraire* (Paris, 1912), p. 39; *Oeuvres Complètes de Clemont Marot* (Paris, 1883). Vol. 2, p. 138.

23. C. F. Bühler, "The Assembly of Gods and Christine de Pisan," *English Language Notes* 4 (1967), pp. 251–254.

24. R. Thomassy, *Ecrits Politiques,* p. 98.

25. R. Thomassy, pp. lxxxiii–lxxxiv.

26. *Fais et Bonnes Meurs,* Vol. 1, p. xcix.

27. S. Solente, *Histoire de la Littérature Française,* Vol. 40, p. 87.

28. *Essai sur les Moeurs* (Paris, 1829), cited by M. Laigle, p. 42.

29. S. Solente, *Histoire de la Littérature Française,* vol. 40, pp. 87–88 and G. Mombello, *Studi Francesi* 46, 5–25.

30. C. C. Willard, "The Remarkable Case of Clothilde de Surville," *L'Esprit Créateur* 6 (1966), 108–116.

31. S. Solente, *Histoire de la Littérature Française,* pp. 166–167.

32. *L'Avision,* pp. 144–145.

33. *Littérature Française: Le Moyen Age, 1300–1480* (Paris, 1971), p. 206.

34. *Le Champion des Dames,* Brussels, Bibl. Roy. Ms. 9281, fol. 151.

❦

Bibliography

I. Modern Editions of the Works

L'Avision-Christine. Ed. Sister Mary Louise Towner (Washington, D. C., 1932).

Ballades, Rondeaux and Virelais. Ed. Kenneth Varty (Leicester, U. K. 1965).

Cent Ballades d'Amant et de Dame. Ed. Jacqueline Cerquiglini (Paris, 1982).

Christine de Pisan. Ed. Jeanine Moulin (Paris, 1962).

La Ditié de Jeanne d'Arc. Eds. Angus J. Kennedy and Kenneth Varty (Oxford, 1977).

Le Débat sur le Roman de la Rose. Critical edition, with introduction translations, and notes by Eric Hicks (Paris, 1977).

Epistre de la prison de vie humaine. Partially edited by S. Solente in "Un Traité Inédit de Christine de Pisan," *Bibliothéque de l'Ecole des Chartes* 85 (1924), pp. 263–301.

La Lamentacion sur les maux de la France. In *Mélanges de Langue et Littérature Françaises du Moyen Age et de la Renaissance Offerts à Charles Foulon,* ed. Angus J. Kennedy. Vol. 1 (Rennes, 1980), pp. 177–185.

Lettre à Isabeau de Bavière. In *Anglo-Norman Letters and Petitions from All Souls Ms. 182,* Ed. M. Dominica Legge (Oxford, 1971).

Le Livre du Chemin de Long Estude. Ed. Robert Püschel (Berlin, 1881).

Le Livre du Corps de Policie. Ed. Robert H. Lucas (Geneva, 1967).

Le Livre des Fais et Bonnes Meurs du Sage Roy Charles V. Ed. Suzanne Solente. 2 vols. (Paris, 1936–1941).

Le Livre de la Mutacion de Fortune. Ed. Suzanne Solente. 4 vols. (Paris, 1959–1966).

Le Livre de la Paix. Ed. Charity Cannon Willard (The Hague, 1958).

Oeuvres Poétiques. Ed. Maurice Roy. 3 vols. (Paris, 1886–1896).

Sept Psaumes Allegorisés. Ed. Ruth Ringland Rains (Washington, D. C., 1965).

II. Translations

The Boke of the Cyte of Ladyes. Trans. Brian Anslay (London, 1521). Reprinted in *Distaves and Dames: Renaissance Treatises for and about Women.* Ed. Diane Bornstein (Delmar, N. Y., 1978).

The Book of the City of Ladies. Trans. Earl Jeffrey Richards (New York, 1982).

Caxton, William, *The Book of Fayttes of Armes and of Chyvalrye*. Ed. A. T. P. Byles (London, 1932, rev. 1937).

The Book of the Duke of True Lovers. Trans. Alice Kemp-Welch; the Ballads rendered into the original meter by Lawrence Binyon and Eric D. Maclagen (London, 1908).

The Fayt of Armes and of Chyvalrie. Facsimile of Caxton's 1489 edition (Amsterdam-New York, 1968).

La Ditié de Jehanne d'Arc. Ed. and trans. Angus J. Kennedy and Kenneth Varty (Oxford, 1977), pp. 41–50.

Das Buch von den Drei Tugenden in Portugiesischer Ubersetzung. Ed. Dorotee Carstens-Groken-berger (Münster, 1961).

O Espelho de Cristina. Ed. Maria Manuela de Silva Nunes Ribeiro Cruzeiro. 2 vols. (Lisbon, 1965).

The Epistle of Othéa to Hector. Ed. James D. Gordon. Trans. Anthony Babington (Philadelphia, 1942).

Sir Stephen Scrope, The Epistle of Othéa. Ed. Curt F. Bühler (London, 1970).

"The Letter of Cupid" in *Hoccleve's Works: The Minor Poems*. Ed. I. Gollancz (London, 1925).

The Letter of Cupid in the Bahbatyne Manuscript. Ed. W. Todd Ritchie (Edinburgh–London, 1930).

The Middle English Translation of Christine de Pisan's Livre du Corps de Policie. Ed. Diane Bornstein (Heidelberg, 1977).

Morale Proverbes of Chrystine. Facsimile of Caxton's 1478 edition of Anthony Woodville's translation. (Amsterdam-New York, 1970).

La Querelle de la Rose: Letters and Documents. Ed. Joseph L. Baird and John R. Kane (Chapel Hill, 1978).

III. Biographical Studies

Boldingh-Goemans. *Christine de Pizan (1364–1430) Haar Tijd, Haar Leven, Haar Werken*. (Rotterdam, 1948).

Du Castel, Françoise. *Damoiselle Christine de Pizan, veuve de M. Etienne de Castel* (Paris, 1972).

———. *Ma Grand-mère Christine de Pizan* (Paris, 1936).

Kemp-Welch, Alice. *Of Six Medieval Women* (London, 1913).

McLeod, Enid. *The Order of the Rose. The Life and Ideas of Christine de Pizan* (London, 1976).

Nys, Ernest. *Christine de Pisan et Ses Principales Oeuvres* (Brussels, 1914).

Pernoud, Régine. *Christine de Pisan* (Paris, 1982).

Pinet, Marie-Josèphe. *Christine de Pisan, 1364–1430. Etude Biographique et Littéraire* (Paris, 1927).

Solente, Suzanne. *Christine de Pisan*. Extract of *L'Histoire Littéraire de la France*. Vol. 40 (Paris, 1969).

IV. Critical Studies

Avril, François. "La Peinture Française au Temps de Jean de Berry," *Revue de l'Art* 28 (1975), pp. 40–52.

Ballet-Lynn, T. "The Ditié de Jeanne d'Arc: Its Political, Feminist and Aesthetic Significance," *Fifteenth Century Studies* 1 (1978), pp. 149–157.

Beck, Jonathan and Gianni Mombello, eds. *Segonda Miscellanea di Studi e Ricerche sul Quattrocento Francese*. Ed. Franco Simone (Chambéry-Turin, 1981).

Bornstein, Diane. "French Influence on Fifteenth-Century English Prose as Exemplified by the Translation of Christine de Pizan's *Livre du corps de policie*," *Medieval Studies*, 39 (1977), pp. 369–386.

———. "Humanism in Christine de Pizan's *Livre du corps de policie*," *Les Bonnes Feuilles* 3 (1975), pp. 100–115.

Bornstein, Diane, ed. *Ideals for Women in the Works of Christine de Pizan*, Michigan Consortium for Medieval and Early Modern Studies I, (1981).

Bossuat, André. "Jean Castel, Chroniqueur de France," *Le Moyen Age* 64 (1958), pp. 283–304; 499–538.

Bozzolo, Carla. "Il *Decameron* come Fonte del *Livre de la Cité des Dames* de Christine de Pisan" in *Miscellanea di Studi e Ricerche sul Quattrocento Francese* (Turin, 1967), pp. 3–24.

Brunelli, G. A. "Jean Castel et *Le Mirouer des Dames*," *Le Moyen Age* 62 (1956), pp. 93–117.

Bühler, Curt F. "The 'Assembly of Gods' and Christine de Pisan," *English Language Notes*, 4 (1967), pp. 251–254.

———. "Sir John Fastolf's Manuscript of the *Epître d'Othéa* and Stephan Scrope's translation of this Text," *Scriptorium*, 3 (1949), pp. 123–128.

Bumgardner, George H. "Christine de Pizan and the Atelier of the Master of the Coronation," *Segonda Miscellanea di Studi e Ricerche sul Quattrocento Francese*, pp. 35–52.

Campbell, P. G. C. "Christine de Pisan en Angleterre," *Revue de Littérature Comparée*, 5 (1925), 659–670.

———. *L'Epître d'Othéa: Étude sur les Sources de Christine de Pisan* (Paris, 1924).

Cigada, Sergio. "Il Tema Arturiano del Château Tournant: Chaucer e Christine de Pisan," *Studi Medievali* 3d ser. 2 (1961), pp. 567–606.

Curnow, Maureen C. "*The Boke of the Cyte of Ladyes*, an English Translation of Christine de Pisan's *Le Livre de la Cité des Dames*," *Les Bonnes Feuilles* 3 (1974), pp. 116–137.

De Winter, Patrick M. "Christine de Pizan et ses enlumineurs," *Actes du 104ᵉ Congrès National des Sociétés Savantes* (1979) (Paris, 1982), pp. 336–75.

Dow, Blanche H. *The Varying Attitude toward Women in French Literature of the Fifteenth Century: The Opening Years* (New York, 1936).

Dulac, Liliane. "Christine de Pisan et le Malheur des *Vrais Amans*," *Mélanges de Langue et de Littérature Médiévales Offerts à Pierre-Le Gentil* (Paris, 1973), pp. 223–233.

———. "Inspiration mystique et savoir politique: les conseils aux veuves chez Francesco da Barberino et chez Christine de Pizan." In *Mélanges à la Mémoire de Franco Simone*, J. Beck and G. Mombello, eds. (Geneva, 1980), pp. 113–141.

————. "Un écrit Militant de Christine de Pizan: La Ditié de Jehanne d'Arc." In *Aspects of Female Existence*. Proceedings from the St. Gertrude Symposium "Women in the Middle Ages," Copenhagen, 1978 (Cyldebdal, Denmark, 1980), pp. 115–134.

————. "Un Mythe Didactique chez Christine de Pizan, Semiramis ou la Veuve Héroique," *Mélanges de Philologie Romane Offerts à Charles Campoux*. Vol. 1, (Montpellier, 1978), pp. 315–343.

Durley, Maureen S. "The Crowned Dame, Dame Opinion and Dame Philosophy: The Female Characteristics of Three Ideals in Christine de Pizan's *L'Avision-Christine*." In *Ideals for Women in the Works of Christine de Pizan*, Michigan Consortium for Medieval and Early Modern Studies I (1981), pp. 29–50.

Finkel, Helen R. "The Portraits of the Women in the Works of Christine de Pisan," *Les Bonnes Feuilles* 3 (1975), pp. 138–151.

Fraioli, Donna. "The Literary Image of Joan of Arc: Prior Influences," *Speculum* 56 (1981), pp. 811–830.

Françon, Marcel. "Sur les Rondeaux de Christine de Pizan," *Studi Francesi* 46 (1972), pp. 68–70.

Gabriel, Astrik L. "The Educational Ideas of Christine de Pisan," *Journal of the History of Ideas* 16 (1955), pp. 3–21.

Gauvard, Claude. "Christine de Pisan, a-t-elle Eu une Pensée Politique?" *Revue Historique* 1250 (1973), pp. 417–430.

Hicks, Eric C. "The 'Querelle de la Rose' in the *Roman de la Rose*," *Les Bonnes Feuilles* 3 (1974), pp. 152–163.

————. "La Tradition Manuscrite des Epîtres sur la Rose," in *Segonda Miscellanea di Studi e Ricerche sul Quattrocento Francese*, pp. 95–123.

Hicks, Eric C. and Ezio Ornato. "Jean de Montreuil et le Débat sur le *Roman de la Rose*," *Romania* 98 (1977), pp. 34–64; 186–219.

Hindman, Sandra. "The Composition of the Manuscript of Christine de Pizan's Collected Works in the British Library: A Reassessment," *The British Library Journal* 9 (1983), pp. 93-123.

Ignatius, Mary A. "Christine de Pizan's *Epistre d'Othéa*. An Experiment in Literary Form," *Medievalia et Humanistica*, NS 9 (1979), pp. 127–142.

————. "A Look at the Feminism of Christine de Pizan," *Proceedings of the Pacific Northwest Conference on Foreign Languages* 29 (1978), pp. 18–21.

Jeanroy, Alfred. "Boccace et Christine de Pisan: Le 'De Claris Mulieribus' Principal Source du 'Livre de la Cité des Dames,'" *Romania* 48 (1922), pp. 92–105.

Kennedy, Angus J., *Christine de Pizan: A Bibliographical Guide*, (London, 1984).

Laidlaw, James C. "Christine de Pizan—An Author's Progress," *The Modern Language Review* 78 (1983), pp. 532–550.

————. "Christine de Pizan, The Earl of Salisbury and Henry IV," *French Studies* 36 (1982), pp. 130–143.

Laigle, Mathilde. *Le Livre des Trois Vertus de Christine de Pisan et Son Milieu Historique et Littéraire* (Paris, 1912).

Lecoy, Félix, "Notes sur Quelques Ballades de Christine de Pisan." In *Fin du Moyen Age et Renaissance, Mélanges de Philologie Française offerts à Robert Guiette* (Antwerp, 1961), pp. 107–114.

LeGentil, Pierre. "Christine de Pisan, Poète Méconnu." In *Mélanges d'Histoire Littéraire Offerts à Daniel Mornet* (Paris, 1961), pp. 1–10.

Margolis, Nadia. "The Human Prison: The Metamorphoses of Misery in the Poetry of Christine de Pizan, Charles d'Orléans, and François Villon," *Fifteenth Century Studies* 1 (1978), pp. 185-192.

Meiss, Millard. "Atropos-Mors: Observations on a Rare Early Humanist Image," in *Florilegium Historiale: Essays Presented to Wallace K. Ferguson* (Toronto, 1971), pp. 152–159.

————. "The Exhibition of French Manuscripts of the XIIIth to the XVIth Centuries at the Bibliothèque Nationale," *Art Bulletin* 38 (1956), pp. 187–196.

————. *French Painting in the Time of Jean de Berry: The Limbourgs and Their Contemporaries* (New York, 1974).

Mombello, Gianni. "Quelques Aspects de la Pensée Politique de Christine de Pizan d'après ses Oeuvres Publiées" in *Culture et Politique en France à l'Epoque de l'Humanisme et de la Renaissance* (Turin, 1974), pp. 43–153.

————. "J. M. L. Couppé e Horace Walpole: Gli Amori di Christine de Pizan," *Studi Francesi*, 46 (1972), pp. 5–25.

————. "Recherches sur l'Origine du Nom de la Déesse Othéa," *Atti della Accademia delle Scienze di Torino*, 103 (1968–1969), 1–33.

————. *La Tradizione Manoscritta dell 'Epistre Othea di Christine de Pizan* (Turin, 1967).

————. "Per un'Edizione Critica dell'Epistre Othea di Christine de Pizan," *Studi Francesi* 24 (1964), pp. 401–417.

Nicolini, Elena. "Christina da Pizzano, l'Origine e il Nome," *Cultura Neolatine* 1 (1941), pp. 143–150.

Ouy, Gilbert and Christine M. Reno. "Identification des Autographes de Christine de Pizan," *Scriptorium* 34 (1980), 221–238.

Picherit, Jean-Louis. "Christine de Pisan et le *Livre des faits du bon Messire Jean Le Maingre, dit Boucicaut, maréchal de France et gouverneur de Gennes,*" *Romania* 103 (1982), 300–331.

Potansky, Peter. *Der Streit um den Rosenroman* (Munich, 1972).

Reno, Christine M. "Feminist Aspects of Christine de Pizan's *Epistre d'Othéa à Hector,*" *Studi Francesi* 71 (1980), pp. 271–276.

————. "Virginity as an Ideal in Christine de Pizan's *Cité des Dames.*" In *Ideals for Women in the Works of Christine de Pizan,* Diane Bornstein, ed. (Michigan Consortium for Medieval and Early Modern Studies I, 1981), pp. 69–90.

Richardson, Lula M. *The Forerunners of Feminism in French Literature of the Renaissance: Part I. From Christine de Pisan to Marie de Gournay* (Baltimore, 1929).

Rigaud, Rose. *Les Idées Féministes de Christine de Pisan* (Neuchâtel, 1911).

Schaeffer, Lucie. "Die Illustrationen zu den Handschriften der Christine de Pizan," *Marburger Jahrbuch für Kunstwissenschaft* 10 (1938), pp. 119–209.

Schilperoort, Johanna C., *Guillaume de Machaut et Christine de Pisan: Étude Comparative* (The Hague, 1936).

Thomas, Antoine. "Documents sur la Vie de Jean Castel," *Romania* 21 (1892), pp. 273–274.

Thomassy, Raimond. *Essai sur les Écrits Politiques de Christine de Pisan* (Paris, 1838).

Wilkins, Nigel, "The Structure of Ballades, Rondeaux and Virelais in Froissart and in Christine de Pisan," *French Studies* 23 (1969), pp. 337–348.

Willard, Charity C. "Christine de Pizan's *Cent Ballades d'Amant et de Dame:* Criticism of Courtly Love." In *Court and Poet.* Ed. G. S. Burgess (Liverpool, 1981). pp. 357–364.

———. "Christine de Pizan's 'Dit de la Pastoure.'" In *Mélanges de Langue et Littéraire Françaises du Moyen Age et de la Renaissance Offerts à Charles Foulon.* Vol. 2 (Liège, 1981), pp. 293–300.

———. "Lovers' Dialogues in Christine de Pizan's Poetry from the *Cent Ballades* to the *Cent Ballades d'Amant et de Dame,*" *Fifteenth Century Studies* 4 (1981), pp. 167–180.

———. "Christine de Pizan and the Order of the Rose" in *Ideals for Medieval Women in the Works of Christine de Pizan,* Diane Bornstein, ed. (Michigan Consortium for Medieval and Early Modern Studies I, 1981), pp. 51–67.

———. "Christine de Pizan: the Astrologer's Daughter," in *Mélanges à la Mémoire de Franco Simone,* J. Beck & G. Mombello, eds. (Geneva, 1980), pp. 95–111.

———. "An Unknown Manuscript of Christine de Pizan's *Livre de la Paix,*" *Studi Francesi* 64 (1978), pp. 90–97.

———. "A Fifteenth-Century View of Women's Role in Medieval Society." In *The Role of Women in the Middle Ages* (Albany, N.Y., 1975), pp. 90–120.

———. "A Re-Examination of the 'Débat de Deux Amants'," *Les Bonnes Feuilles* 3 (1974), pp. 73–88.

———. "Christine de Pizan's Treatise on the Art of Medieval Warfare." In *Essays in Honor of Louis Francis Solano,* R. Cormier and U. T. Holmes, eds. (Chapel Hill, 1970), pp. 179–191.

———. "The Manuscript Tradition of the *Livre des Trois Vertus* and Christine de Pizan's Audience," *Journal of the History of Ideas* 27 (1966), pp. 433–444.

———. "A New Look at Christine de Pizan's *Epistre au Dieu d'Amours.*" In *Segonda Miscellanea di Studi e Ricerche sul Quattrocento Francese* (Turin, 1967), pp. 71–92.

———. "A Portuguese Translation of Christine de Pisan's *Livre des Trois Vertus,*" *PMLA* 78 (1966), pp. 433–444.

———. "Christine de Pisan's 'Clock of Temperance,'" *L'Esprit Créateur* 2 (1963), pp. 149–156.

Yenal, Edith. *Christine de Pizan. A Bibliography of Writings by Her and About Her* (Metuchen, New Jersey—London, 1982).

V. General Background

Andreas Capellanus. *The Art of Courtly Love.* Translated with notes and introduction by John Jay Perry (New York, 1944; rpt. 1979).

Anne de Beaujeu. *Les Enseignements d'Anne de France à sa fille Suzanne de Bourbon.* Original text published by A.-M. Chazaud. (Moulins, 1878).

Avril, Françis. *L'Enluminure du XIVe Siècle à la Cour de France* (Paris, 1978).

————. "Trois Manuscrits Napolitains des Collections de Charles V et de Jean de Berry," *Bibliothèque de l'Ecole des Chartes* 127 (1969), pp. 291–328.

Badel, Pierre-Yves. *Le Roman de la Rose au XIVe Siècle; Étude de la réception de l'Oeuvre* (Geneva, 1980).

Barker, John W. *Manuel II Palaeologus, 1391–1425: A Study in Late Byzantine Statesmanship* (New Brunswick, N. J., 1969).

Bishop, Morris. *Petrarch and His World* (Bloomington, 1963).

Born, E. K. "The Perfect Prince," *Speculum* 3 (1928), pp. 470–504.

Bortolotti, Luigi. *I Comuni della Provincia de Bologna nella Storia e nell'Arte* (Bologna, 1964).

Bozzolo, Carla, and Hélène Loyan. *La Cour Dite Amoureuse de Charles VI, Etude et Edition Critique des Sources Manuscrites* (Paris, 1981).

Boucicaut, Jean Le Maingre. "Le Livre des Faits du Bon Messire Jean Le Maingre, dit Bouciquaut." In *Les Chroniques de Jean Froissart.* Ed. J. A. C. Bouchon (Paris, 1835). Vol. 3, pp. 557–695.

Braustein, P. and R. Delort. *Venise, Portrait Historique d'une cité* (Paris, 1971).

Brereton, Georgine E. and Janet M. Ferrier. eds. *Le Ménagier de Paris,* (Oxford, 1981).

Bühler, Curt F. *The Fifteenth Century Book* (Philadelphia, 1960).

Bullough, Vern L. "Marriage in the Middle Ages: Five Medical and Scientific Views of Women," *Viator* 4 (1973), pp. 485–501.

Castelnau, Jacques Th. de. *Le Paris de Charles V, 1364–1380* (Paris, 1930).

Castiglione, Baldassare. *The Book of the Courtier,* trans. Charles S. Singleton (New York, 1959).

Caxton, William. *An Exhibition to Commemorate the Quincentenary of the Introduction of Printing to England.* The British Library Reference Division, 24 September 1976–31 January 1977 (London, 1976).

Cecchetti, Dario. "Un'Egloga Inedita di Nicolas de Clamanges" in *Miscellanea de Studi e Ricerche sul Quattrocento Francese,* pp. 27–57.

Les Cent Ballades, Poème du XIVe Siècle Composé par Jean le Sénéschal, Publié par G. Raynaud (Paris, 1905).

Chabannes, Hedwige de and Isabelle de Linarès. *Anne de Beaujeu* (Paris, 1955).

Champeaux, A. de and R. Gauchery. *Les Travaux d'Art Exécutés pour Jean de France, Duc de Berry avec une Étude Biographique sur les Artistes Employés par ce Prince* (Paris, 1894).

Champion, Pierre. *La Librairie de Charles d'Orléans* (Paris, 1910).

————. *Histoire Poétique du Quinzième Siècle.* 2 vols. (Paris, 1923; rpt. 1966).

————. ed. *Charles d'Orléans, Poésies.* 2 vols. (Paris, 1966).

Chartier, Alain. *La Belle Dame sans Merci et les Poésies Lyriques* (Lille-Geneva, 1949).

————. *Le Quadriloque Invectif.* Ed. E. Droz (Paris, 1923).

Chronique du Religieux de Saint-Denis. Ed. B. Bellaguet. Vols. 1–3 (Paris, 1839–1841).

Chartularium Universitatis Parisiensis. Eds. Henri Denifle and Emile Chatelain. 4 vols. (Paris, 1889–1893).

Coopland, George W. *Nicole Oresme and the Astrologers* (Cambridge, Mass., 1952).

Coopland, George W., ed. *The Tree of Battles of Honoré Bonet. An English Version with Introduction* (Liverpool, 1949).

Cosneau, E. *Le Connétable de Richemont (Arthur de Bretagne, 1393–1458)* (Paris, 1886).

Courcelle, Pierre. *La Consolation de Philosophie dans la Tradition Littéraire* (Paris, 1967).

Coville, Alfred. *Les Cabochiens et l'Ordonnance de 1413* (Paris, 1888).

————. *Jean Petit et la Question du Tyrannicide au Commencement du XVᵉ Siécle* (Paris, 1932).

Crane, Thomas F. *Italian Social Customs of the Sixteenth Century* (New Haven, 1920).

Crombie, A. C. *Augustine to Galileo* (Cambridge, Mass., 1979).

Dahlberg, Charles. "Love and the *Roman de la Rose*," *Speculum* 44 (1969), pp. 568–584.

Delachenal, Roland. "La Date de la Naissance de Charles V," *Bibliothèque de l'Ecole des Chartes* 64 (1903), pp. 94–98.

————. *Histoire de Charles V.* 5 vols. (Paris, 1909–1931).

Delaissé, L. M. J. *Miniatures Médiévales dans la Librairie de Bourgogne au Cabinet des Manuscrits de la Bibliothèque Royale de Bruxelles* (Brussels, 1969).

Delisle, Léopold. *Recherches sur la Librairie de Charles V,* 2 vols. (Paris, 1907).

Deschamps, Eustache, *Oeuvres.* Eds. Queux de Saint-Hilaire and G. Raynaud. 11 vols. (Paris, 1873–1903).

Destrez, Jean. *La "Pecia" dans les Manuscrits Universitaires du XIIIᵉ et du XIVᵉ Siècle* (Paris, 1935).

De Winter, Patrick J. "Jean de Marville, Claus Sluter et les Statues de Philippe le Hardi et Marguerite de Flandre au Château de Germolles," *Actes du 101ᵉ Congrès National des Sociétés Savantes* (1976) (Paris, 1978), pp. 215–232.

Dufour, Antoine. *Les Vies des Femmes Célèbres.* Ed. J. Jeanneau, with notes and comments (Geneva-Paris, 1970).

Eder, Robert. "Tignonvillana inédita," *Romanische Forschungen* 33 (1915), pp. 851–1022.

Fantuzzi, G. *Notizie degli Scrittori Bolognesi* (Bologna, 1789).

Les Fastes du Gothique: le Siècle de Charles V. Catalogue of the exhibition at the Galeries Nationales du Grand Palais. 9 October 1981–1 February 1982 (Paris, 1981).

Febvre, Lucien and Martin, Henri-Jean. *L'Apparition du Livre* (Paris, 1958).

Fleming, John V. "Hoccleve's 'Letter to Cupid' and the 'Quarrel' over the *Roman de la Rose*," *Medium Aevum* 40 (1970), pp. 21–40.

————. *The Roman de la Rose: A Study in Allegory and Iconography* (Princeton, 1967).

Fondazione Giorgio Cini. *La Civiltà Veneziana del Trecento* (Florence, 1955).

Gallet-Guerne, Danielle. *Vasque de Lucène et la Cyropédie à la Cour de Bourgogne* (Geneva, 1974).

Gilmore, Myron R. *Humanists and Jurists* (Cambridge, Mass., 1963).

Gottfried, Robert L. *The Black Death, Natural and Human Disaster in Medieval Europe* (New York-London, 1983).

Grand, R. and R. Delatouche. *L'Agriculture au Moyen Age de la Fin de l'Empire Romain au XVIe Siècle* (Paris, 1950).

Gunn, Alan M. *The Mirror of Love. A Reinterpretation of the Romance of the Rose* (Lubbock, Texas, 1952).

Hindman, Sandra. "The Iconography of Isabeau de Bavière (1410–1415): An Essay in Method," *Gazette des Beaux Arts* 102 (1983), pp. 102–110.

Jorga, N. *Philippe de Mézières, 1326–1405, et la Croisade au XIVe Siècle* (Paris, 1896).

Juvenal des Ursins, Jean. *Histoire de Charles VI.* Ed. J. A. C. Buchon (Paris, 1875).

Kervyn de Lettenhove. *Oeuvres Complètes de Froissart.* 28 vols. (Brussels, 1867–1877).

Kohl, Benjamin G. and Ronald G. Witt. *The Earthly Republic; Italian Humanists on Government and Society* (Manchester, 1978).

Kristeller, Paul O. "Learned Women of Early Modern Italy: Humanists and University Scholars." In *Beyond Their Sex: Learned Women of the European Past.* Ed. P. H. Labalme (New York, 1980).

———. *Renaissance Thought II; Papers on Humanism and the Arts* (New York, 1965).

Krynen, Jacques. *Idéal du Prince et Pouvoir Royal en France à la Fin du Moyen Age (1380–1441)* (Paris, 1981).

Laborde, A. de. *Les Manuscrits à Peintures de la Cité de Dieu* (Paris, 1909).

Lacroix, P., ed. *Le Bon Berger ou le Vrai Régime et Gouvernement des Bergers et Bergères Composé par le Rustique Jean de Brie* (Paris, 1879).

Lane, Frederic C. *Venice, A Maritime Republic* (Baltimore, 1973).

Le Fèvre de Ressons, Jean. *Les Lamentations de Mathéolus et le Livre de Leese . . . Poèmes Français du XIVe Siècle.* Ed. A. G. Van Hamel. 2 vols. Critical edition including the original text of *Les Lamentations* from the unique Utrecht Ms. With an introduction, notes and two glossaries (Paris, 1905).

Lieberman, Max. "Chronologie Gersonienne," *Romania* 83 (1962), pp. 71–73.

La Librairie de Charles V (Paris, 1968).

Le Roux de Lincy, L. and L. M. Tisserand. *Paris et Ses Historiens aux XIVe et XVe Siècles* (Paris, 1867).

Lièvre, M. "Evrart de Tremaugon et le *Songe du Verger,*" *Romania* 101 (1980), 527–530.

———. "Notes sur le Manuscrit Original du *Songe du Verger,*" *Romania* 77 (1956), pp. 532–560.

Le Livre du Chevalier de la Tour Landry pour l'Enseignement de ses Filles. Ed. A. de Montaiglon. (Paris, 1854).

Lorris, Guillaume de and Jean de Meun. *The Romance of the Rose.* trans. Harry W. Robbins (New York, 1962).

Marot, Clément. *Oeuvres Complètes* (Paris, 1883).

Mary, André, ed. *Journal d'un Bourgeois de Paris sous Charles VI et Charles VII* (Paris, 1929). With preface and notes.

Meiss, Millard and Off, Sharon. "The Bookkeeping of Robinet d'Estampes and the Chronology of Jean de Berry's Manuscripts," *Art Bulletin* 53 (1971), pp. 225–235.

Meiss, Millard. *French Painting in the Time of Jean de Berry: The Late XIV Century and the Patronage of the Duke* (London, 1962).

Mézières, Philippe de. *Le Songe du Vieil Pèlerin.* Ed. G. W. Coopland. 2 vols. (Cambridge, U.K., 1969).

Montreuil, Jean de. *Opera.* Vol. 1, *Epistolario.* Ed. Ezio Ornato (Turin, 1963). Vol. 2, *L'Oeuvre Historique et Polémique.* Eds. Nicole Grévy et al. (Turin, 1975).

Mirot, Léon. *Etudes Lucquoises* (Paris, 1930).

Mitchell, Jerome. *Thomas Hoccleve, A Study in Early Fifteenth-Century English Poetic* (Urbana, 1968).

Monfrin, Jacques. "La Connaissance de l'Antiquité et le Problème de l'Humanisme en Langue Vulgaire dans la France du XVe Siècle." In *The Late Middle Ages and the Dawn of Humanism Outside Italy,* M. C. Verbeber and J. Ijsewijn, eds. (Louvain–The Hague, 1972).

Morel, Octave. *La Grande Chancellerie Royale et l'Expédition des Lettres Royaux de l'Avènement de Philippe de Valois à la Fin du XIVe Siècle.* (Paris, 1900).

Mourin, Louis. *Jean Gerson, Prédicateur Français* (Bruges, 1952).

Neal, Young A. *Le Chevalier Poète, Jehan de Garencières, 1375–1450* (Paris, 1953).

Nordberg, Michael. *Les Ducs et la Royauté; Étude sur la Rivalité des Ducs d'Orleans et de Bourgogne, 1392–1407* (Uppsala, 1964).

Nys, Ernest, ed. *L'Arbre des Batailles, Publié d'après le Ms. 9097 de la Bibliothèque Royale de Bruxelles* (Brussels-Leipzig, 1883).

Oresme, Nicole. *Le Livre du Ciel et du Monde,* eds. A. D. Menut and A. J. Denomy (Madison, 1968).

———. *Le Livre de Ethiques.* Ed. A. D. Menut (Paris, 1940).

Origo, Iris. *Le Marchand de Prato: Francesco di Marco Datini,* trans. J. Fillion, (Paris, 1959).

Ouy, Gilbert. "Paris, l'un des Principaux Foyers de l'Humanisme en Europe au Début du XVe Siécle," *Bulletin de la Société d'Histoire de Paris et de l'Ile-de-France* (1967–1968), pp. 71–98.

———. "Le 'Pastorium Carmen', Poème de Jeunesse de Gerson et la Renaissance de l'Eglogue en France à la Fin du XIVe Siècle," *Romania* 88 (1967), pp. 175–231.

———. "Honoré Bouvet (appelé à tort Bonet), Prieur de Selonnet," *Romania* 85 (1959), pp. 255–259.

Painter, George D. *William Caxton. A Quincentenary Biography of England's First Printer* (London, 1976).

Pannier, Louis. "Les Joyaux du Duc de Guyenne, Recherches sur les Goûts Artistiques et la Vie Privée du Dauphin Louis, Fils de Charles VI," *Revue Archéologique* 26 (1873), pp. 158–170; 209–225; 306–320; 384–395, and 27 (1874), 31–42.

Patch, Howard R. *The Goddess Fortuna in Medieval Literature* (Cambridge, Mass., 1927; rpt. New York, 1967).

Perret, P.-M. *Histoire des Relations de la France avec Venise du XIIIe à l'Avènement de Charles VIII* (Paris, 1896).

Piaget, Arthur. "Ballades de Guillebert de Lannoy et de Jean de Werchin," *Romania* 39 (1910), pp. 324–368.

———. "Le Songe de la Barge de Jean de Werchin, Sénéchal de Hainaut (1404)," *Romania* 38 (1909), pp. 70–110.

———. "La Cour Amoureuse, Dite de Charles VI," *Romania* 20 (1891), pp. 416–454.

Picard, E. "Le Château de Germolles et Marguerite de Flandre," *Mémoires de la Société Éduenne,* NS 40 (1912), pp. 147–218.

Poirion, Daniel. *Littérature Française: Le Moyen Age, 1300–1480* (Paris, 1971).

———. *Le Roman de la Rose* (Paris, 1973).

———. *Le Poète et Prince, l'Évolution du Lyrisme Courtois de Guillaume de Machaut à Charles d'Orléans* (Paris, 1965).

Predelli, R. ed. *I libri Commemoriali della Republica di Venezia, Registri,* in *Monumenti Storici Pubblicata della Deputazione Veneta di Storia Patria.* Ser. 1 (Venice, 1976 ff.).

Prost, B. *Inventaires Mobiliers et Extraits des Comptes des Ducs de Bourgogne et de la Maison de Valois (1363–1477)* (Paris, 1902).

Quillet, Jeannine. *Charles V, le Roi Lettré. Essai Sur la Pensée Politique d'un Règne* (Paris, 1984).

Les Quinze Joies de Mariage. Ed. Joan Crow (Oxford, 1969).

Richmond, C. F., "The War at Sea." In *The Hundred Years War,* ed. K. Fowler (London, 1971).

Robertson, D. W., Jr. *A Preface to Chaucer* (Princeton, 1962).

Roncière, Charles de la. *L'Histoire de la Marine Française,* 6 vols. (Paris, 1899–1934).

Samaran, Charles. "Pierre Bersuire, Prieur de Saint-Eloi de Paris," *Histoire de la Littérature Française,* XXXIX (1962), pp. 259–433.

Scherrer, Margaret R. *The Legends of Troy in Art and Literature* (New York, 1963).

Scott, E., and Gilliods van Severen, ed. *Documents pour servir à l'histoire des relations entre l'Angleterre et la Flandre. Le Cotton Ms. Galba B-I* (Brussels, 1896).

Seznec, Jean. *The Survival of the Pagan Gods: The Mythological Tradition and its Place in Renaissance Humanism and Art.* Trans. by B. F. Sessions (New York, 1961).

Sherman, Claire R. "Some Visual Definitions in the Illustrations of Aristotle's Nicomachean Ethics and Politics in the French Translation of Nicole Oresme," *Art Bulletin* 69 (1977), pp. 320–330.

———. "Representations of Charles V of France (1338–1380) as a Wise Ruler," *Medievalia et Humanistica,* NS 2 (1971), pp. 83–96.

———. *The Portraits of Charles V of France, 1338–1380* (New York, 1969).

Simone, Franco, ed. *Miscellanea di Studi e Recerche sui Quattrocento Francese* (Turin, 1967).

Simone, Franco. *Il Rinascimento Francese, Studi e Ricerche* (Turin, 1961).

Thibault, Marcel. *Isabeau de Bavière, Reine de France. La Jeunesse, 1370–1405* (Paris, 1903).

Thomas, Antoine. *Jean de Gerson et l'Éducation des Dauphins de France* (Paris, 1930).

———. "Jacques de Longuyon, Trouvère," *Histoire de la Littérature Française* 36 (1924), pp. 1–35.

———. "Bernard Gui, Frère Prêcheur," *Histoire de la Littérature Française* 35 (1921), pp. 139–232.

———. "Alain Chartier, Chanoine de Notre-Dame de Paris," *Romania* 33 (1904), pp. 387–402.

———. "Un Manuscrit de Charles V au Vatican. Notice Suivie d'une Étude sur les Traductions de Bernard Gui." In *Mélanges d'Archéologie et d'Histoire de l'Ecole Française de Rome.* Vol. 1 (Paris, 1881), pp. 259–283.

Thomas, Marcel. *La Visite de l'Empereur Charles IV en France d'après l'Exemplaire des "Grands Chroniques" Exécuté pour Charles V.* Proc. of the 6th Congrès International des Bibliophiles, Vienna, 29 September–5 October (Vienna, 1971), 85–89.

Thorndike, Lynn. *A History of Magic and Experimental Science.* 8 vols. (New York, 1923–1958).

Toynbee, Paget. "Christine de Pisan and Sire John de Maundville," *Romania* 21 (1922), pp. 228–239.

Tuetey, A., ed. *Journal de Nicolas de Baye, Greffier du Parlement de Paris, 1406–1417.* 2 vols. (Paris, 1885–1888).

Tuve, Rosemond. *Allegorical Imagery: Some Medieval Books and Their Posterity* (Princeton, 1966).

Vale, Malcolm G. A. *Charles VII* (Berkeley, 1974).

———. *War and Chivalry* (London, 1981).

Vaughan, Richard. *Philip the Bold: The Formation of the Burgundian State* (Cambridge, Mass., 1962).

———. *John the Fearless: The Growth of Burgundian Power* (London, 1966).

Verdon, Jean. *Isabeau de Bavière* (Paris, 1981).

Wilkins, Ernest H. *The Life of Petrarch* (Chicago, 1963).

Wilkins, Nigel. *One Hundred Ballades, Rondeaux and Virelais* (Cambridge, U. K., 1969).

Willard, Charity C. "The Remarkable Case of Clothilde de Surville," *L'Esprit Créateur* 6 (1966), pp. 108–116.

———. "The Duke of Berry's Multiple Copies of the *Fleur des Histoires d'Orient*" in *From Linguistics to Literature, Romance Studies Offered to Francis M. Rogers* (Amsterdam, 1981), pp. 281–292.

Wright, N. A. R. "The Tree of Battles of Honoré Bouvet and the Laws of War." In *War, Literature and Politics in the Late Middle Ages.* Ed. C. T. Allmand (Liverpool, 1976), pp. 12–31.

Ziegler, Philip. *The Black Death* (London, 1970).

Index